The Santiago Campaign

Truly Your friend
Jos Wheeler

THE

SANTIAGO CAMPAIGN

1898

BY

Major-General

JOSEPH WHEELER

COMMANDING FOURTH CORPS, UNITED STATES ARMY

LATE COMMANDER OF CAVALRY DIVISION
IN SANTIAGO CAMPAIGN

BOOKS FOR LIBRARIES PRESS
FREEPORT, NEW YORK

First Published 1898
Reprinted 1970

INTERNATIONAL STANDARD BOOK NUMBER:
0-8369-5539-0

LIBRARY OF CONGRESS CATALOG CARD NUMBER:
75-130566

PRINTED IN THE UNITED STATES OF AMERICA

TO

The Brave Officers and Soldiers

OF THE

CAVALRY DIVISION, ARMY OF SANTIAGO,

I DEDICATE THIS BOOK

TO THEIR SUPERB COURAGE IN BATTLE, AND THEIR ENDURANCE AND
FORTITUDE WHEN SUBJECTED TO THE DISCOMFORT, DISEASES,
AND HARDSHIPS OF THE TROPICAL CLIMATE OF CUBA,
IS LARGELY DUE THE GLORY ACHIEVED BY
AMERICAN ARMS IN THE CAMPAIGN
OF SANTIAGO

THEIR GOOD CONDUCT IN BIVOUAC, UPON THE MARCH, AND IN
BATTLE, HAS NEVER BEEN SURPASSED BY ANY SOLDIERS;
AND I SHALL REMEMBER EACH AND ALL OF THEM
WITH EVER INCREASING GRATITUDE
AND ADMIRATION

TABLE OF CONTENTS

Below synopsis of each chapter will be found, by way of Index, the running heads on right-hand pages.

PART I.

THE CAMPAIGN.

PART II.

DESPATCHES ON THE FIELD.

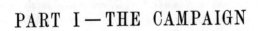

PART I—THE CAMPAIGN

Note. — *The exact wording of official Reports has been followed here; and also the spelling of proper names in the Reports, even where it differs from the spelling in Addendas A and B to Part I., which aims to be correct. Throughout the book, I have preferred "Daiquiri," as the common local spelling; though "Baiquiri" has good usage.*

THE SANTIAGO CAMPAIGN

CHAPTER I

MY APPOINTMENT — REPORT FOR DUTY TO GENERAL
WADE, COMMANDING AT TAMPA — GENERAL SHAFTER
TAKES COMMAND OF THE EXPEDITION — EMBARKING
FOR CUBA — DIARY EN ROUTE

THE initial campaign of the Spanish War is over. The surrender of the eastern province of Santiago, together with all their forts and twenty-three thousand Spanish soldiers, is completed, and the flag of our country floats over the palace of an historic city three hundred and eighty-two years old. The Spanish army, which had fought gallantly in the defence of Santiago, is now disarmed and encamped in the fields to the east of the city which they had so bravely defended, awaiting the arrival of ships to take them to Spain.

I will begin by stating that on the night of April 26th President McKinley wrote me that he would like to see me at half-past eight that evening. I was prompt in complying, and was ushered into a room where I found the President, the Attorney-General, the Secretary of War, Major Webb Hayes, of Ohio, and Major Hastings and ex-Congressman Thompson, of the same State. After some pleasant interchanges the President said, " General, I have sent for you to ask if you want to go, and if you feel able to go." I replied that, while I was sixty-one years old, I felt as strong and capable as when I was forty, or even much younger, and that I desired very much to have another opportunity to serve my country. He said, "I have got to appoint fifteen major-generals; and it would have given you great pleasure to have heard the pleasant things said about you while we were discussing the matter yesterday." After a little more conversation he took me into a separate room, where we had a little private talk.

On the evening of May 2d, I received a notice from the War Department that my appointment had been made out. The Senate did not meet on the 3d, but on the 4th it was received by that body and at once confirmed. Late in the evening of May 9th I received the following order:

WAR DEPARTMENT, ADJUTANT-GENERAL'S OFFICE,
WASHINGTON, D.C., May 9, 1898, 6.18 P.M.
MAJOR-GENERAL JOSEPH WHEELER,
Washington:
Under instructions from the Secretary of War, the Major-General Commanding Army directs, as necessary for public service, that you proceed to Camp George

H. Thomas, Chickamauga, Ga., and report in person to Major-General John R. Brooke for assignment to duty. Prompt action imperative.

H. C. CORBIN,
Adjutant-General.

I immediately packed my trunk and left on the first through train, reporting to General Brooke early on the morning of May 11th. I was very much pleased with General Brooke; he is a large, handsome man, and impressed me very favorably. The next day at 2 o'clock I received the following telegram:

WAR DEPARTMENT, ADJUTANT-GENERAL'S OFFICE,
WASHINGTON, D.C., May 12, 1898, 1.38 P.M.

MAJOR–GENERAL JOSEPH WHEELER,
Chickamauga Battlefield, Ga., care of
General Brooke:

With approval of Secretary of War, Major-General Commanding directs you report at Tampa, Fla., to command the cavalry in the expedition now leaving. General Miles leaves here to-night. You should meet him at Tampa soon as possible after his arrival.

H. C. CORBIN,
Adjutant-General.

I hastened to the depot in time to take the 2.07 train; and reached Tampa the next day, and telegraphed to Washington of my arrival there. I reported to General Wade; who informed me that he had not received any instructions about my duties, and would have to wait until they arrived. General Wade is a thorough soldier: he is the son of the distinguished Senator and Acting Vice-President Benjamin F. Wade, of Ohio. He has spent his life in the army, and has an excellent military reputation. Some two or three days later, General Wade was ordered upon other duties, and General Shafter was placed in command. I confess that when I met this officer I was struck with his bearing, and what I interpreted as his force of character. His head and face are not unlike those of President Cleveland; and I readily saw that he possessed administrative ability, and that he was fitted for an important command. When orders from Washington were received assigning me to the command of the Cavalry Division, I immediately pitched my tent with the command, and devoted myself to inspection and other means of becoming familiar with the officers and men. In less than three days I had looked squarely in the face of every man in the command. I attended the drills, and soon saw that the command was one of which I could be justly proud.

About 9 o'clock of the night of June 7th, an officer of General Shafter's staff came to me and stated that orders from Washington made it imperative that the command should embark at daylight the next morning, and that a train of cars to take the division to Port Tampa — a distance of nine miles — would be ready for us at 11 o'clock that night. Immediately all was bustle. Camps were struck, everything hauled alongside of the railroad; the cars finally came, and shortly after they arrived we reached Port Tampa. We embarked with all speed. But a second telegram from Washington directed a delay until the following Monday. We understood that the sudden order which caused us to leave that night was occasioned by a telegram from Admiral Sampson stating that if ten thousand men were promptly sent to Santiago he could capture Cervera's fleet and the garrison in the city. That message, as since verified, reads:

MOLE, HAYTI, June 7, 1898.

SECRETARY OF NAVY, Washington:

Bombarded forts at Santiago 7.30 A.M. to 10 A.M. to-day, June 6th. Have silenced works quickly, without injury of any kind, though stationary within 2,000 yards. If 10,000 men were here, city and fleet would be ours within forty-eight hours. Every consideration demands immediate army movement. If delayed, city will be defended more strongly by guns taken from fleet.

SAMPSON.

I cannot do better than to insert here a brief diary of the details of our trip, from the night we left Tampa, June 7th, until we came within sight of our landing-place, near Santiago, on June 20th. It is as follows :

At 9 o'clock Tuesday, June 7th, despatches from Admiral Sampson indicated immediate necessity for troops. We promptly broke camp;

and, by daylight, had traveled nine miles and reached the transports at Port Tampa. My cavalry troops embarked upon the steamships *Alleghany*, *Rio Grande*, *Miami*, and *Yucatan*, with orders to sail immediately. When all on board, telegrams were received to delay, and we remained in port until the morning of Tuesday, June 14th. After many delays, we succeeded in pushing down Tampa Bay. The channel is a difficult one, — our ships drawing 18 feet, and the channel at the deepest place, which is narrow, being only 23 feet. There were nearly fifty transports, and there were only four pilots, which accounted for some of the delay.

Wednesday, June 15. — The sky in the evening is perfectly beautiful, the stars very bright, and appear much more numerous than in more northern latitudes. At dusk we see Tortugas Light, and pass, leaving it to our right.

Thursday, June 16. — At daylight we find ourselves under the escort of a number of warships. The entire fleet, including the naval vessels, numbers some fifty-five ships. We sail in three columns, the columns being about one thousand yards apart. My ship, the *Alleghany*, leads the right column, the one nearest to Cuba. The war-ship *Indiana* sails some thousand or more yards to our front and right. The other naval ships are approximately as laid down in the official table showing the order of sailing of the cruisers and transports, as follows:

Order of Cruising.

International Signal, T.C.F.

Vesuvius. ☉ 1600 yds. ☉ *Scorpion.*

1600 yds. 1600 yds.

Annapolis. Castine. Helena. Indiana.
☉ 800 yds. ☉ 800 yds. ☉ 1600 yds. ☉

400 yds. 400 yds.

About 20 miles.

◇ 1 ◇ 9 ◇ 17 *Alleghany.*

◇ 2 ◇ 10 ◇ 18 1st Div.

1600 yds. ◇ 3 ◇ 11 ◇ 19 1600 yds.

◇ 4 ◇ 12 ◇ 20

Panther. *Yosemite.*
☉ 1600 yds. ◇ 5 ◇ 25 ◇ 30 ☉

800 yds. 800 yds.

Bancroft. *Detroit.*
☉ ☉ 800 yds. ☉ 800 yds. ☉ ☉

400 yds. 400 yds.

◇ 26 ◇ 28 ◇ 22

◇ 7 ◇ 15 ◇ 23 2d Div.

◇ 8 ◇ 16 ◇ 24 1600 yds.

◇ 27 ◇ 29 ◇

Wompatock. *Eagle.*
☉ 1600 yds. ◇ 6 ◇ 14 ◇ 21 ☉

1600 yds.
Wasp. ☉

During all of Thursday we sailed in an easterly direction bearing south, keeping nearly parallel to the coast of Cuba. Of course it is very warm, but not so intolerable as one would imagine. We occasionally see a strange sail, which generally turns out to be a despatch boat or a freight vessel. I think we have seen but one of the latter kind; the danger of capture is too great for merchantmen to take the risk.

Friday, June 17. — Soon after daylight the fleet turned southward, and by 8 o'clock we were running parallel to and in sight of the shore of Cuba, about opposite the western end of Puerto Principe. We are compelled to regulate our speed by that of the slowest vessel, and hardly make more than nine or ten knots an hour. At 10 o'clock we are passing the Cuban light-house at Paradone Principe. We can plainly see the barracks that are occupied by Spanish soldiers, and some contend they can see the men standing in front of the buildings. At 2 P.M. we are passing Lopos Light-house, leaving it to our left, or north of us. This light-house is on one of the most southern of the Bahama Islands. It is English, of course. It is only about fourteen miles from Cuba. A ship sailing midway of the channel is in sight of both the English and Cuban shores. I can now see high ground in Cuba, and the Lopos Light-house on Bahama Islands cannot be more than about four miles distant.

Five P. M. — See very high ground in Cuba. The sea has been very blue, quite as blue as blue indigo. At night the signalling of the war-ships is very interesting. Bright and varied colors are displayed, by which communications are held.

Saturday, June 18. — Remained at a standstill several hours this morning, for slow ships to catch up. At 2 P.M. we are passing Cape Lucretia, about the middle (measured east and west) of the province of Santiago de Cuba, and almost north of the city of Santiago de Cuba. We see high hills on the Cuban coast, estimated at from twelve hundred to fifteen hundred feet high. Towards night we take direct course to the English island called Inagua Island. It is just north of what is called Windward Channel. This is the channel between Cuba and Haiti or St. Domingo.

Sunday, June 19. — At about nine o'clock, approaching Matthew Town on Inagua Island. We can plainly see the light-house. When within about fifteen miles of the island, we turn sharply south towards the Windward Channel. The sea is getting quite rough. At 3 P.M. the sea has become more calm, and we are in sight of Cape Maisa. The shore seems to be lined with high hills or mountains, say from one thousand to fifteen hundred feet. We see clouds of smoke; very possibly Spaniards preparing to retreat to Santiago. We are now about one hundred and twenty miles from that place. Sunday night, 9 P.M., we have rounded the eastern end of the Island of Cuba, and are now sailing west to Santiago.

Monday, June 20. — At daylight, we are about thirty miles east of Santiago. We see high mountains on the shore, probably two thousand feet high.

Will close this before reaching landing-place, as we must pack up for disembarkation.

CHAPTER II

WITH the aid of our glasses we could see the town of Daiquiri, the place selected for our landing. The place has no harbor, but as it was a shipping-point for iron-ore, General Shafter and the naval officers concluded we could safely land the army by the use of the small-boats belonging to the fleet and the transports. There is a strongly built iron pier extending out some distance from the shore, but we readily saw this could not be used by us. It extended very high above the water, it being constructed for the purpose of dumping iron-ore from the cars into lighters. It was, therefore, evident that we would be obliged to land on the beach, or else at the end of a small dock that extended some twenty yards from the shore.

On the 21st, General Shafter and his staff had a meeting with General Castillo; and on the

22d, all the generals were directed to visit General Shafter. Here we were informed that a landing would be effected the next day. Shortly after daylight the navy commenced a heavy bombardment on to the shore, which lasted about an hour; after which the disembarkation commenced. I should have mentioned that, in order to take this trip, it was necessary for us to leave our horses behind, as we had no way of transporting them to Cuba. This made it necessary to leave a squadron of every regiment to take care of the horses, so that my entire division which entered into the expedition was as tabulated on the opposite page.

The disembarkation was attended with serious difficulties. The high surf dashed several of the strong naval boats to pieces. The mules, artillery, and private horses of officers were pushed overboard, several being drowned in attempting to swim to the shore.

General Lawton's Division was given the honor to be the first to disembark; but on purpose to prepare for my troops I went ashore personally, and directed Colonel Wood, of my command, to send a man to the top of an eminence, upon which a Spanish block-house and flag-staff had been erected, and to hoist his regimental flag upon the flag-staff. This was promptly done; and it was responded to by shrill whistles from the entire fleet. I rode forward some three and a half miles to

Strength of the Cavalry Division that sailed from Tampa for Cuba, June 14, 1898.

ORGANIZATIONS.	OFFICERS.	MEN.
Major-General Wheeler and Staff .	12	
FIRST BRIGADE (Sumner's) :		
Brigadier-General and Staff. . .	3	
3d Regular Cavalry	22	420
6th Regular Cavalry	16	437
9th Regular Cavalry	21	410
SECOND BRIGADE (Young's) :		
Brigadier-General and Staff . .	6	
1st Regular Cavalry	25	540
10th Regular Cavalry	21	465
1st U.S. Volunteer Cavalry . .	32	550
TOTALS	158	2,822

examine the country, and when I returned it was late at night. The next morning General Shafter sent for me, and directed that I go to Juragua to throw forward pickets to Juraguacito, more commonly called Siboney. I rode rapidly to this place, followed by two squadrons of Colonel Wood's Regiment and one squadron each of the 1st and 3d Regulars, and three Hotchkiss guns. When I reached Juraguacito, or Siboney, I found that the enemy had taken their men out of the block-house in that vicinity the midnight preceding, and at daylight had started in the direction of Sevilla, followed by some two hundred Cubans. I rode rapidly to the front, and found that the enemy had halted in a strong position three miles from Siboney; the Cubans having engaged their rear, in which action nine of them were wounded. I saw one dead Spaniard, but do not know what other casualties they suffered. Hoping that my troops would be up that night, I hastened back to Siboney; and at 8 o'clock the troops of my command above mentioned had arrived. With the aid of General Castillo I learned the features of the country; and determined to attack as early as possible next morning, General Castillo promising that he would go with me and assist.

In order to march with more rapidity, it was arranged with Colonel Wood to march with his regiment, five hundred strong, by a left-hand or westerly road; while the Hotchkiss guns and the squadrons of the 1st and 10th Cavalry, and the dynamite gun, which we momentarily expected, were to march on what is called the main Santiago road. General Castillo was also to march with us on this road with two hundred Cubans. At a designated point Colonel Wood was to file to the right, forming line on the right of the road which he was to travel; which would cause his right flank to connect with the left flank of the regular cavalry, which was to march on the other road; the distance between the two roads at the point of formation being about seven hundred or eight hundred yards. Unfortunately, neither General Castillo nor the dynamite gun reached us at all, and we were compelled to make the fight without them.[1] We were up before daylight, and by sun-up both columns were on the march; but I cannot do better in describing what occurred than to incorporate here my official report of this affair, which I take

[1] I was very much disappointed at the failure of my dynamite gun to reach me, as my plans of the engagement contemplated its aid; but I desire specially to exonerate Sergt. Hallet A. Borrowe from any neglect in this matter. The day previous, before leaving Daiquiri, I successfully devoted myself to procuring horses for this gun, and then, with the aid of Sergeant Borrowe and Major Jacobs, harnesses of various kinds were procured, which by the industry and ingenuity of Sergeant Borrowe were adjusted to haul the gun. Sergeant Borrowe then started with commendable promptitude on his march of eleven miles to Siboney; but before reaching that place he was stopped at dark on the 23d by an infantry commander, and was compelled to go into camp, and was not permitted to pass the infantry lines until the next morning, after the sounds of the battle reached that point. I desire to say here that Sergeant Borrowe's management of this gun, and conduct in all respects, were worthy of high commendation.

verbatim from the "Army and Navy Journal" of July 23d, its publication having been authorized or directed by General Shafter.

The report is as follows:

CAMP, SIX MILES EAST OF SANTIAGO DE CUBA,
June 26, 1898.
ADJUTANT–GENERAL 5TH ARMY CORPS,
S.S. Segurança:

SIR: I have the honor to report that, in obedience to instructions from the Major-General commanding, given to me in person on June 23d, I proceeded to Siboney (Juraguacito). The enemy had evacuated the place at daylight that morning, taking a course toward Sevilla. A body of about 100 Cubans had followed, and engaged the enemy's rear-guard. About 9 of them were wounded.

I rode out to the front, and found the enemy had halted and established themselves at a point about three miles from Siboney. At night the Cubans returned to the vicinity of the town.

At 8 o'clock on that evening (the 23d) General Young reached Siboney with eight troops of Colonel Wood's Regiment, A, B, D, E, F, G, K, and L, — five hundred strong; Troops A, B, G, and K, of the 1st Cavalry, — in all, two hundred and forty-four; and Troops A, B, E, and I, of the 10th Cavalry, — in all, two hundred and twenty men: making the total force nine hundred and sixty-four men, which included nearly all of my command which had disembarked. These troops had marched from Daiquiri, eleven miles. With the assistance of General Castillo, a rough map

of the country was prepared and the position of the
enemy fully explained, and I determined to make an
attack.

At daylight on the 24th, Wood's Regiment was sent
by General Young, accompanied by two of his staff
officers, Lieuts. Tyree R. Rivers and W. R. Smedberg, jr., to approach the enemy on the left-hand, or
more westerly, road, while General Young, myself,
and the troops of the 1st and 10th Cavalry, with three
Hotchkiss mountain guns, approached the enemy on
the regular Sevilla road. We expected also to take
the dynamite gun with us, but unfortunately it did
not reach Siboney.

General Young and myself examined the position
of the enemy ; the lines were deployed, and I directed
him to open fire with the Hotchkiss guns. The enemy
replied, and the firing immediately became general.
Colonel Wood had deployed his regiment, his right
nearly reaching the left of the Regulars. For an hour
the fight was very warm, the enemy being very lavish
in the expenditure of ammunition, most of their firing
being by volleys.

Finally the enemy gave way and retreated rapidly,
our line keeping well closed upon them. Our men
being physically exhausted by both their exertions
and the great heat, were incapable of maintaining the
pursuit.

I cannot speak too highly of the gallant and excellent conduct of the officers and men throughout the
command. General Young deserves special commendation for his cool, deliberate, and skilful management.

I also specially noticed his Acting Adjutant-General,
Lieut. A. L. Mills, who, under General Young's direc-

tion, was at various parts of the line, acting with energy and cool courage.

The imperative necessity of disembarking with promptitude had impelled me to leave most of my staff to hasten this important matter, and, unfortunately, I had with me only Major Beach and Mr. Mestre, a Cuban Volunteer Aid, — both of whom, during the engagement, most creditably and bravely performed their duties. I am especially indebted to Maj. W. D. Beach for his cool and good judgment.

Colonel Wood's Regiment was on the extreme left of the line, and too far distant for me to be a personal witness of the individual conduct of his officers and men ; but the magnificent and brave work done by the regiment, under the lead of Colonel Wood, testifies to his courage and skill. The energy and determination of this officer had been marked from the moment he reported to me at Tampa, Fla. ; and I have abundant evidence of his brave and good conduct on the field, and I recommend him for consideration of the Government.

I must rely upon his report to do justice to his officers and men, but I desire personally to add that all that I have said regarding Colonel Wood applies equally to Lieutenant-Colonel Roosevelt.

I was immediately with the troops of the 1st and 10th Regular Cavalry, dismounted, and personally noticed their brave and good conduct, which will be especially mentioned by General Young.

I personally noticed the good conduct of Capt. W. H. Beck, Robert P. P. Wainwright, and Jacob G. Galbraith, Maj. James M. Bell, Capt. Thomas T. Knox, and Lieut. George L. Byram. The last three were wounded.

Major Bell, as he lay on the ground with a broken leg, said, "I only regret I can't go on with you farther."

Captain Knox, though severely wounded, continued as long as possible to exercise command, and insisted to me that he was not much hurt; and Lieutenant Byram also made light of his wound to me, and continued upon the line until he fainted. I recommend these officers for favorable consideration of the Government.[1]

I cannot state positively as to the size of the Spanish force which we engaged, or the extent of their casualties, further than that the force was much greater than ours, and that the information I had would indicate that their killed and wounded very far exceeded the

[1] At the Front, on the Rio Guamo, Second Crossing, June 28, 4 P.M., by Despatch Boat *Dauntless* to Port Antonio, June 29. — Preparations for a general advance of the American troops on Santiago are being pushed steadily forward, and troops of all branches of the service are being hurried to the front. General Kent's Division, consisting of the brigades of General Hawkins, Colonel Pearson, and Colonel Worth, has joined General Lawton's Division, and, with the Cavalry Division of General Wheeler and four batteries of light artillery, will now be strung out in the rear of General Lawton's Division.

The military telegraph line has been completed as far as General Wheeler's headquarters, thus placing the front in direct communication with General Shafter, who still maintains his headquarters on board the *Segurança*, where he can keep in close touch with Rear-Admiral Sampson. It is probable, however, that he will establish his headquarters at Juragua to-morrow or Thursday.

It is reported here to-night, on apparently good authority, that the water supply of Santiago de Cuba has been cut off.

General Wheeler to-day forwarded his official report of the encounter between the Spaniards and Colonel Young's and Colonel Wood's commands. The officers are highly complimented for their dash and courage. The general says there is absolutely no warrant for the statement that our troops were ambuscaded. He says the attack was deliberately planned from knowledge in his possession the night before. — *The New York " Press," Thursday, June 30, 1898.*

losses which our troops sustained; but our estimates on these points can be verified only when we have access to the reports of the Spanish commanders.

The engagement inspirited our troops and must have had a bad effect upon the spirits of the Spanish soldiers. It also gave our army a beautiful and well-watered country, in which we have established our encampments. It has also given us a full view of Santiago and the surrounding country, and enabled us to reconnoiter close up to the fortifications of that place.

The strength of my command, and the casualties in the engagement, were as follows:

ORGANIZATIONS.	STRENGTH.	KILLED.	WOUNDED.
1st U.S. Volunteer Cavalry . .	500	8	34
1st Regular Cavalry	244	7	8
10th Regular Cavalry	220	1	10
TOTALS	964	16	52

Very respectfully,

Jos. Wheeler,

Maj.-Gen. U.S. Vols., Commanding.

List of the Killed in the Engagement at Las Guasimas,
June 24, 1898.

NAMES.	TROOP.	ORGANIZATIONS.
Private JESSE K. STARK	A	1st Regular Cavalry.
Private OTTO KRUPP	B	" "
Corp. ALEXANDER SLEMERE	K	" "
Private EMEL BJORK	K	" "
Private GUSTAVE KOLBE	K	" "
Private PETER H. DIX	K	" "
Private JACK BERLIN	K	" "
Corp. WM. L. WHITE	E	10th Regular Cavalry.
Capt. ALLYN K. CAPRON	. .	1st U.S. Vol. Cavalry.
Private EDWARD LEGGETT	A	" "
Corp. GEO. H. DOUGHERTY	A	" "
Private WM. T. IRVINE	F	" "
Sergt. MARVIN RUSSELL	G	" "
Private HARRY HEFFNER	G	" "
Sergt. HAMILTON FISH, JR.	L	" "
Private TILDON DAWSON	L	" "

CHAPTER III

THE official report of Brigadier-General
S. B. M. Young, of the same battle, is as
follows:

HEADQUARTERS 2D CAVALRY BRIGADE, U.S.A.
CAMP NEAR SANTIAGO DE CUBA, June 29, 1898.

ADJUTANT-GENERAL CAVALRY DIVISION:

SIR: By direction of the major-general commanding the Cavalry Division, I have the honor to submit
the following report of the engagement of a part of
this brigade with the enemy at Guasimas, Cuba, on the
24th inst., accompanied by detailed reports from the
regimental and other commanders engaged, and a list
of the killed and wounded.

After debarking at Daiquiri on the afternoon of the
23d inst., I received verbal orders from Major-General
Wheeler, the division commander, to move out with
three days' rations in haversacks to a good camping-
place between Juraguacito and Siboney, on the road
leading to Santiago de Cuba.

In obedience thereto, at 4.30 P.M. I moved from my bivouac near the landing, with brigade headquarters, the 1st Volunteer Cavalry (Wood's), one squadron of the 1st U.S. Cavalry (Bell's), one squadron of the 10th U.S. Cavalry (Norvell's), and the Hotchkiss Mountain Gun Battery (4 guns — Capt. Watson, 10th Cavalry, temporarily commanding), all dismounted. The remainder of the brigade was ordered to follow early the following morning on receiving its rations.

I arrived at Siboney with the head of the column at about 7 P.M., where I bivouacked for the night with the 1st Volunteer Cavalry ; the two squadrons of the 1st and 10th U.S. Cavalry and the battery being delayed by the crowded condition of the trail and the difficulty of following through the jungle after night.

I reported to General Wheeler, and from him learned of an engagement between Cubans and Spaniards in that vicinity during the day, resulting in the repulse of the former with some loss. Later I met General Castillo, the commander of the Cuban forces, who gave me a full description of the topography of the country, and much information regarding the Spanish troops, their manner of fighting, and so forth. General Castillo expressed the belief that the Spaniards, though successfully resisting his attack, would fall back to Santiago during the night ; but he also stated that he had received information that they were being reinforced.

Deeming it essential that positive information should be obtained as to the position and movements of the enemy in our front, I asked and obtained authority to make a reconnaissance in force for this purpose,

General Castillo having promised to assist and co-operate with me with a force of 800 effective Cubans.

Leading from Siboney there are two roads, or, more properly, trails, one to the eastward, the other to the westward of the little town, which unite about one mile before reaching Sevilla and a little in advance of the scene of the Cuban-Spanish engagement. The trails are at no point more than one and one-half miles apart. I concluded to move by the two trails, General Castillo having informed me his outposts covered both. I consequently directed Colonel Wood to move with his regiment by the western route, cautioning him to keep a careful lookout, and to attack any Spaniards he might encounter; connecting in the latter event, by his right flank, with the other column, while trying to gain the enemy's right flank. Col. Wood marched about six A. M., the 24th inst., and I sent my personal aids, 1st Lt. F. R. Rivers, 3d Cav., and 2d Lt. W. R. Smedberg, 4th Cav., to accompany his column. The other, the right column, marched at 5.45 A. M. I moved with it, accompanied by Capt. A. L. Mills, Ass't Adj't-General. I proposed to attack the enemy in front, and on his left if I found him in position.

At 7.30 A. M., the right column being massed in an open glade, Captain Mills with a patrol of two men advanced and discovered the enemy located, as described by General Castillo, in a locality called Guasimas, from trees of that name in the vicinity.

After having carefully examined the enemy's position, I prepared to develop his strength. Canteens were ordered filled; the Hotchkiss Battery was placed in position in concealment at about 900 yards, and Bell's Squadron was deployed, and Norvell's in support.

On discovering the enemy, I had sent a Cuban guide to warn Colonel Wood ; and knowing that his column had a more difficult route, and would require a longer time to reach the position, I delayed the attack some time in order that the development on both flanks should begin simultaneously. During this delay General Wheeler arrived, and was informed of my dispositions, plan of attack, and intentions. After examination of the position by him, and his approval of my action, I ordered the attack ; and it was executed in a manner winning the admiration of the Division Commander, and all present who witnessed it. The Spanish forces occupied a range of high hills in the form of obtuse angles, with the salient towards Siboney, and with an advance party on the trail on which I had been moving. The attack of both wings was simultaneous ; and the junction of the two lines occurred near the apex of the angle on the ridge, which had been fortified with stone breastworks flanked by block-houses. The Spanish were driven from their position and fled precipitately toward Santiago. The attacking force numbered 950 men ; while that of the enemy, at first estimated at 2,000, has since been learned from Spanish sources to have been 2,500. The Cuban military authorities claim the Spanish strength was 4,000. It has also been reported that Lieutenant-General Linares, commanding the Spanish forces in Eastern Cuba, and two other general officers were present, and witnessed the action. The fire of the enemy was almost entirely by volleys, executed with the precision of parade. For an account of the operations of the left column, attention is invited to the enclosed report of Col. Wood, marked "A." The ground over which the right column advanced was a mass of jungle growth, with wire fences not to be seen until encountered, and precipitous heights as the ridge was approached. It was impossible for the troops to keep touch along the front, and they could only judge the enemy from the sound and direction of his fire. However, had it not been for this dense jungle, the attack would not have been made against an overwhelming force in such a position. Headway was so difficult that advance and support became merged, and moved forward under a continuous volley-firing supplemented by that of two rapid-firing guns. Return firing, by my force, was only made as here and there a small clear spot gave a sight of the enemy. The fire discipline of these particular troops was almost perfect. The ammunition expended by the two squadrons, engaged in an incessant advance for one hour and fifteen minutes, averaged less than ten rounds per man. The fine quality of these troops is also shown by the fact that there was not a single straggler; and in not one instance was an attempt made by any soldier to fall out in the advance, to assist the wounded or carry back the dead. The fighting on the left flank was equally creditable; and was remarkable, and I believe unprecedented, in volunteer troops so quickly raised, armed, and equipped.

Our total losses were 1 officer and 15 men killed; 6 officers and 46 men wounded. Forty-two dead Spanish soldiers were found, the bodies of nearly all of whom had been thrown into the jungle for concealment. Spanish newspapers of Santiago the day after the battle gave their loss as 77 killed. It is known that many wounded were carried into the city. Every possible attention was given to the wounded, and the

medical officers were unremitting in their efforts to
alleviate their sufferings. Circumstances necessarily
limited their appliances to the First Aid order. The
wounded were carried in improvised litters to Siboney,
and the dead were carefully buried on the battlefield,
a proper record of their burial being kept. Finding,
when the ridge was carried, that many of my men had
become exhausted by the excessive heat and exertion,
I ordered a halt, and occupation of the captured position. Had I had at hand at the time of the assault a
force of mounted cavalry, the fruits of our victory
would have been more apparent. General Castillo
did not appear on the field, nor did any of his troops
come to the front until the firing had ceased. No other
troops than those mentioned were engaged in the action.
Three troops of the 9th U.S. Cavalry arrived on the
left after the firing had stopped, and were posted as
pickets until relieved by General Chaffee's Brigade of
General Lawton's Division, which then took the advance.
The action of all officers and men, so far as my personal observation extended, was superb; and I can
only at this time mention the names of those whose
conduct was personally observed by me as being
highly conspicuous in gallantry and daring, and evi-
dencing a firm intention to do everything within the
power and endurance of humanity and the scope of
duty. Capt. Knox, after being shot through the
abdomen, and seeing his Lieutenant and 1st Sergeant
wounded, gave necessary orders to his troop, and refused to allow a man in the firing-line to assist him to
the rear. Lieutenant Byram, after having his scalp-
wound dressed, and knowing his Captain (Knox) to
be wounded, assumed command of his troop, but fell

fainting while pushing to the front. Capt. Mills, the
only member of my staff present with me on this part
of the field, was most conspicuous for his daring and
unflagging energy in his effort to keep troops in touch
on the line, and in keeping me informed of the progress
made in advancing through the jungle.

In connection with the conduct of the officers, attention is called to Col. Wood's report*on the conduct of
Captain Capron, Major Brodie, Captain McClintock,
Lieutenant Thomas, Lieut.-Colonel Roosevelt, Captain
McCormick (7th U.S. Cavalry), and my personal
Aids, Lieutenants T. R. Rivers and Smedberg. I
cannot speak too highly of the efficient manner in
which Colonel Wood handled his regiment, and of his
magnificent behavior on the field. The conduct of
Lieut.-Col. Roosevelt, as reported to me by my Aids,
deserves my highest co mmendation. Both Col. Wood
and Lieut.-Col. Roosevelt disdained to take advantage
of shelter or cover from the enemy's fire while any
of their men remained exposed to it; — an error of
judgment, but happily on the heroic side. I beg leave
to repeat that the behavior of all men of the regular
and volunteer forces engaged in this action was simply superb, and I feel highly honored in the command
of such troops. I desire to express my admiration of
the fine soldierly qualities, and conduct on the march
and after meeting the enemy, of Major Norvell, 10th
Cavalry, and Major Bell, 1st Cavalry, commanding
squadrons; their quick and rapid execution of orders
and instructions was admirable and gratifying. Major
Bell received a serious wound in the early part of the
engagement, and was succeeded in the command of his
squadron by Captain Wainwright, whose management

of the right wing of the advance firing-line was all that
I could desire or hope for, and more than I could under
such opposing conditions confidently expect.   Captains
Beck and Galbraith and Lieutenants Wright and Fleming also deserve equal praise for the manner in which
they manœuvered and controlled their troops in attacking the precipitous heights before them.   Captain
Ayres' performance of the duties assigned to his troop
was highly commendable, as was also Captain Watson's
fine work with his battery.   Attention is invited to the
enclosed reports of troop commanders regarding the
conduct of their subordinates and their men.   Ass't
Surgeon Fuller and Acting Ass't Surgeon Delgardo,
also Ass't Surgeon J. R. Church, 1st Vol. Cavalry,
deserve special mention for their gallant action in personally carrying and assisting in carrying wounded
men from the field under heavy fire.

The chief results following from this action with the
Spaniards are : A test of the valor of the opposing
forces ; the spirit of superiority I believe it has fixed
in our own ; the opening of the gates of Santiago de
Cuba ; and the gaining of a beautiful camping-ground
for our army on the heights overlooking that city,
which can now easily be taken at our leisure.

Very respectfully,

S. B. M. YOUNG,
Brigadier-General U.S. Vols.

[*Endorsement:*]
Respectfully forwarded. Calling special attention to commendation of Capt. Knox, Capt. Miller, Lt. Byram, Capt. Capron, Major Brodie, Capt. McClintock, Lt. Thomas, Lt.-Col. Roosevelt, Capt. McCormick [7th Cav'y], Lt. T. R. Rivers, Lt. Smedberg, Capt. Wainwright, Capt. Beck, Capt. Galbraith, Lt. Wright, Lt. Fleming, Capt. Ayers, Capt. Watson, Ass't Surg. Fuller, Surg. Delgardo, Surg. J. R. Church. I personally observed the conduct of many of these officers, and join heartily in General Young's commendation of them.

JOS. WHEELER,
Major-Gen'l U.S. Vols., Commanding.

Colonel Leonard Wood made the following report of the part taken by the 1st U.S. Volunteer Cavalry (Rough Riders) in this battle:

HEADQUARTERS 1ST U.S. VOL. CAVALRY,
IN CAMP AT GUASIMAS, CUBA, June 25, 1898.
BRIG.-GENERAL YOUNG,
Comm'd'g 2d Brigade, Cavalry Division:
SIR : I have the honor to submit the following report of the action at Guasimas, about nine (9) miles from Santiago, on the morning of June 24, 1898.

I left camp at the sea-coast at 5.40, proceeding by trail in the direction of the town of Caverita. On reaching the top of the mesa, an advance guard was thrown out, and every precaution taken against surprise, as we had positive information that the enemy was ahead of us in force. The character of the country was such that reconnoitering was extremely difficult, as the dense growth of underbrush rendered the rapid movement of flanking parties practically impossible. At 7.10 our advanced point discovered what they believed to be signs of the immediate presence of the enemy. The command was halted and the troops deployed to the right and left, in open skirmish order, and the command ordered to advance carefully. The firing began almost immediately, and the extent of firing on each flank indicated that we had encountered a very heavy force. Two additional troops were deployed on the right and left, thus leaving only three (3) troops in reserve. It was soon apparent that their lines were overlapping us on both flanks. Two (2) other troops were rapidly deployed, one on the right and one on the left, which gave our line a length about equal to their own. The firing about this time was exceedingly heavy, much of it at very short range, but on account of the heavy undergrowth comparatively few men were injured at this time. It was about this time that Capt. Capron was mortally wounded. The firing on his immediate front was terrific.

The remaining troop was sent to the front, and the order given to advance very slowly. Men and officers behaved splendidly, and advanced slowly, forcing back the enemy on the right flank. We captured a small block-house and drove the enemy out of a very strong position in the rocks. We were now able to distinguish their line, which had taken a new position about 800 or 1,000 yards in length and about 300 yards in front of us. The firing was exceedingly heavy here again, and it was here that we had a good many men wounded and several officers. Our men continued to advance in very good order, and steadily forced the Spanish line back. We now began to get a heavy fire from a ridge on our right, which enfiladed our line (this ridge was the position which was being attacked by two squadrons of the regular cavalry), and was held in very strong force by the Spanish in small rock forts along its entire length, supported by two machine-guns. Having cleared our right flank, we were able to pay some attention to the Spanish on the above-mentioned ridge, and centered upon it the fire of two troops. This fire, with the attacking force on the other side, soon completed the evacuation of this end of the ridge, and the regular assault completed the evacuation along the entire length of the ridge. Of the Spaniards who retreated from the ridge some few fell into line, but apparently remained there only a moment when large masses of them were seen to retreat rapidly, and we were able to distinguish parties carrying litters of wounded men. At this time my detached troops had moved out to the left to take the right end of the Spanish line in flank. This was successfully accomplished; and as soon as this troop gained its position, "Cease firing and advance" was ordered. Our men advanced within 300 yards of the enemy, when we again opened heavy fire. The Spanish broke under this fire and retreated rapidly. We advanced to the last position held by them and halted, having established before this a connection on the right with the regular troops, who had successfully carried the ridge before mentioned. This left us in complete possession of the entire Spanish position. Our troops were too much exhausted and overcome with heat and hard work of the 2 preceding days to continue the pursuit. Had we had many mounted men or even fresh foot troops I think we could have captured a large portion of their forces, as they seemed completely disheartened and dispirited. About 30 minutes after the firing had ceased, three troops of the 9th U.S. Cavalry under Captain Dimmock reported to me and I advanced them, forming a heavy line of outposts covering our entire front at a distance of about 800 yds. from our line.

About two hours after the fight was over, a number of Cubans came up and made a short reconnaissance as far as Cevitas, and reported that the Spanish had apparently fled into Santiago, as they found no evidence of them. They reported a quantity of blood along the trail and a quantity of abandoned equipments, and every evidence of a complete rout from the point of their break in our front to above-named town (Cevitas).

In regard to the conduct of the officers and men, I can only say that one and all of them behaved splendidly. Captain Capron died shortly after the termination of the fight. I cannot say enough in commendation of the gallant conduct of this officer. His troop was in advance and met the enemy in very heavy force, and resisted them and drove them back, and it was in the performance of this duty that the captain was mortally wounded. The service he performed prior to his death, and the work of his troop subsequently to it, were of the very greatest value in contributing to the success of this engagement. Captain Capron's loss is an irreparable one to this regiment.

Major Brodie was shot through the arm while on the firing-line. Captain McClintock had both bones of his leg broken, also on the firing-line. Lieut. Thomas, Captain Capron's 1st Lieutenant, was shot shortly after the fall of Capt. Capron. We found no wounded Spaniards, but all along the line we found their abandoned equipments; and there is every evidence of a large number of wounded. To the best of my knowledge we discovered in the neighborhood of 40 dead Spaniards. There may be some mistake in the figures owing to the jungle character of the country, and it is probable that a careful search will reveal many more. Mr. Marshall, of the New York "Journal," was shot through the spine while on the firing-line witnessing the action. His conduct was extremely courageous.

The 1st Squadron was under the command of Lieutenant-Colonel Theodore Roosevelt, and the 2d under Major Alex. O. Brodie : both of these officers deserve great credit for the intelligence and courage with which they handled their men. In this particular it is only fair to say that this remark would apply to all officers.

I desire to express my appreciation of the gallant and effective services of Capt. McCormick, 7th Cav., attached to my regiment for any duty to which I might assign him ; also of Capt. Rivers and Lieut. Smedberg of your staff, whose services were of the greatest value and performed under heavy fire.

Very respectfully,
Your obedient servant,

LEONARD WOOD,
Comdg 1st U.S. Vol. Cav., of 2d Brig. Cav. Div.

P.S. — Richard Harding Davis was with Col. Roosevelt during almost the entire action.

[*Endorsement :*]

Respectfully forwarded. Calling special attention to commendation of Captain Capron, Major Brodie, Capt. McClintock, Lieut. Thomas, Lt.-Col. Roosevelt, Capt. McCormick, Lt. Rivers, Lt. Smedberg, Mr. Marshall, and Mr. Richard Harding Davis, in all of which I join.

JOS. WHEELER,
Major-Gen'l U.S. Vols., Comdg.

The "España" of the 25th of June — a paper published in Santiago — has this to say of their affair with the Cubans on the 23d, and the fight of Las Guasimas on the 24th:

"June 24th. The column of General Rubin, under the command of the general-in-chief of the 4th Army Corps (Lieutenant-General Linares), was attacked yesterday afternoon. This morning large forces of the enemy with artillery attacked said column anew. Their attack was made with vigor and they fought without being under cover. They were repulsed with heavy losses which were seen by us."

The New York "Times" of July 1st contains an editorial which states that a Spanish despatch puts the Spanish forces in that battle at four thousand, and their loss at two hundred and sixty-five. The article is as follows:

The more the facts come to light about the fight of last Friday, the more clearly appear the coolness and bravery of the volunteer cavalrymen. General Shafter puts it humorously in saying that "reports from Spanish sources from Santiago say we were beaten, but persisted in fighting, and they were obliged to fall back."

As to the comparative number engaged, we now know exactly what the numbers were. The Spanish report is that four thousand Spaniards were attacked by ten thousand Americans and driven back with a loss of two hundred and sixty-five. The estimate of the American force is a loose Castilian exaggeration, but the statement of the Spanish force is doubtless accurate. On the other hand, General Wheeler reports that we had nine hundred and sixty-four men engaged, almost equally divided between regulars and volunteers, and that the total loss was sixteen killed and fifty-two wounded. It is evident that the volunteers behaved as well as the regulars, although their loss happened to be somewhat heavier. Of the sixteen killed they lost eight, and of the fifty-two wounded, thirty-four. It is really an amazing showing. Of course it will not do to reckon upon a repetition of that which has no precedent. Though not disciplined soldiers, these were picked men, and their performance shows that in extreme cases men of high individual courage, intelligence, and self-reliance, led by men like themselves, may be as efficient a fighting force as an equal number of men who have been drilled to respond to orders with the precision of a machine.

CHAPTER IV

THE SPANISH FORCES ENGAGED — EL CANEY'S DEFENCES — BATTLE OF SAN JUAN — SENIOR IN COMMAND ON THE LINE — THE QUESTION OF FALLING BACK AFTER THE HILLS WERE GAINED

THE next day after the engagement at Las Guasimas, General Miles telegraphed from his office in the War Department as follows:

WASHINGTON, D.C., June 25.

GENERAL SHAFTER,
        Daiquiri, Cuba:

Congratulations on success attained thus far. Regret most deeply to hear of the loss of your heroic men.

MILES,
                Major-General.

General Shafter sent the following despatch:

DAIQUIRI, CUBA, June 26.

MAJOR–GENERAL MILES,
        Commanding Army, Washington:

Thanks for congratulations. Nine hundred and sixty-four men only engaged on our side. But it was very decisive in our favor, and the enemy retreated precipitately. Lack of cavalry only prevented their capture. Reports from Spanish sources from Santiago say we were beaten, but persisted in fighting, and they were obliged to fall back. Deeply regret the loss of so many brave men.

SHAFTER.

The civil governor of this province told me personally that the force which Lieutenant-General Linares had on the 24th was 4,000. Gen. José Toral told me that this was a mistake, and that they had but 2,000; he afterwards said a little less than 2,000 ; and he also said that their losses were about 250. When I mentioned the figure 265, he said, Yes, but that included the losses of the two preceding days. Lieutenant-General Linares told me that the force engaged on the twenty-fourth was 1,400; and General Escario told me that the losses that day were about 200.

The moment General Lawton and the commander of his leading brigade, General Chaffee, heard the noise of my engagement, they promptly struck camp and marched to the front; but as the enemy broke and was in full retreat in a little more than an hour, they did not reach me until some time after the action was over.

That evening I received letters from General Shafter expressing his pleasure at the good news of the fight, and telling me that he would send me reinforcements if needed; and at dark I received another letter from him reiterating offers of reinforcements, and saying : " Your news is excellent." I also that evening received orders to take command of all the troops on shore, and to put them in camp as they came up, in favorable positions for defence as well as convenience; but he instructed me very positively not to move forward so as to become engaged with the enemy, as he did not wish any further engagement to take place until we could advance with the entire force. I therefore devoted myself to reconnoitering the country, and selected camps with convenient water for the various divisions as they arrived. I also used large forces in repairing the road, so that we got it in very fair condition.

On the 26th, I again received instructions not to advance. On the same day, General Shafter sent me this telegram from the President, thanking the troops for their victory at Las Guasimas:

The President directs me to send his thanks to you and your army for the gallant action of yesterday, which I gladly do.

R. A. ALGER,
Secretary of War.

I reconnoitered close up to El Caney, and learned that there were not more than five hundred Spaniards at that place. I described the defences to General Shafter, and urged that I be permitted to attack the place with a large force of artillery; my argument being that the fire from a number of guns upon the forces at El

Caney would soon make their position untenable; and that a division of infantry or dismounted cavalry being placed between El Caney and Santiago, would catch the Spaniards as they attempted to retreat. General Shafter admitted the feasibility of this plan, but after two interviews and some correspondence informed me that he had determined to entrust this work to General Lawton. This officer was instructed to make the attack on El Caney at daylight on July 1st, while the Cavalry Division, and the Infantry Division under Brigadier-General Kent, were ordered forward; General Shafter's intention being for Lawton to take El Caney, which he thought could be accomplished in half an hour or an hour, and then for him to move toward Santiago and support the attack of my own and Kent's Divisions upon the main Spanish army. Unfortunately, only a few guns were opened upon the forces at Caney, and it was not until three o'clock that the place was taken. In the meantime, the Cavalry Division and Kent's Division had crossed the San Juan River, and formed in line of battle, — the left of the cavalry resting on the main Santiago road, and the right of Kent's Division joining the cavalry's left.

There were two hills in our front: one called San Juan Hill, or San Juan House, from the fine farmhouse on its summit, which was directly in front of the cavalry line of battle, but did not extend to the line occupied by Kent's Division.

Upon this hill a body of the enemy were favorably positioned, but not strongly fortified; while several hundred yards nearer Santiago the main Spanish forces were intrenched along the crest of the other hill, called Fort San Juan.

A large balloon was elevated not far above the main road, attached by a rope to the reel in its wagon; and while forming our troops, the enemy concentrated a warm fire of both artillery and infantry upon our whole line, especially concentrating the fire upon the main road, which was indicated to them by the balloon.

I had been directed by Colonel McClernand, General Shafter's adjutant-general, to give directions to General Kent in these movements; and I informed him that General Shafter desired the whole command to move forward. My former instructions and the general custom of the service made it proper that I should exercise this control over the whole line, which was fully appreciated by General Kent. I explained to him in person the orders, and this gallant officer moved his division forward in magnificent order. My staff officers devoted themselves to the Cavalry Division, which, in forming that morning, had been temporarily under the control of Gen. S. S. Sumner; the two brigades being commanded, the first by Lieut.-Col. Henry Carroll, and the second by Col. Leonard Wood, of the 1st Volunteer Cavalry. I also gave directions to General Sumner, and, through my staff officers, to Colonel Carroll and Colonel Wood.

After the line was formed it was quite evident that the enemy had our range very accurately established,[1] and that it would not increase our casualties to charge; but would shorten the time spent by our troops subject to galling fire.

The Cavalry Division charged up San Juan Hill in the face of a heavy fire, and descended to the plain below; where the left of the line joined the right of Kent's Division. The plain was then rapidly crossed by the entire force, also under heavy fire. The hill of Fort San Juan was charged, and the battle of July 1st was won.

The enemy started in well, and fought with great vigor until they saw the determination of our men. The main Spanish line retreated from their works soon after our troops reached the foot of San Juan Hill; but squads of skirmishers had selected positions where they were partly screened, and kept up their fire upon us; but when the crest was reached, the whole Spanish force was in retreat down the western slope of the ridge, under a warm fire from our entire line.

---

[1] That the assault on Santiago had begun, was known by the receipt in Washington, at 9 o'clock in the morning, of the following:

CAMP AT SEVILLA, CUBA, July 1.
SECRETARY OF WAR, Washington:

Action now going on, but firing light and desultory. Begun on right, near Caney, Lawton's Division. He will move on northeast part of town of Santiago. Will keep you continually advised of progress.

SHAFTER, *Major-General Commanding.*

It is hard to conceive of any more gallant conduct than was displayed by these troops in this
engagement. They had waded the San Juan
River, formed line under fire, advanced upon the
enemy with nothing to shelter them from a deadly
fire, charged over one hill and to the crest of
another, and taken works which the Spaniards
felt confident were impregnable. They were then
exhausted. They numbered not more than six
thousand men that morning: nearly a thousand
had been killed or wounded; they had been
compelled to throw down everything but their
guns and ammunition in their advance, and were
able to procure little food except rice and other
articles which the Spaniards had left at the
trenches. Yet these gallant men were uncom-
plaining. Many of them had marched all the
preceding night; they had been in line of battle
fighting the entire day; and yet they cheerfully
fell to work erecting breastworks, — they improvised litters to carry their numerous wounded to
the rear, and made large details to perform the
melancholy duty of burying their dead. These
details, and the depletion of the ranks from absolute exhaustion, so reduced this force that it is
doubtful if there were more than three thousand
men on the ridge at midnight; but still they
worked, and by daylight had constructed breastworks sufficiently strong to enable them successfully to repulse an attack. All this was done
under fire from the enemy, who were but a few

hundred yards off. It was not surprising that the bravest of the brave men in their exhausted condition were apprehensive. They knew they had but some three thousand men on the ridge; they knew that a force of some seven thousand were in line of battle before them; and appeals of the strongest character were made for the army to withdraw for fear an attack would drive them in a rout from their position. I discountenanced this in every way possible. I reminded them that we had met the enemy at Las Guasimas on the 24th, — attacked and defeated them, driving them before us; and that here again we had successfully charged and taken their breastworks, driving them from a very strong position. I said: "These facts will convince the Spaniards that we will continue our attack upon their next line; and with that expectation it is unreasonable and not to be expected that they will return and attack us in the strong position we now hold." I also sent members of my staff along the line, reassuring officers and men in this manner.

I felt quite convinced that the numerous and powerful appeals which had been made to me, in favor of withdrawing the army from San Juan ridge to some point in the rear, were without doubt being made to General Shafter with equal if not greater force; and a little later I received information that my apprehensions in this regard were correct, and that General Shafter was assured that unless the army withdrew there was

great danger of its being driven from the ridge
in a disgraceful rout. I therefore wrote to General Shafter telling him of these appeals to me,
and also informing him that I was discountenancing these apprehensions as far as it was in my
power. I also told him, in my letter,[1] that to fall
back from the position gained would result in a
great loss of prestige.

That portion of the main road extending from
my headquarters — situated under the crest of
the hill some 150 yards behind the firing-line,
to those occupied by General Shafter — some five
miles in the rear, was one of the worst pieces of
highway it has ever been my lot to encounter.
Large rocks and stones were there in abundance,
which made it very difficult for the wagons
conveying supplies from the ships to make even
fair progress; and it was especially hard for the
ambulance-wagons, which were constantly employed conveying the wounded from the front
back to the Division Hospital. Especially after
the various heavy rains, this road was practically
impassable, and traveling its length during the
active prosecution of hostilities was by no means
without danger. This for a two-fold reason :
First, because the bullets from the Spanish
Mausers, which the Spaniards had shot too high
to injure the men in our trenches, and which
passed harmlessly over their heads, fell with their
first force spent, into this road below; and again,

[1] For this letter, see Part II., p. 274.

there were quite a number of sharp-shooters hidden in the branches of the trees lining this road, whose object it was to shoot down, from their place of refuge, any solitary officer or man who had the misfortune to travel unattended. I was informed that some of them had sewn on their clothing small leaves and branches of trees so as to lessen their chances of detection.

It was somewhat amusing and yet very pitiful to witness the abject fear and trepidation of the prisoners captured by us. They were marched to General Shafter's headquarters, promptly disarmed, and anything with which they could inflict injury taken from them. They gazed about them with staring eyes, watching closely every movement of their guards, and whenever a body of these latter entered and were drawn into line, they confidently thought their time had come, and that they were to be shot down in a body.

At such times they would alternately shriek for mercy and endeavor to pacify their captors by shouting " Viva los Americanos! " Unmistakable, therefore, were their expressions of surprise and delight, and frantic their gesticulations when they were made to lie down on the grass, were spoken to kindly by the Americans' interpreters, and were given a more substantial meal than they had probably had since leaving their native land.

CHAPTER V

A T midnight of the first, General Bates
reached me and reported his brigade en
route. At half-past two, the leading regiment
reached the foot of the ridge; and at daylight
on July 2d, I had it placed upon the ridge to
the left of our line.

General Lawton arrived during the morning of July 2d, and the leading brigade of his
division was placed in line about noon, and was
deployed upon the right of the cavalry. Before
daylight, I had placed the artillery under Major
Dillenback in position on the ridge to open fire
in conjunction with the infantry when day
dawned. This was done, but the artillery found
themselves subjected to a very warm infantry
fire from the Spanish lines, and finally withdrew
to a position which they said was more favor-

able. From early in the morning of July 2d, a tolerably brisk and almost continuous fire was kept up by the two armies ; but as our line was favorably located and fairly protected by breast-works, the casualties on our side were not severe. I directed the officers to reassure the men; and after Bates and Lawton were placed on the line, I directed that the men be told that they were in twice as strong a position and twice as strong in numbers as they were the preceding day. I did not intend speaking of this matter at all; but it appears that the New York newspapers of July 4th made mention of this, and it also appears that General Shafter's telegram which reached Washington July 3d stated that he might find it necessary to fall back to a stronger position while awaiting the arrival of reinforcements. It seems that this part of General Shafter's despatch was not made public at the time, but later in the day was given out by the Secretary of War. I copy the following statement upon this question from the second page, fourth column, of the New York " Sun " of July 4th :

The despatches received here to-day from Major-General Shafter show that he is holding his own at Santiago. That is all that can be said for the American army at this time, and the conditions are not likely to change until the army has been reinforced. There has been no reverse to the American ,arms, — in fact, General Shafter has had a series of successes; and while it is true that some of his troops may be obliged to fall back to better positions, the wait will not be long, and Santiago will be in possession of the United States forces within a very short time. In the expressive words of Major-General Miles to the "Sun" reporter: "General Shafter has done well, but the situation has developed conditions which prevent us from taking the city."

The failure to make public the full text of General Shafter's telegram of this morning has caused some thoughtless criticism. Secretary Alger frankly said, in explanation of giving out an expurgated copy of the message, that it would not be policy to make public all it contained, as General Shafter included mention of his plans. It is known that General Shafter said in the despatch, that he might find it necessary to fall back to a stronger position while awaiting the arrival of reinforcements, and that he also reported his illness.

Immediately after these events I made an official report to General Shafter, which is as follows:

HEADQUARTERS CAVALRY DIVISION,
BEFORE SANTIAGO, CUBA, July 7, 1898.

ADJUTANT-GENERAL 5TH ARMY CORPS:

SIR: After the engagement of June 24th I pushed forward my command through Sevilla into the valley, Lawton's and Kent's commands occupying the hills in the vicinity of that place. After two days' rest Lawton was ordered forward, and on the night of the 30th instructions were given by Major-General Shafter to this officer to attack Caney while the Cavalry Division and Kent's Division were ordered to move forward on the regular Santiago road. The movement commenced on the morning of July 1st. The Cavalry Division advanced, and formed its line with its left near the Santiago road; while Kent's Division formed its line with the right joining the left of the Cavalry Division.

Colonel McClernand, of General Shafter's staff, directed me to give instructions to General Kent, which I complied with in person, at the same time personally directing General Sumner to move forward. The men were all compelled to wade the San Juan River to get into line. This was done under very heavy fire of both infantry and artillery. Our balloon, having been sent up right by the main road, was made a mark of by the enemy. It was evident that we were as much under fire in forming the line as we would be by an advance, and I therefore pressed the command forward from the covering under which it was formed. It merged into open space in full view of the enemy, who occupied breastworks and batteries on the crest of the hill which overlooks Santiago, — officers and men falling at every step. The troops advanced gallantly, soon reached the foot of the hill, and ascended, driving the enemy from their works and occupying them on the crest of the hill. To accomplish this required courage and determination, on the part of the officers and men, of a high order, and the losses were very severe.

Too much credit cannot be given to General Sumner and General Kent, and their gallant Brigade Commanders — Colonel Wood and Colonel Carroll of the Cavalry, Gen. Hamilton S. Hawkins, commanding

1st Brigade, Kent's Division, and Colonel Pearson, commanding 2d Brigade. Colonel Carroll and Major Wessells were both wounded during the charge; but Major Wessells was enabled to return and resume command. General Wyckoff, commanding Kent's 3d Brigade, was killed at 12.10. Lieutenant-Colonel Worth took command, and was wounded at 12.15. Lieutenant-Colonel Liscum then took command, and was wounded at 12.20; and the command then devolved upon Lieutenant-Colonel Ewers, 9th Infantry.

Upon reaching the crest, I ordered breast works to be constructed, and sent to the rear for shovels, picks, spades, and axes. The enemy's retreat from the ridge was precipitate, but our men were so thoroughly exhausted that it was impossible for them to follow. Their shoes were soaked with water by wading the San Juan River, they had become drenched with rain, and when they reached the crest they were absolutely unable to proceed further. Notwithstanding this condition, these exhausted men labored during the night to erect breastworks, and furnished details to bury the dead and carry the wounded back in improvised litters.

I sent word along the line that reinforcements would soon reach us, and that Lawton would join our right, and that General Bates would come up and strengthen our left. After reaching the crest of the ridge General Kent sent the 13th Regulars to assist in strengthening our right. At midnight General Bates reported, and I placed him in a strong position on the left of our line. General Lawton had attempted to join us from Caney; but when very near our lines he was fired upon by the Spaniards and turned back, but joined us next day at noon by a circuitous route.

During all the day, on July 2d, the Cavalry Division, Kent's Division, and Bates' Brigade were engaged with the enemy, being subjected to a severe fire and incurring many casualties; and later in the day Lawton's Division also became engaged.

During the entire engagement my staff performed their duties with courage, judgment, and ability. Special credit is due to Lieut.-Colonel J. H. Dorst, Maj. William D. Beach, Capt. Joseph E. Dickman, and Lieut. M. F. Steele. I desire also to say that Lieuts. James H. Reeves and Joseph Wheeler, junior, Capt. Wm. Astor Chanler, Major E. A. Garlington, Mr. Aurelius E. Mestre, and Corp. John Lundmark also deserve high commendation for courage and good conduct. Major West, my quartermaster, deserves special commendation for his energy and good conduct during the campaign; and Maj. Valery Havard and Mr. Leonard Wilson have also done their full duty. Captain Hardie and 1st Lieut. F. J. Koester, with Troop 6, 3d Cavalry, were detailed with headquarters, and conducted themselves handsomely under fire. The superb courage displayed by the officers and men will be specially mentioned in the reports of subordinate commanders.

Our aggregate strength, and our losses, were as follows:

Strength and Casualties of the Cavalry Division, U.S. Army, in the Battle of San Juan,[1] Cuba.

FIRST BRIGADE.

ORGANIZATIONS.	KILLED.		WOUNDED		AGGRE-GATE.	STRENGTH.	
	Offi-cers.	Men.	Offi-cers.	Men.		Offi-cers.	Men.
3d Cavalry		3	6	47	56	22	420
6th Cavalry		4	4	50	58	16	427
9th Cavalry	2	2	2	17	23	12	207
TOTALS	2	9	12	114	137	50	1,054

SECOND BRIGADE.

Attached			3		3		
1st Cavalry	1	13	1	47	62	21	501
10th Cavalry	2	6	9	66	83	22	450
1st Volunteer Cavalry .	1	12	5	72	90	25	517
TOTALS	4	31	18	185	238	77	1,468
GRAND TOTALS . .	6	40	30	299	375	127	2,522

One man in First United States Volunteer Cavalry reported missing.

[1] Two engagements — San Juan Hill, and Fort San Juan — together formed the Battle of San Juan. San Juan Hill was the name of one hill taken, and Fort San Juan the name of another with a fort on it.

Strength and Casualties, Kent's Infantry Division, U.S. Army, in the Battle of San Juan, Cuba.

ORGANIZATIONS.	PRESENT FOR DUTY, JULY 1.		KILLED.		WOUNDED.		MISS- ING.
	Offi- cers.	Men.	Offi- cers.	Men.	Offi- cers.	Men.	Officers and Men.
Division Commander and Staff	6	3	. .	. .	1	1	. .
1st Brigade, Com- mander and Staff .	5	. .	2	. .	1	. .	. .
2d Brigade, Com- mander and Staff .	. .	. .	. .	. .	. .	. .	. .
3d Brigade, Com- mander and Staff .	. .	. .	1	. .	. .	. .	. .
1st BRIGADE:							
6th U.S. Infantry .	29	435	4	13	7	99	2
16th U.S. Infantry .	23	607	1	13	6	105	3
71st N.Y. Volunteer Infantry . . .	43	915	. .	13	1	59	43
2d BRIGADE:							
2d U.S. Infantry . .	18	601	. .	6	4	48	2
10th U.S. Infantry .	21	450	1	5	5	37	2
21st U.S. Infantry .	25	442	. .	6	1	33	1
3d BRIGADE:							
9th U.S. Infantry .	18	469	1	3	. .	28	. .
13th U.S. Infantry .	24	436	2	17	5	84	1
24th U.S. Infantry .	23	511	2	11	6	69	5
TOTALS . . .	235	4,869	14	87	37	563	59

Officers of the Cavalry Division Killed and Wounded in the Battle of San Juan, Cuba.

OFFICERS KILLED.

NAMES.	ORGANIZATIONS.
Lieut.-Col. JAMES N. HAMILTON	9th Cavalry.
Major ALBERT G. FORSE . . .	1st Cavalry.
Capt. W. O. O'NEIL	1st U.S. Vol. Cavalry.
1st Lieut. WILLIAM N. SHIPP .	10th Cavalry.
1st Lieut. W. N. SMITH . . .	10th Cavalry.
Acting Assistant Surgeon H. W. DANFORTH	9th Cavalry.

OFFICERS WOUNDED.

NAMES.	ORGANIZATIONS.
Lieut.-Col. HENRY CARROLL . .	6th Cav. (Com'd'g First Brigade.)
Major HENRY W. WESSELLS, JR.	3d Cavalry.
Major T. J. WINT	10th Cavalry.
Major and Assistant Surgeon H. LA MOTTE	1st U.S. Vol. Cavalry.
Major W. C. HAYES	1st Ohio Vol. Cavalry.
Capt. J. B. KEER	6th Cavalry.
Capt. GEORGE A. DODD . . .	3d Cavalry.
Capt. GEORGE K. HUNTER . .	3d Cavalry.
Capt. C. W. TAYLOR	9th Cavalry.
Capt. A. P. BLOCKSAM	6th Cavalry.
Capt. JOHN BIGELOW, JR. . . .	10th Cavalry.
Capt. M. T. HENRY	Com'd'g 1st U.S. Vol. Cavalry.
1st Lieut. A. L. HILLS	1st Cavalry, Captain and Act'g Adj.-Gen. Vols.
1st Lieut. M. H. BARNUM . .	10th Cavalry.

[Continued on next page.

Wounded, — concluded.

NAMES.	ORGANIZATIONS.
1st Lieut. ARTHUR THAYER . .	3d Cavalry.
1st Lieut. O. B. MEYER . . .	3d Cavalry.
1st Lieut. W. S. WOOD . . .	9th Cavalry.
1st Lieut. A. C. MURRILLAT . .	3d Cavalry.
1st Lieut. E. D. ANDERSON . .	10th Cavalry.
1st Lieut. R. C. LIVERMORE . .	10th Cavalry.
1st Lieut. CARR	1st U.S. Vol. Cavalry.
1st Lieut. DAVID J. LEAHEY . .	1st U.S. Vol. Cavalry.
2d Lieut. WILLIARD	10th Cavalry.
2d Lieut. WALTER C. SHORT . .	6th Cavalry.
2d Lieut. F. R. McCOY . . .	10th Cavalry.
2d Lieut. T. A. ROBERTS . . .	10th Cavalry.
2d Lieut. H. K. DEVEREAUX . .	1st U.S. Vol. Cavalry.
2d Lieut. H. C. WHITEHEAD . .	10th Cavalry.
1st Lieut. R. C. DAY	1st U.S. Vol. Cavalry.
Cadet L. K. HASKELL	1st U.S. Vol. Cavalry.

General Kent's report of casualties of officers has been forwarded.

The strength given in tabulated statements[1] above, is the aggregate strength of the command; but as there were many details, above figures are about 15 per cent. greater than the forces actually engaged in battle.

The command has been active in strengthening their position, and commanders and their staffs have thoroughly informed themselves as to the topographical features of the country and the situation of the enemy.

Very respectfully,

JOS. WHEELER,
Major-General Vols., Commanding.

[1] See pp. 55 and 56.

CHAPTER VI

THE BATTLE OF SAN JUAN (CONCLUDED) — OFFICIAL REPORTS OF GENERAL KENT, COLONEL LEONARD WOOD, OF THE "ROUGH RIDERS," AND THEODORE ROOSEVELT, LIEUTENANT-COLONEL COMMANDING

FOLLOWING is the official report by Brig.-Gen. J. F. Kent, of the part taken by his command in the Battle of San Juan:

HEADQUARTERS 1ST DIVISION, 5TH ARMY CORPS,
IN THE FIELD, FORT SAN JUAN,
NEAR SANTIAGO DE CUBA, July 7, 1898.

THE ASSISTANT ADJUTANT-GENERAL, FIFTH ARMY CORPS:

SIR: I have the honor to submit the following report of the operations of my command in the battle of July 1:

On the afternoon of June 30, pursuant to orders given me verbally by the corps commander at his headquarters, I moved my second and third brigades (Parson and Wikoff) forward about two miles to a point on the Santiago road near corps headquarters. Here the troops bivouacked, the First Brigade (Hawkins) remaining in its camp of the two preceding days, slightly in rear of corps headquarters.

On the following morning (July 1) at 7 o'clock, I rode forward up the hill where Capt. Grimes' Battery was in position. I here met Lieut.-Col. McClernand, Assistant Adjutant-General Fifth Corps, who pointed out to me a green hill in the distance, which was to be my objective on my left, and either he or Lieutenant Miley of Major-Gen. Shafter's staff gave me directions to keep my right on the main road leading to the city of Santiago. I had previously given the necessary orders for Hawkins' Brigade to move early; to be followed in turn by Wikoff and Parson.

Shortly after Grimes' Battery opened fire, I rode down to the stream, and there found Gen. Hawkins at the head of his brigade at a point about 250 yards from the El Poso sugar-house. Here I gave him his orders. The enemy's artillery was now replying to Grimes' Battery. I rode forward with Hawkins about 150 yards, closely followed by the 6th Infantry, which was leading the First Brigade. At this point I received instructions to allow the cavalry the right of way, but for some unknown reason they moved up very slowly, thus causing a delay in my advance of fully forty minutes. Lieutenant Miley, of Gen. Shafter's staff, was at this point, and understood how the division was delayed; and repeated several times that he understood I was makin gall the progress possible. Gen. Hawkins went forward, and word came back in a few minutes that it would be possible to observe the enemy's position from the front. I immediately rode forward with my staff. The fire of the enemy's sharp-shooters was very distinctly felt at this time. I crossed the main ford of the San Juan River, joined General Hawkins, and with him observed the enemy's position from a point some distance in advance of the ford. General Hawkins deemed it possible to turn the enemy's right at Fort San Juan, but later, under the heavy fire, this was found impracticable for the First Brigade, but was accomplished by the Third Brigade, coming up later on Gen. Hawkins' left. Having completed the observation, with my staff I proceeded to join the head of my division, just coming under heavy fire. Approaching the First Brigade, I directed them to move alongside the cavalry (which was halted). We were already suffering losses caused by the balloon, near by, attracting fire and disclosing our position.

The enemy's infantry fire, steadily increasing in intensity, now came from all directions, not only from the front and the dense tropical thickets on our flanks, but from sharp-shooters thickly posted in trees in our rear, and from shrapnel apparently aimed at the balloon. Lieut.-Colonel Derby, of Gen. Shafter's staff, met me about this time, and informed me that a trail or narrow way had been discovered from the balloon, a short distance back, leading to the left of a ford lower down the stream. I hastened to the forks made by this road, and soon after the 71st New York Regiment of Hawkins' Brigade came up. I turned them into the by-path indicated by Lieut.-Col. Derby, leading to the lower ford, sending word to Gen. Hawkins of this movement. This would have speedily delivered them in their proper place on the left of their brigade, but under the galling fire of the enemy the leading battalion of this regiment was thrown into confusion and recoiled in disorder on the troops in the rear. At this critical moment the officers of my staff practically formed a cordon behind the panic-stricken men, and urged them to again go forward. I finally ordered them to lie down in the thicket and clear the way for others of their own regiment, who were coming up behind. This many of them did, and the Second and Third Battalions came forward in better order and moved them along the road toward the ford.

One of my staff officers ran back waving his hat to hurry forward the Third Brigade, who, upon approaching the forks, found the way blocked by men of the 71st New York. There were other men of this regiment crouching in the bushes, many of whom were encouraged by the advance of the approaching column to arise and go forward. As already stated, I had received orders some time before to keep in rear of the Cavalry Division. Their advance was much delayed, resulting in frequent halts, presumably to drop their blanket-rolls, and due to the natural delay in fording a stream. These delays under such a hot fire grew exceedingly irksome, and I therefore pushed the head of my division as quickly as I could toward the river, in column of files of twos, paralleled in the narrow way by the cavalry. This quickened the forward movement, and enabled me to get into position as speedily as possible for the attack. Owing to the congested condition of the road, the progress of the narrow column was, however, painfully slow. I again sent a staff officer at a gallop to urge forward the troops in the rear.

The head of Wikoff's Brigade reached the forks at 12.20 P.M., and hurried on the left, stepping over prostrate forms of men of the Seventy-first. This heroic brigade, consisting of the 13th, 9th, and 24th

United States Infantry, speedily crossed the stream and was quickly deployed to the left of the lower ford. While personally superintending this movement, Col. Wikoff was killed, — the command of the brigade then devolving upon Lieut.-Colonel Worth, 13th Infantry, who immediately fell, severely wounded; and then Lieut.-Col. Liscum, 24th Infantry, who five minutes later also fell under the withering fire of the enemy. The command of the brigade then devolved upon Lt.-Col. E. P. Ewers, 9th Infantry. Meanwhile I had again sent a staff officer to hurry forward the Second Brigade, which was bringing up the rear. The 10th and 2d Infantry, soon arriving at the forks, were deflected to the left to follow the Third Brigade; while the 21st was directed along the main road to support Hawkins.

Crossing the lower ford a few minutes later, the 10th and 2d moved forward in column, in good order, toward the green knoll already referred to as my objective on the left. Approaching the knoll, the regiments deployed, — passed over the knoll, and ascended the high ridge beyond, driving back the enemy in the direction of his trenches. I observed this movement from the Fort San Juan Hill. Colonel E. P. Pearson, 10th Infantry, commanding the Second Brigade, and the officers and troops under his command, deserve great credit for the soldierly manner in which this movement was executed. I earnestly recommend Col. Pearson for promotion. Prior to this advance of the Second Brigade, the Third, connecting with Hawkins' gallant troops on the right, had moved toward Fort San Juan, sweeping through a zone of most destructive fire, scaling a steep and difficult hill, and assisting in capturing the enemy's strong position, Fort San Juan, at 1.30 P.M. This crest was about 125 feet above the general level, and was defended by deep trenches and a loopholed brick fort surrounded by barbed-wire entanglements. Gen. Hawkins, some time after I reached the crest, reported that the 6th and 16th Infantry had captured the hill, which I now consider incorrect. The credit is almost equally due the 6th, 9th, 13th, 16th, and 24th Regiments of Infantry. Owing to Gen. Hawkins' representations, I forwarded the report sent to corps headquarters about 3 P.M., that the 6th and the 16th Infantry had captured the hill.

The 13th Infantry captured the enemy's colors waving over the fort, but unfortunately destroyed them, distributing the fragments among the men, because, as was asserted, " it was a bad omen," two or three men having been shot while assisting private Arthur Agnew, Company H, 13th Infantry, the captor. All fragments which could be recovered are submitted with this report. The greatest credit is due to the officers of my command, — whether company, battalion, regiment, or brigade commanders, who so admirably directed the formation of their troops, unavoidably intermixed in the dense thicket, and made the desperate rush for the distant and strongly defended crest. I have already mentioned the circumstances of my Third Brigade's advance across the ford, where in the brief space of ten minutes it lost its brave commander (killed), and the next two ranking officers by disabling wounds. Yet, in spite of these confusing conditions, the formations were effected without hesitation, although under a stinging fire ; companies acting singly in some circumstances and by battalions and regiments in others, rushing through the jungle across the stream, waist-deep, and over the wide bottom thickly set with barbed-wire entanglements. At this point I wish to particularly mention First Lieut. Wendell L. Simpson, Adjutant 9th Infantry, Acting Assistant Adjutant-General Third Brigade, who was noticeably active and efficient in carrying out orders which I had given him to transmit to his brigade commander, who no longer existed.

The enemy having retired to the second line of rifle-pits, I directed my line to hold their position and intrench. At ten minutes past 3 P.M. I received almost simultaneously two requests, — one from Col. Wood, commanding Cavalry Brigade, and one from General Sumner, asking for assistance for the cavalry on my right, as they were hard-pressed. I immediately sent to their aid the 13th Infantry; who promptly went on this further mission, despite the heavy losses they had already sustained.

Great credit is due to the gallant officer and gentleman, Brig.-Gen. H. S. Hawkins, who, placing himself between the two regiments leading his brigade, — the 6th and 16th Infantry, — urged and led them by voice and bugle-calls to the attack so successfully accomplished. My earnest thanks are due to my staff officers present at my side and under my personal observation on the field, especially to Major A. C. Sharpe, Assistant Adjutant-General, Major Philip Reade, Inspector-General, Capt. U. G. McAlexander, Chief Quartermaster; and my Aids, 1st Lieutenant George S. Cartwright, 24th Infantry, and 1st Lieutenant William P. Jackson, 2d Infantry; — also to

Mr. Adolfo Carlos Munez; the latter a Volunteer Aid, subsequently wounded in the fight of the 2d inst., who richly merits a commission for his able assistance given without pay.

The officers enumerated should at least be breveted for gallantry under fire. I also personally noticed the conduct of 1st Lieut. T. J. Kirkpatrick, Assistant Surgeon, United States Army, on duty with 24th Infantry, giving most efficient aid to the wounded under fire. I observed several times 1st Lieut. J. D. Miley, 5th Artillery, Aid to Gen. Shafter, who was conspicuous throughout the day for his coolness under fire, delivering instructions with apparent unconcern.

The bloody fighting of my brave command cannot be adequately described in words. The following list of killed, wounded, and missing, tells the story of their valor:

Report of the Killed, Wounded, and Missing, — 1st Division, 5th Army Corps, — July 1, 1898.

FIRST BRIGADE.

ORGANIZATIONS.	KILLED.		WOUNDED.		MISS-ING.
	Offi-cers.	Men.	Offi-cers.	Men.	
16th Infantry	1	13	5	82	6
6th Infantry . . , ...	4	13	7	95	. .
71st N.Y. Vol. Infantry . . .	. .	12	1	47	43
TOTALS	5	38	13	224	49

Report of July 1st, — concluded.

SECOND BRIGADE.

ORGANIZATIONS.	KILLED.		WOUNDED.		MISS-ING.
	Offi-cers.	Men.	Offi-cers.	Men.	
10th Infantry	1	4	5	21	. .
21st Infantry	. .	5	1	25	. .
2d Infantry	. .	1	4	16	. .
TOTALS	1	10	10	62	. .

THIRD BRIGADE.

Brigade Commander	1	. .	. .	. .	. .
9th Infantry	1	3	. .	23	1
13th Infantry	2	16	5	81	1
24th Infantry	2	10	4	73	7
TOTALS	6	29	9	177	9
GRAND TOTALS	12	77	32	463	58

At daylight on the morning of July 2d, the enemy resumed the battle, and firing continued throughout the day, part of the time in a drenching rain. At nightfall the firing ceased, but at 9 P.M. a vigorous assault was made all along our lines. This was completely repulsed, the enemy again retiring to his trenches. The following morning, firing was resumed, and continued until near noon, when a white flag was displayed by the enemy, and firing was ordered to cease.

The casualties in these two days (July 2d and 3d) are as follows:

Report of the Killed, Wounded, and Missing, — 1st Division, 5th Army Corps, — July 2, 1898.

FIRST BRIGADE.

ORGANIZATIONS.	KILLED.		WOUNDED.		MISS-ING.
	Offi-cers.	Men.	Offi-cers.	Men.	
Division Staff	. .	. .	1[1]	. .	. .
General Officers	. .	. .	1	. .	. .
16th Infantry	. .	1	. .	21	1
6th Infantry	. .	. .	. .	2	. .
71st N.Y. Vol. Infantry . . .	1	. .	. .	7	. .
TOTALS	1	1	2	30	1

SECOND BRIGADE.

10th Infantry	. .	1	. .	14	3
21st Infantry	. .	1	. .	7	. .
2d Infantry	. .	4	. .	31	. .
TOTALS	. .	6	. .	52	3

[1] Mr. A. C. Munoz, Volunteer Aid to Division Commander.

Report of July 2d, — continued.

THIRD BRIGADE.

ORGANIZATIONS.	KILLED.		WOUNDED.		MISS-ING.
	Offi-cers.	Men.	Offi-cers.	Men.	
9th Infantry	. .	. .	. .	4	. .
13th Infantry	. .	. .	. .	3	. .
24th Infantry	. .	1	2	1	. .
TOTALS	. .	1	2	8	. .
GRAND TOTALS	. .	9	4	90	4

Report of the Killed, Wounded, and Missing, — 1st Division, 5th Army Corps, — July 3, 1898.

FIRST BRIGADE.

ORGANIZATIONS.	KILLED.		WOUNDED.		MISS-ING.
	Offi-cers.	Men.	Offi-cers.	Men.	
16th Infantry	. .	. .	. .	1	. .
6th Infantry	. .	. .	. .	2	. .
71st N.Y. Vol. Inf.	. .	. .	. .	4	. .
TOTAL	. .	. .	. .	7	. .

Report of July 3d, — concluded.

SECOND BRIGADE.

ORGANIZATIONS.	KILLED.		WOUNDED.		MISS- ING.
	Offi- cers.	Men.	Offi- cers.	Men.	
10th Infantry	. .	. .	. .	. .	. .
21st Infantry	. .	. .	. .	. .	. .
2d Infantry	. .	1	. .	. .	. .
TOTAL	. .	1	. .	. .	. .

THIRD BRIGADE.

	KILLED.		WOUNDED.		MISS- ING.
9th Infantry	. .	. .	. .	. .	. .
13th Infantry	. .	. .	. .	1	. .
24th Infantry	. .	. .	. .	. .	. .
TOTALS	. .	. .	. .	1	. .
GRAND TOTAL	. .	1	. .	8	. .
GRAND TOTALS: July 1, 2, 3, 1898	12	87	36	561	62

One Hospital Corps man attached to the 10th Infantry, killed, not included in above report.

I desire, in conclusion, to express my gratitude to Major-Gen. Joseph Wheeler for his courteous conduct to me, and through me to my division, under the trying circumstances enumerated. Though ill and suffering, Gen. Wheeler was so perfectly at home under fire that he inspired all of us with assurance.

Attention is invited in this connection to the report of brigade and subordinate commanders, and of my Inspector-General, herewith. I cordially indorse their recommendations. Very respectfully,

J. FORD KENT,
Brigadier-General U.S.A., Commanding.

The report of Col. Leonard Wood, commanding Second Brigade, Cavalry Division, of the same battle, was as follows:

HEADQUARTERS 2D CAVALRY BRIGADE,
IN TRENCHES ABOUT SANTIAGO DE CUBA, July 6, 1898.

ADJ.-GENERAL, CAV. DIVISION, 5TH ARMY CORPS:

SIR: I have the honor to submit the following report relative to the 2d Cavalry Brigade in the assault on the works to the east of Santiago de Cuba, and the action on the heights, during the afternoon and night of the 1st of July. The brigade was composed of Troops A, B, C, D, E, F, G, and I; also Headquarters and Band of 10th U.S. Cavalry, under command of Lieut.-Colonel T. A. Baldwin, 10th Cavalry; Troops A, B, C, D, E, G, I, and K, 1st U.S. Cavalry, under command of Lieut.-Colonel C. D. Viele, 1st Cavalry; and Troops A, B, D, E, F, G, K, and L, 1st U.S. Volunteer Cavalry, under command of Lieut.-Colonel Theodore Roosevelt, 1st U.S. Volunteer Cavalry.

On the morning of July 1, 1898, the brigade was camped at El Pozo, about three miles from Santiago de

Cuba, in support of Grimes' Battery of artillery, which
was in position on a ridge just above the old sugar-
mill.   Early in the morning we received orders to
prepare for a move to the front in support of a move
which Lawton's Division was making upon Santiago
by way of Caney.   At 7 a.m., Capt. Grimes' Battery
opened fire on the Spanish works; which fire was
rapidly returned by Spanish artillery, using smokeless
powder, with the result that they promptly located our
position by the clouds of smoke from our guns, and
inflicted quite a severe loss upon both the brigade and
battery, — the 1st Vol. Cavalry being principal sufferers.

The brigade moved down the road toward Santiago,
in rear of the 1st Cavalry Brigade, with instructions
to deploy to the right after crossing the San Juan, and
continue to extend to the right, reaching out toward
General Lawton's left and holding ourselves in rear of
the First Brigade as a support.   On reaching the stream
the 1st Volunteer Cavalry, which was in lead, crossed
the stream with comparatively slight loss and deployed
to the right in good order; but at about this time a
captive balloon was led down the road in which the
troops were massed, and finally anchored at the crossing of the stream.   The approach and anchoring of the
balloon served to indicate the line of approach of our
troops, and to locate the ford; and the result was a
terrific converging artillery and rifle fire on the ford,
which resulted in severe loss of men.   Under this fire
the 1st U.S. Cavalry and the 10th U.S. Cavalry
crossed the stream and deployed to the right, where
they were placed in position in rear of the First Brigade.

We lay in this position some time, partially covered by small rises of ground, but generally speaking

exposed to a heavy dropping fire from the forts and block-houses. After remaining in this position for about an hour and one-half, the order to advance was given, and the brigade advanced in as good order as possible, but more or less broken up by the masses of brush and heavy grass and cactus; passing through the lines of the First Brigade, mingling with them, and charging the hill in conjunction with these troops, as well as some few infantry who had extended to the right. Our first objective was the hill with small red-roofed house on it. This was promptly taken, and after short delay the brigade went forward to the right of the main hill covered with heavy intrenchments, and took it under very heavy fire, swinging around to the right, and flanking and taking the angle to the right of the hill; our right finally resting about 800 yards to the right of the road passing into Santiago de Cuba.

Here we held on under heavy fire all night, the enemy making repeated and fierce attempts to regain this lost position and works. The brigade intrenched itself as best it could, and before morning had covered itself fairly well. All during the 2d, and a portion of the 3d, the enemy kept up a constant fire, and made repeated attempts to regain this lost position on our front.

In regard to the conduct of the brigade as a whole, I can only say that it was superb. That dismounted cavalry should have been able to charge regular infantry in strong position, supported by artillery and the general lay of the land, seems almost incredible; yet this is exactly what the Cavalry Division of the 5th Army Corps did in this fight, passing over a long zone of fire, and charging steep hills topped with works and

block-houses. Some idea of the severity of the enemy's
fire may be gained from the fact — that of the five officers
of the brigade staff, four were killed or wounded and
one exhausted by the intense heat.

In an action where every one so well performed his
full duty, it is difficult to select cases of especial merit.
I desire, however, to mention the following: Lt. W.
E. Shipp, Brigade Quartermaster, killed while leading
a charge; Capt. M. J. Henry, shot through the leg
while delivering an order; Capt. A. L. Mills, shot
through the head while assembling men for a second
charge; Lt. J. H. Parker, 13th U.S. Infantry, for
marked gallantry while in charge of the Gatling Gun
Battery; Lt. J. B. Hughes, 10th Cavalry, for conspicuous gallantry in handling his Hotchkiss Battery;
Lt.-Col. Theodore Roosevelt for conspicuous gallantry
in leading a charge on one of the hills; Hugo Wm.
Brittain, Troop G, 1st U.S. Cavalry, for great gallantry
in supporting and waving the regimental standard to
encourage and lead on the 1st under heavy fire, he
having been wounded; Cadet E. Haskell, U.S.M.A.,
for gallantry in action, coolness, and courage, after
being shot through the body.   Lt.-Col. Viele and Lt.-
Col. Baldwin handled their regiments with skill and
courage, and by their example encouraged and steadied
their men.   Major Wint, 10th Cavalry, displayed
great courage, and was severely wounded while
repelling a charge on our front during the night of
the 1st of July.

I have the honor to submit herewith reports from Lt.-
Col. Viele, Lt.-Col. Baldwin, and Lt.-Col. Roosevelt;
also reports from one of the surgeons and various company commanders of the regiments composing brigade.

I desire also to invite attention to the coolness, courage, and gallantry of Captain Wm. O. O'Neil, 1st U.S. Volunteer Cavalry, killed in action. This officer had already been recommended for a medal of honor, for gallant service in attempting to rescue some drowning men of the 10th Cavalry at Daiquiri during the landing. Major Webb Hayes, 5th Ohio Volunteer Cavalry, temporarily on duty with the brigade, did gallant service, — was cool and collected under fire. He was slightly wounded.

The brigade took into action 75 officers and 1,446 men; and lost 21 officers killed and wounded, and 217 men killed and wounded, — a loss of 26 per cent. of officers, and 15 per cent. of enlisted men.

I desire also to state that Capt. McCormack, 7th U.S. Cavalry, on temporary duty with 1st Volunteer Cavalry, rendered efficient and gallant service during the action until finally overcome by heat. The intense heat of the day and almost entire absence of wind added much to the difficulty of the work.

Very respectfully,

LEONARD WOOD, *Col. 1st U.S. Vol. Cavalry,*
Comm'd'g 2d Brigade, Cav. Div.

[*Endorsement :*]

HEADQUARTERS CAVALRY DIVISION, U.S. ARMY,
BEFORE SANTIAGO, CUBA, July 10, 1898.

Respectfully forwarded. Colonel Wood commanded the 2d Brigade during the fight of July 1st and 2d. He showed energy, courage, and good judgment. I heretofore recommended him for promotion to a Brigadier-General. He deserves the highest commendation. He was under the observation and direction of myself and of my staff during the battle.

JOS. WHEELER,
Maj.-Gen. U.S. Vols., Comm'd'g.

Lieutenant-Colonel Theodore Roosevelt reported as follows, concerning the part taken by his command in this battle:

TRENCHES OUTSIDE SANTIAGO, July 4, 1898.

COL. LEONARD WOOD,
Commanding 2d Cavalry Brigade:

SIR: On July 1st the regiment with myself in command was moved out by your orders, directly following the First Brigade. Before leaving the camping-ground several of our men were wounded by shrapnel. After crossing the river at the ford we were moved along and up its right bank, under fire, and were held in reserve at a sunk road. Here we lost a good many men, including Captain O'Neil killed and Lieutenant Haskell wounded.

We then received your order to advance and support the regular cavalry in the attack on the intrenchments and block-houses on the hills to the left. The regiment was deployed on both sides of the road, and moved forward until we came to the rearmost lines of the regulars. We continued to move forward until I ordered a charge; and the men rushed the block-house and rifle-pits on the hill to the right of our advance. They did the work in fine shape, though suffering severely; the guidons of Troops E and G were first planted on the summit, though the first men up were some A and B troopers who were with me. We then opened fire on the intrenchments on a hill to our left, which some of the other regiments were assailing, and which they carried a few minutes later. Meanwhile we were under a heavy rifle fire from the intrenchments along the hills to our front, from which they

also shelled us with a piece of field artillery until
some of our marksmen silenced it.   When the men
got their wind we charged again, and carried the
second line of intrenchments with a rush.   Swinging
to the left, we then drove the Spaniards over the brow
of the chain of hills fronting Santiago.   By this time
the regiments were much mixed, and we were under a
very heavy fire, both of shrapnel and fine rifles, from
the batteries, intrenchments, and forts immediately in
front of the city.

On the extreme front I now found myself in command, with fragments of the six cavalry regiments of
the two brigades under me.   The Spaniards made one
or two efforts to retake the line, but were promptly
driven back.   Both General Sumner and you sent me
word to hold the line at all hazard, and that night we
dug a line of intrenchments across our front, using the
captured Spanish intrenching-tools.   We had nothing
to eat except what we captured from the Spaniards;
but their dinner had fortunately been cooked, and we
ate theirs with relish, having been fighting all day.
We had no blankets or coats, and lay by the trenches
all night.

The Spaniards attacked us once in the night, and at
dawn they opened a heavy artillery and rifle fire.
Very great assistance was rendered us by Lieutenant
Parker's Gatling Battery at critical moments; he
fought his guns at the extreme front of the firing-line
in a way that repeatedly called forth the cheers of my
men.

One of the Spanish batteries which was used
against us was directly in front of the hospital, so that
the Red Cross flag flew over the battery, saving it
from our fire for a considerable period.   The Spanish

Mauser bullets made clean wounds; but they also used a copper-jacketed or brass-jacketed bullet which exploded, making very bad wounds indeed.

Since then we have continued to hold the ground. The food has been short, and until to-day we could not get any blankets, coats, or shelter-tents; while the men lay all day under the fire from the Spanish batteries, intrenchments, and guerillas in trees, and worked all night in the trenches, never even taking off their shoes; but they are in excellent spirits, and ready and anxious to carry out any orders they receive.

At the end of the first day the eight troops were commanded, two by captains, three by 1st lieutenants, two by 2d lieutenants, and one by the sergeant whom you made acting lieutenant. We went into the fight about 490 strong; 86 men were killed or wounded, and there are still half a dozen missing. The great heat prostrated nearly forty men, some of them among the best in the regiment. Besides Captain O'Neil and Lieutenant Haskell, Lieutenants Leaby, Devereux, and Carr were wounded. All behaved with great gallantry.

As for Captain O'Neil, his loss is one of the severest that could have befallen the regiment. He was a man of cool head, great executive capacity, and literally dauntless courage.

The guerillas in trees not only fired at our troops, but seemed to devote themselves especially to shooting at the surgeons, the hospital assistants with Red Cross badges on their arms, the wounded who were being carried on litters, and the burying-parties. Many of these guerillas were dressed in green uniforms. We sent out a detail of sharp-shooters among those in our rear, along the line where they had been shooting the wounded, and killed thirteen.

To attempt to give a list of the men who showed signal valor, would necessitate sending in an almost complete roster of the regiment. Many of the cases which I mention stand merely as examples : Captain Jenkins acted as major, and showed such conspicuous gallantry and efficiency that I earnestly hope he may be promoted to major as soon as a vacancy occurs. Of the rest, not as exceptions, Captains Lewellen, Muller, and Luna led their troops throughout the charges, handling them admirably. At the end of the battle Lieutenants Kane, Greenwood, and Goodrich were in charge of their troops, immediately under my eye, and I wish particularly to commend their conduct throughout. Lieutenant Franz, who commanded his troop, also did well. Corporals Waller and Fortescue, and trooper McKinley of Troop E, Corporal Rhoads of Troop D, troopers Albertson, Winter, McGregor, and Ray Clark of Troop F, troopers Rugbee, Jackson, and Waller of Troop A, Trumpeter McDonald of Troop L, Sergeant Hughes of Troop B, and trooper Gerien, G Troop, all continued to fight after being wounded, some very severely ; most of them fought until the end of the day. Trooper Oliver B. Norton of B, who with his brother was by my side throughout the charging, was killed while fighting with marked gallantry. Sergeant Ferguson, Corporal Lee, and troopers Bell and Carroll of Troop K, Sergeant Dame of Troop E, troopers Goodwin Campbell and Dudley Dean and Trumpeter Foster of B, and troopers Greenwald and Bardshas of A, are all worthy of special mention for coolness and gallantry ; they merit promotion when the opportunity comes.

But the most conspicuous gallantry was shown by trooper Rouland. He was wounded in the side in our first fight, but kept in the firing-line; he was sent to the hospital next day, but left it and marched out to us, overtaking us, and fought all through this battle with such indifference to danger that I was forced again and again to rate and threaten him for running needless risk.

Great gallantry was also shown by four troopers whom I cannot identify, and by trooper Winston Clark of G. It was after we had taken the first hill. I had called out to rush the second, and, having by that time lost my horse, climbed a wire fence and started towards it. After going a couple of hundred yards under a heavy fire, I found that no one else had come: as I discovered later, it was simply because in the confusion, with men shooting and being shot, they had not noticed me start. I told the five men to wait a moment — as it might be misunderstood if we all ran back — until I ran back and started the regiment; and as soon as I did so the regiment came with a rush. But meanwhile the five men coolly lay down in the open, returning the fire from the trenches. It is to be wondered at that only Clark was seriously wounded; and he called out as we passed again to lay his canteen where he could get it, but to continue the charge and leave him where he was. All the wounded had to be left until after the fight, for we could spare no men from the firing-line.

Very respectfully,

THEODORE ROOSEVELT,

Lieut.-Col. U.S. Volunteer Cav.

[*Endorsement :*]   HEADQUARTERS CAVALRY DIVISION,
                NEAR SANTIAGO DE CUBA.

Respectfully forwarded. Col. Roosevelt and his entire command deserve high commendation. I call special attention to Col. Roosevelt's recommendation regarding Capt. O'Neil; Lieuts. Haskell, Leaby, Devereaux and Carr. Also his commendation of Capt. Jenkins, Lieuts. Kane, Greenwood, Goodrich, and Franz. Also Corpls Waller and Fortesque, and Pvte McKinley, Troop E; Corpl Rhoads, troopers Albertson, Winter, McGregor, and Ray Clark of Troop F; troopers Rugbee, Jackson, and Waller, Troop A; Trumpt. McDonald, Troop L; Sgt Hughes, Troop B; Gerien, Troop G; Oliver B. Norton, Troop B; Sgt Ferguson, Corpl Lee, troopers Bell and Carroll, Troop K; Sgt Damy, Troop E; troopers Goodwin, Campbell and Dudley Dean, Trpt. Foster, Troop B; troopers Greenwald and Bardshas, Troop A; and special commendation of troopers Rouland and Winston Clark of Troop G. I concur in these recommendations.

JOSEPH WHEELER,
Major-General U.S. Vols., Commanding.

General Kent's report of his entire strength the day before the battle of July 1st, was 235 officers and 4,869 men. The strength of the Cavalry Division was 127 officers and 2,522 men: making the entire strength of the command which fought the Battle of San Juan, 362 officers and 7,391 men. The balance of the army, — consisting of Lawton's Division, 5,280 men ; Bates' Brigade, 1,064 men ; artillery and mounted cavalry, 150 men, and some 400 Cubans: in all, 6,889 men, — were fighting under General Lawton at El Caney. The rest of the Cubans, some 4,000 strong, had marched off to meet the Spanish force under General Escario.

CHAPTER VII

CONCERNING THE REGULARS AND THE VOLUNTEERS IN
ACTION — " HARPER'S WEEKLY " ON DUE CREDIT
TO THE PERMANENT OR THE TEMPORARY SOLDIER —
CONDUCT OF THE SEVENTY-FIRST NEW YORK

MUCH has been said regarding the action of the volunteers and the regulars. We must be fair, just, and honest in this thing. The volunteers deserve great credit for abandoning, as many of them did, high positions with large salaries, and comfortable and in many cases luxurious homes, and coming to the front to serve their country. They were brave, determined, and chivalrous men, but the truth impels me to say that in effectiveness in battle they could not be expected to be equal to trained regular soldiers. These men had been superbly drilled. They and their officers had been trained to estimate distances with wonderful accuracy, which enabled them to adjust their sights; and, having been drilled as marksmen, they had become experts to a wonderful degree. Consequently, when the battle commenced, each regular moved forward with precision, and halted on his knee at every favorable opportunity. They were told by the officers the distance of the enemy, and every shot from them was from an expert and accurate marksman. The consequence was, that their fire was most deadly and effective. Many of the Rough Riders were also good marksmen, but they had not been drilled to use the kind of rifles with which they were armed; and it is also true that many of them had never shot a rifle of any kind in their lives, and, while they went forward with courage and determination, their fire was not as effective as that of the regulars.

"Harper's Weekly" of July 9th contains an editorial which treats this subject in a fair and conservative manner. It is as follows:

There is no desire on our part to lessen in the smallest degree the great credit that is due the volunteer soldiers, and which is always theirs whenever the country engages in war, for our citizens make good soldiers quickly. Crying injustice, however, is done to the regular army by the press and the war-correspondents, as well as by the politicians. The country has received splendid service from the regular army in every war, and our officers who have won the greatest distinction have, in most instances, been the graduates of West Point. These instructed soldiers show their education at the very outset of the war, and while the volunteers are learning the wisdom of prudence by hard experience, the regulars are practising it. To read the accounts of the battle on the

heights of Sevilla, one would think that none but the
"Rough Riders" had been engaged in it; but the regulars were doing just as effective work, and doing it in
a more businesslike and prudent way. We would not
for a moment wish that any word which has been said
in praise of the volunteers had been left unsaid; but if
those who are writing of this war could only know the
bitter discouragement of the regular officers, who devote their whole lives to the service of their country,
due to the manner in which they are treated by the
newspapers and the politicians, we think they would
dwell a little more on the deeds of the regulars. It is
not in human nature to remain content under such injustice as is habitually done to the regular army. We
know, of course, why politicians and their favorites
succeed in securing commissions for themselves and
their civilian relatives and friends in preference to de-
serving soldiers, but why is it that the newspapers and
their correspondents refuse to give credit to the regulars? It will not cause the volunteers any grief, we
know, if their professional brethren receive what they
earn. Why not be just to the American soldier,
whether he be serving the country permanently or
temporarily?

The 71st New York was composed of most
magnificent material, including some of the leading people of the city of New York.

Gen. Frank Green told me that more than
three hundred of that regiment had never fired a
rifle or gun of any kind. They were armed
with the Springfield rifle, which we now call an
inferior weapon. An uninstructed soldier, by

failing to adjust properly the sight of this gun, might aim accurately at an enemy twelve hundred yards off and yet the bullet would strike the ground six hundred yards short of the mark. This shows the difficulty undrilled marksmen would have in using this gun effectively. What made matters worse was that all the volunteer infantry regiments were furnished with black-powder ammunition, which creates a dense smoke, thereby disclosing your position to the enemy.

I append as a note an article defending this regiment.[1] It is from the New York "Herald" of July 14th, and is a reply to some unfriendly

[1] Officers and men of the 71st New York Regiment are intensely mortified by the reports sent from here by some correspondents, reflecting adversely on the conduct of the regiment in action, and particularly branding some of the officers for cowardice.

I am perfectly familiar with the circumstances upon which these charges were founded, and unhesitatingly pronounce them unjustified. In the first general engagement before Santiago, the 71st was among the first regiments deployed in the wooded valley which was swept by fire from the San Juan block-house and trenches, but afterward carried by our troops. When shrapnel from the Spanish artillery suddenly commenced bursting over our troops, they were crowded along the narrow road which wound through underbrush.

Just then I passed through the lines of the 71st while seeking a road to get to El Caney, where the sound of artillery announced that the action had already begun. Thus the conduct of the regiment at this time, on which the criticism is based, came directly under my observation. It is true that one battalion showed nervousness. It was the first time it had been under fire, and it showed an inclination to get out of the range of shrapnel without waiting for orders, and began to retire. This confusion was only momentary, and the battalion quickly regained presence of mind and marched forward into the thick of the fight. The other battalions never wavered. In fact, the conduct of the leading battalion throughout the battle excited the warm commendation of regular army officers the next day. General Kent, with whose division the 71st is connected, praised the regiment and its criticisms regarding the conduct of this regiment in the battle of July 1st. That a portion of the regiment acted in a most creditable and gallant manner will be gladly testified to by all who were in that part of the field during the engagement.

conduct while speaking to me, and said that in the next engagement it would equal the regulars.

There is no denying that after the battle many privates of the 71st severely criticised the conduct of some of their own officers. This criticism, from what I learned the day after the battle while canvassing the subject thoroughly, might have been justified in some instances relative to the handling of troops under fire, but it is decidedly unfair to make a charge of cowardice.

On the whole the 71st behaved creditably, and will do even better in the future. It now occupies an advanced position on our right, where the heavy fighting is most likely to occur. It is armed with Springfield rifles and it is at a decided disadvantage, but the average material in the regiment is as good as any in the army. — *From the "Herald's" Special Correspondent, with the Army before Santiago.*

CHAPTER VIII

THE defences of Santiago were certainly
constructed with commendable engineering
skill. Immediately following the fight of July
1st and 2d, I made a most careful investigation
of the forts which defended the city. With a
very powerful glass I viewed them from every
possible point, to accomplish which I selected
places from which to view them on all sides of
the city. This investigation convinced me, and
I so reported, that to take the city by assault
would cost us at least three thousand men. An
examination of the works after having taken the
city fully confirmed me in this; and General
Shafter, in his report regarding the works, after
the city was captured, informed the War Department that an assault would have cost us five
thousand men.

The batteries in the harbor were also constructed with commendable engineering skill. The Punta Gorda Battery is built upon a high promontory, three sides of which are upon the sea and the fourth side upon a low, marshy place which at high tides is also covered with water. The battery consists of two 16-centimeter breech-loading modern guns and two small breech-loading guns of the same character. These guns point directly down the bay, and they could concentrate their fire upon anything approaching, for some two or three miles. The approach by land is defended by very strong breastworks on the top of the hill, and also upon the swamp. If properly defended, a successful assault would have been very difficult.

The Socapa Battery is also built upon a high promontory, which is a peninsula; its armament consists of two modern 16-centimeter breech-loading guns and three very large rifle muzzle-loading mortars. They all face south, directly out to sea. The approach to this from the regular landing is guarded by forts armed with rapid-fire guns, and the approach from the west is guarded by a block-house surrounded by strong earthworks; and further on and nearer the battery is another line of very strong breastworks. This fort, if properly defended, could be held against anything except the most determined attack. Wire entanglements are also used for the defence of this position.

The ridge upon which our army was situated was very favorably located. We overlooked the city and could readily see their fortifications and the barbed-wire fences which they had put up as an additional means of defence. San Juan River and other streams ran back of and parallel to a great part of the ridge and adjacent to all parts of it, so that we were abundantly supplied with water for all purposes. I therefore advocated the plan of extending our right around the city, which was done in the first instance by thinning our lines and continually spreading them to the right; and finally the arrival of reinforcements enabled us to lengthen the line by placing the new troops in position.

The enemy very soon perceived that the gradual increase of our forces would make this inclosure so complete that escape would be impossible, and this would place their army and their fleet under Admiral Cervera at our mercy. General Blanco and Admiral Cervera both seemed to realize this, and in order to save their fleet it sailed out on Sunday morning, July 3d. The utter destruction of the fleet by our navy was most magnificently accomplished.

The Spanish fleet was here composed of the armored cruisers *Almirante Oquendo*, *Infanta Maria Teresa*, *Vizcaya*, *Cristobal Colon*, the *Reina Mercedes*, and the torpedo-boat destroyers *Furor*, *Terror*,[1] and *Pluton*. The armored cruisers were 7,000-ton ships, all of them larger and in

[1]The torpedo-boat destroyer *Terror* had left Spain with Cervera's fleet, but was stopped at San Juan de Puerto Rico, and never reached Santiago harbor.

some respects more powerful than the battleship *Maine*. Their speed was twenty knots an hour, their armament was of the best; and taking them all in all they were classed among the best battleships in the world. The torpedo-boat destroyers were the highest order of ships of that character. The *Pluton* ran thirty knots an hour, and the *Furor* and *Terror* had attained the speed of twenty-eight knots. The *Terror* had been previously destroyed, and the *Pluton* and *Furor* were sunk on July 3d.

In order to give the reader a fuller description of the character of the ships which composed the fleet of Admiral Cervera, I incorporate the following item from the New York "Sun" of July 4, 1898:

Cervera's squadron was made up of four armored cruisers, three torpedo-boat destroyers, and several other vessels, when he left Spain. The most formidable vessels were the four armored cruisers, fine examples of the armored-cruiser type. They were the *Almirante Oquendo*, the *Infanta Maria Teresa*, the *Vizcaya*, and the *Cristobal Colon*. The first three were sister ships, built at Bilboa, Spain, and launched in 1890 and 1891. Their cost was given as $3,000,000 each.

These cruisers were 7,000-ton ships, somewhat larger than the battleship *Maine*. Their water-line length was 340 feet, beam 65 feet, maximum draught 21 feet 6 inches, indicated horse-power 13,000, and speed 20 knots. This speed they attained in their trial speeds, but when inefficient Spanish engineers took hold of them they could not develop any such speed as this. Their normal coal supply was 12,000 tons, and their complement 500 men each.

Heavy armor protected the machinery of the cruisers. They had steel water-line belts 315 feet long, 5½ feet broad, and from 10 to 12 inches thick. The two turrets on each ship were constructed of 9-inch steel. The gun positions of the broadside guns were protected by armor 10½ inches thick, and the deck-plating was 3 inches thick. In armor these ships were far superior to our armored cruisers *New York* and *Brooklyn*. The *Brooklyn's* thickest belt armor is 7 inches thick, and on the gun positions the thickest is 8 inches.

This trio of cruisers carried heavy armaments. In turrets, forward and aft, each ship mounted 11-inch breech-loading rifles. In addition, each mounted ten 5½-inch guns. The *Oquendo* and *Maria Teresa* 5½-inch guns were Hontoria guns, but the *Vizcaya* had rapid-fire guns. Each ship carried a number of small guns, and was equipped with six torpedo-tubes. Spain had trouble in buying torpedoes before the war opened, — the country has no facilities for making torpedoes, — and it is doubtful if the ships in Santiago de Cuba harbor were adequately equipped with torpedoes.

The *Cristobal Colon* was one of the newest ships in the Spanish navy. She was built at Sestri Potente by the Italian government, and launched in 1896. Her name was then the *Giuseppe Garibaldi II.*, replacing a previous ship by that name. Spain paid several million dollars for her, and named her the *Cristobal*

Colon in memory of the cruiser by that name lost near Cape San Antonio, Cuba, in October, 1895. She was a 6,840-ton ship, 388 feet on the water-line, 59 feet 8 inches beam, and 24 feet draught. Her indicated horse-power was 14,000, her trial speed 20 knots, maximum coal supply 1,000 tons, and complement 450 men.

The *Cristobal Colon's* armament consisted of two 10-inch turreted guns, ten 6-inch rapid-fire guns, and six 4.7-inch, ten 2.2-inch, ten 1.4-inch, and two machine guns. She also carried four torpedo-tubes. Her armor consisted of a 6-inch water-line belt, 6 inches on the gun positions, and a 1½-inch deck. The heavy armor was of Harveyized steel.

The torpedo-boat destroyers were fine Clyde-bank boats — the *Furor* and *Terror*, launched in 1896, and the *Pluton*, launched last year. The first two were capable of developing the remarkable speed of 28 knots an hour, and the *Pluton* was credited with 30 knots. No boats in the American navy now in commission approached them in speed. The *Furor's* and *Terror's* principal dimensions were : Length, 220 feet ; beam, 22 feet ; draught, 5.6 feet ; displacement, 300 tons ; coal capacity, 100 tons ; complement, 67 men ; armament, two 12-pounders, two 6-pounders, and two 1-pounders. The *Pluton* was a larger boat, registering 400 tons and having an indicated horse-power of 7,500, — 1,500 greater than the others.

The naval battle commenced about 9.30 Sunday morning, July 3d. The torpedo-boat destroyers were foundered, the tops of their masts sinking below the surface. The *Reina Mercedes* already lay in the harbor-mouth, almost submerged, where she had been sunk by our navy. The *Infanta Maria Teresa* and *Almirante Oquendo* kept up a running fight westward about five miles, when they succumbed, turned towards the shore, the fire streaming from their decks; they surrendered, and our navy devoted itself to saving the lives of the Spanish sailors. The *Vizcaya* ran some six miles further; but being unable to continue the fight, yielded to the same fate as her sister ships. The *Cristobal Colon*, by virtue of her great speed, escaped for a while, but after a run of fifty miles was overtaken and captured. A few days afterwards I visited all these ships except the *Cristobal Colon*.[1] It is generally conceded that the *Reina Mercedes* cannot be raised and repaired to advantage. The *Infanta Maria Teresa*, although completely burnt out, has already been floated by the " Merritt Wrecking Company," and will be repaired sufficiently to become an American man-of-war.[2] The *Cristobal Colon* will also be constructed into an American ship; but the *Vizcaya* and *Almirante Oquendo* are structurally injured to such an extent that the only use that can be made of them would be to place them in some harbor as hospital ships or as historical monuments.

[1] For an account of this visit, see pp. 184–187.

[2] Others have since been raised, or will soon be raised by the skilful plans of Lieutenant Hobson, who now (October 10th) has the work in charge.

Admiral Sampson telegraphed the Secretary of the Navy as follows:

SIBONEY, July 3.

SECRETARY OF THE NAVY:

The fleet under my command offers the Nation as a Fourth of July present the destruction of the whole of Cervera's fleet. Not one escaped. They attempted to escape at 9.30 this morning. At 2, the last ship, the *Cristobal Colon*, had run ashore sixty miles west of Santiago and had let down her colors. The *Maria Teresa*, *Oquendo*, and *Vizcaya* were forced ashore, burned, and blown up within twenty miles of Santiago. The *Furor* and *Pluton* were destroyed within four miles of the port. Loss, one killed and two wounded. Enemy's loss probably several hundred, from gunpowder explosions and drowning. About one thousand three hundred prisoners, including Admiral Cervera. The man killed was George H. Ellis, Chief Yeoman of the *Brooklyn*.   SAMPSON.

To which the President and the Secretary of the Navy replied as follows:

EXECUTIVE MANSION, July 4, 12.30 P.M.

ADMIRAL SAMPSON:

You have the gratitude and congratulations of the whole American people. Convey to your noble officers and crews, through whose valor new honors have been added to the American navy, the grateful thanks and appreciation of the Nation.

WILLIAM McKINLEY.

NAVY DEPARTMENT, July 4.

ADMIRAL SAMPSON:

The Secretary of the Navy sends you and every officer and man of your fleet, remembering equally your dead comrades, grateful acknowledgment of your heroism and success. All honor to the brave! You have maintained the glory of the American navy.

JOHN D. LONG.

Commander Watson, in charge while Sampson continued the chase, sent the following despatch:

PLAYA DEL ESTE, July 3.

SECRETARY OF THE NAVY,
    Washington, D.C.:

At 9.30 A.M., to-day, the Spanish squadron, seven in all, including one gunboat, came out of Santiago in column, and was totally destroyed within an hour, excepting *Cristobal Colon*, which was chased forty-five miles to the westward by the commander-in-chief, *Brooklyn*, *Oregon*, and *Texas*, surrendering to *Brooklyn*, but was beached to prevent sinking. None of our officers or men were injured except on board *Brooklyn*. Chief Yeoman Ellis was killed and one man wounded. Admiral Cervera, all commanding officers excepting of *Oquendo*, about 70 other officers, and 1,600 men are prisoners. About 350 killed or drowned, and 160 wounded. Latter being cared for on *Solace* and *Olivette*. Have just arrived off Santiago in *Marblehead*, to take charge while commander-in-chief is looking out for *Cristobal Colon*.

WATSON.

I also give the report of Admiral Cervera to his commander, General Blanco:

To the General-in-Chief,
        Havana :

In compliance with your orders, I went out yesterday from Santiago de Cuba with all the squadron, and, after an unequal combat against forces more than triple mine, had all my squadron destroyed by fire; the *Maria Teresa*, *Oquendo*, and *Vizcaya* beached, and the *Colon* fleeing. I accordingly informed the Americans, and went ashore and gave myself up. The torpedo-chasers foundered. I do not know how many people are lost, but it will surely reach six hundred dead and many wounded. Although not in such great numbers, the living are prisoners of the Americans. The conduct of the crew rose to a height that won the most enthusiastic plaudits of the enemy. The commander of the *Vizcaya* surrendered his vessel. His crew are very grateful for the noble generosity with which they are treated. Among the dead is Villamil, and I believe Lazaga, and among the wounded Cancas and Eulate. We have lost all, and are necessarily depressed.

                                CERVERA.

As I was not a personal witness of the naval battle by which Cervera's fleet was destroyed, I will insert the account written by a naval officer who participated; which account appeared in the New York "Herald" of July 7, 1898. It is as follows:

"In anticipation of a great battle between the American fleet and the Cape Verde squadrons, commanded by Admiral Cervera, the 'Herald' secured the services of an expert naval authority on board one of the battleships to write a technical description of the fight when it occurred. The writer is well known to the 'Herald,' and it is therefore able to vouch for its authenticity:

"ON BOARD U.S. S. IOWA, OFF SANTIAGO, July 4.
        BY DESPATCH BOAT TO PORT ANTONIO, July 6.

"On Sunday morning, July 3d, our watching ships lay rolling in the easy surges off the entrance of the harbor of Santiago. Their distances from the guarded haven varied from four to six thousand yards, and there, with an unsparing alertness, they waited for that promised dash which all hoped for, but feared might never come.

"A little after three bells in the forenoon watch the inspection of the ship had been concluded, and as Lieutenant Van Duzer, the officer of the watch, was relieving the navigating officer, Lieutenant Scheutze, then officer of the deck, he heard a quick cry to call the captain, followed by a shout, 'There come the Spaniards out of the harbor!'

"The trained eye of the alert officer had marked the thin trail of drifting smoke, and before the signal 'Clear ship for action" had been given, the bows of the Spanish vessels, rushing in 'Line ahead,' were seen darting around Socapa Point for the open sea.

" In a moment all was bustle and trained energy. Men rushed to their quarters, guns were trained, and in less than twenty seconds the whistling shriek of a rapid-fire gun warned the startled fleet of the hot work awaiting. In two minutes every gun on shipboard was cast loose, manned, loaded, and ready for the long-expected signal to fire.

" At the yard-arm of our battleship a string of signal flags warned the fleet the enemy was trying to escape; but even before the answering pennants of the other ships announced their understanding of the message, every vessel was dashing to the stations long before allotted for the emergency which had come at last.

" It was a splendid spectacle. The Spaniards, with bottled steam, cleared the harbor's mouth seemingly in a moment. Under their eager prows a column of foam whitened the long billows, and their bubbling wakes left a furrow as straight and sharp as a racing yacht making a winning run for the finish line.

" Their course was shaped for the westward ; but fast as they sped in their desperate break for freedom, faster flew the shells of the pursuing Americans. The first heavy shell from the *Iowa's* battery fell short, and then, by a lucky mischance, so did the second ; but afterward the rain of shot fell surely and unsparingly upon the fleeing foe.

"Not a whit behind in this eager fusilade roared the batteries of the Spanish ships. Their port broadsides flamed and grumbled, but it was more a splendid display of fireworks than a successful effort to damage the unharmed targets of the Yankee ships. In fifteen minutes after they were discovered the four Spanish armored cruisers had cleared the wide entrance, and five minutes later the torpedo-boat destroyers, hugging the beach and seeking the sheltering broadside of their sister ships, flew into the turmoil of the action.

"At this time every gun of the American squadron that could be brought to bear was pumping projectiles into the enemy. In an instant, it almost seemed, one ship of the *Vizcaya* class burst into flames, caused, undoubtedly, by a long, sure shot from the *Oregon* or the *Texas*.

"A minute later a 12-inch projectile sent from the *Iowa's* forward turret struck the flagship *Maria Teresa* near her after smoke-pipe. A tremendous explosion followed. Then she was shrouded in smoke and was lighted with lurid flames; and then when the powder-cloud blew down the wind she was seen helm hard a-port rushing for the beach.

"Twenty-five minutes after the first ship had been sighted, half the Spanish fleet had surrendered or was on fire.

"As our vessels rushed toward them every ship was hulled time and again ; and it almost seemed, in the sureness and directness of our batteries, as if it were the target practice of a summer morning, and not the annihilation of a squadron.

" Even this interval would have been shortened measurably, for, aiding them and hindering us, was the cloud of smoke, which concealed and at the best only half revealed the wrecked enemy.

" It was a grand, sad sight, a pathetic one to seamen, who know how much patient thought and patriotic effort had gone into the construction of these splendid vessels, now lying, bruised and burning, on the shores they had hoped to defend.

" There was no time, however, to indulge in emotions of sympathy or of pity, for still rushing eagerly westward, closely followed by the *New York*, and at a further distance by the *Indiana*, came the torpedo-boat destroyers.

" In the hot eagerness of destruction we turned loose our smaller guns on these loudly heralded and ineffective craft, and finally by a lucky hit dropped a 12-inch shell into the bow of the leading destroyer. At the same instant the little *Hist* was rapidly closing upon them, pouring a sickening fire into their fragile hulls.

" The *Gloucester* joined in this splendid assault, and so sure and so effective was their raid of rapid-fire projectiles that both torpedo boats swung their helms hard a-port, ran for the shore, and buried what was left of them among the pitiless rocks of the coast.

"By a quarter past ten we were in full cry after the other Spanish ships, then about four miles ahead, and busy with hot replies to the determined assault of the *Oregon*, *Texas*, and *Brooklyn*.

"Bending every energy to overtake the *Colon*, which was then five miles away and perhaps two miles ahead in a direct line, and a mile and a half further in shore, we picked up the flying *Vizcaya*.

"The game must have seemed up to her then, for with a quick turn to starboard she ran shoreward, and we saw in an instant that she was flaming fore and aft. A beautiful Spanish flag floating from her gaff, and another higher still from her main topmast head, showed her to be the flagship of the second in command. She lagged heavily in the water; no longer did she carry a bone in her teeth, and her foaming wake was gone.

"When we drew near we saw something had gone amiss with her, for just as we swung with a touch of our helm to give her a finishing broadside, the beautiful flags drifted from truck and gaff end and the white flag of surrender went up, and the cheers of our ship went with it.

"We stopped our engines when close aboard, and hoisted out our boats to save her people. We received on board two hundred and fifty of her crew, the *Hist* took another hundred, and that was all that was left of them; for the other hapless sailors were lying dead and wounded on her burning decks.

"The conflagration aboard this ship was astounding; and even now, when the opportunity for calm reflection has come, it is impossible to explain where so much inflammable material could have been collected on board an armored vessel. Through the air-ports and gun-ports of the doomed ship quivering fires shone with a blood-red light upon the light woodwork of the bridge and upper deck, and long tongues of flame licked the towering masts.

"Over the ship a cloud of rosy light hovered, and when, after a time, the explosions of the free powder were added, great volumes of smoke shut out the sky. Several explosions of terrific force followed; but notwithstanding this, and while the flames were still quivering through every outlet and encircling the hull, our boats were busy with the rescue of the unfortunate wounded and those more lucky survivors who had sought the water or the shore as their only refuge from a dreadful death.

"The glorious *Texas*, no longer the 'hoodoo' of the fleet, gave its principal attention to the *Vizcaya*, and one of her 12-inch shells, smashing through the fire-room of the Spaniard, caused her to make that quick turn to the shore which at first we did not understand.

"The *New York* was so far to the eastward that she had a long chase and a stern chase before she got into the action, and she passed us just after the *Vizcaya* surrendered. She made a splendid marine picture as she rushed eagerly by in a hot chase after the *Colon;* and as she shot past, we gave Sampson cheer after cheer, and cheer after cheer came back to us from as gallant a crew as ever served a gun or fed a roaring furnace.

"Some of the crew swam to the beach; but, finding the hostile shores commanded by alert parties of Cuban soldiers, they fought in a mad endeavor to get on board the ships' boats rather than surrender to an enemy whom they knew to be pitiless. Every officer and man on the *Iowa* gave clothes of some sort to the rescued sailors, and their reception must have taught them that the despised Yankee was not the inhuman brute their officers had pictured.

"The paymaster's stores of the ship were drawn on lavishly to clothe the Spanish officers and men; and when after a while they were dried and fed, it was interesting to note the relief all seemed to feel, now that their long suspense of so many weary weeks was over and done.

"When the Spanish captain of the *Vizcaya*, that courteous Eulate of whom we heard so much when his ship was in the harbor of New York, was lifted over the side and half carried aft, he presented his sword to Captain Evans as the symbol; but Evans, gentle as he is brave, declined to receive it, and, waving it back with a friendly gesture, he grasped the hand of the Spaniard and welcomed his brother officer to the hospitality of the ship.

"Much affected by his reception, Captain Eulate asked permission to meet the *Iowa's* officers; and to each he gave a warm grip of his hand and a friendly word of gratitude, before he was carried below.

"The *Oregon* and *Brooklyn* joined in the attack, but were a little too far out to get into the best of it; and their efforts were directed more to head off and catch the *Colon* than to join in the general action. There was a wisdom in this approved of all good sailors; for they knew what work was cut out for them, and in what good hands the other ships were left.

"At one time, the *Iowa* was engaged with all the ships single-handed. The Spanish officers told us later that their orders were to concentrate their fire on her, and every effort must be made to disable her, as she was the most dangerous antagonist of all awaiting them. But, as one of the Spanish officers added, with a fine air of perplexity, 'We found that all the ships were equally dangerous; and that, after all was said and done, it was four ships against four, and one of these, the *Brooklyn*, was much more lightly armored and gunned than any of ours.'

"Reckoning up the data of this memorable fight, which it was our good fortune to take part in, we find, that —

"In less than twenty-five minutes two of their ships were wrecked;

"In less than three-quarters of an hour the third surrendered;

"In fifty-six minutes from the time the first dashing Spaniard was sighted, all hands were piped down, the guns were secured, and our boats were in the water to save what was left of the *Vizcaya's* crew.

"At five o'clock in the afternoon of that memorable Sunday, the *Iowa* arrived off the entrance to Santiago, the *Gloucester* keeping company with us after speaking the *Indiana* and exchanging cheers that made the welkin ring. When alongside the *Indiana*, Captain Evans hailed his brother-in-law, Captain Taylor of that ship, and told him to send Admiral Cervera on board and he would put at his disposal the vacant admiral's-cabin of our ship.

"The gallant but defeated sailor came alongside in the *Gloucester's* boat, and was received with all the honors due his rank and station. The full marine guard was paraded, the bugles flourished a salute; and when the official side was finished the reception accorded him by the captured officers of the *Vizcaya* showed the affectionate regard with which this fearless gentleman was held by those who served under him.

"Captain Eulate wore the sword Captain Evans had refused to accept; and he pointed to it with a pathetic pride as he told of the reception accorded him by the *Iowa's* captain. It was an affecting and a heart-warming sight, and made a fitting close to a day that will be memorable for the glories it yielded to our arms at sea."

While these events were occurring, the Asiatic Squadron, under Admiral Dewey, was engaged in capturing and placing the American flag upon the Ladrone Islands; while at the same time the admiral landed troops and hoisted the American flag at Cavite, Luzon Island. The following cablegrams from Admiral Dewey briefly informed us of these successes:

CAVITE, July 3.
SECRETARY OF THE NAVY,
        Washington:

Three transports, and cruiser *Charleston*, arrived yesterday. Captured Guara, Ladrone Islands. Brought the Spanish officials and the garrison of six officers and fifty-four men to Manila. On June 29th, the Spanish gunboat *Leyte* came out of a river near Manila and surrendered to me; having exhausted ammunition and food repelling attack of insurgents. Had on board 52 officers and 94 men.   DEWEY.

CAVITE, July 4.
SECRETARY OF THE NAVY,
        Washington:

United States troops have landed and have been comfortably housed at Cavite, Luzon Island. Insurgents still active. Aguinaldo proclaimed himself president of the revolutionary republic, July 1st.   DEWEY.

CHAPTER IX

ON the morning of the 4th, the following despatch from General Miles was read to the troops:

> HEADQUARTERS OF THE ARMY,
> WASHINGTON, July 3, 1898.
>
> GENERAL SHAFTER,
>   Cuba:
>
> Accept my hearty congratulations on the record made of magnificent fortitude, gallantry, and sacrifice displayed in the desperate fighting of the troops before Santiago.
>
> I realize the hardships, difficulties, and suffering; and am proud that amidst it all the troops illustrated such fearless and patriotic devotion to the welfare of our common country and flag. Whatever the result to follow, their unsurpassed deeds of valor is already a gratifying chapter of history. Expect to be with you within one week with strong reinforcements.
>
> MILES,
> *Major-General Commanding.*

General Shafter replied to General Miles's telegram in the following words:

HEADQUARTERS 5TH ARMY CORPS,
NEAR SANTIAGO, July 3, 1889.

MAJOR-GENERAL NELSON A. MILES, *Commanding the Army of the United States*, Washington:

I thank you in the name of the gallant men I have the honor to command for splendid tribute of praise which you have accorded them. Your telegram will be published at the head of the regiments, and this morning I feel that I am master of the situation and can hold the enemy for any length of time. I am delighted to know that you are coming, that you may see for yourself the obstacles which this army had to overcome. My only regret is the great number of gallant souls who have given their lives for our country's cause.

SHAFTER.

At the same time the general commanding issued the following order, congratulating the troops upon their victorious achievement:

HEADQUARTERS U.S. FORCES,
SAN JUAN RIVER, July 4, 1898.

GENERAL ORDERS }
No. 21.   }

The general commanding congratulates the army on the results of its first general engagement with the enemy. The strongly fortified outpost and village of Caney was captured after a most stubborn resistance, nearly its entire garrison being killed, wounded, or captured by the 2d Divison, 5th Corps, Brigadier-General Lawton commanding. The heroic valor displayed by these troops adds another brilliant page to the history of American warfare. To Major-General Wheeler, of the Cavalry Division, was probably given the most difficult task, that of crossing a stream under a fire, and deploying under the enemy's rifle-pits. These he almost immediately charged and carried in the most gallant manner, driving the enemy from his strong positions to the shelter of the stronger works in rear. This was only accomplished by the most persevering and arduous efforts, officers and men exposing themselves to the deadly fire of the Spanish troops. In these efforts he was ably seconded by Brigadier-General Kent, with the 1st Division on the extreme left, who also captured the works on his front.

Numerous distinguished acts have been reported, and in due time will be made known to the proper authorities.

.   .   .   .

By command of Major-General Shafter,

E. J. McCLERNAND,
Assistant Adjutant-General.

On the 9th the following from the President was received and read to the troops:

WASHINGTON, D.C., July 8, 1898.

GENERAL SHAFTER,
Playa, Cuba:

Telegram which it appears you did not receive read as follows:

The President directs me to say you have the gratitude and thanks of the Nation for the brilliant and effective work of your noble army in the fight of July 1.

The sturdy valor and heroism of officers and men fill the American people with pride. The country mourns the brave men who fell in battle. They have added new names to our roll of heroes.

R. A. ALGER,
Secretary of War.

The destruction of the Spanish fleet under Admiral Cervera was a terrible blow to the Spanish military commander, General José Toral; Lieutenant-General Linares having been severely wounded about 2 o'clock in the battle of July 1st. On the 5th, General Toral, in reply to a demand for surrender, proposed to withdraw all his forces from the eastern province of Santiago, provided it was stipulated that he should not be molested until he had reached the city of Holguin, some seventy miles to the northwest. This proposition was submitted to the U.S. Government at Washington, and declined. From the 5th to the 10th, the time was divided between flags of truce and some pretty brisk skirmishing along the entire line.

Our losses in these engagements were very small. Besides building quite formidable breastworks and protecting our line by traverses, we had also, by the free and judicious use of sandbags, so thoroughly screened our men from the enemy, that hours of a strong fire from the enemy's works, even at very short range, were almost without effect. The men in the trenches were almost absolutely protected, the only shots of the Spaniards which seemed to have any effect being those which passed over our works and fell among our soldiers who were in the rear. On the 3d, General Shafter sent me the following letter, which I promptly sent forward by a flag of truce:

HEADQUARTERS UNITED STATES FORCES,
NEAR SAN JUAN RIVER, CUBA,
July 3, 1898, 8.30 A.M.

THE COMMANDING GENERAL OF THE SPANISH FORCES,
Santiago de Cuba:

SIR: I shall be obliged, unless you surrender, to shell Santiago de Cuba. Please inform the citizens of foreign countries and all women and children that they should leave the city before 10 o'clock to-morrow morning.

Very respectfully,
Your obedient servant,
W. R. SHAFTER,
Major-General, U.S.A.

General Toral, the Spanish commander, replied as follows:

SANTIAGO DE CUBA, July 3, 1898.

HIS EXCELLENCY THE GENERAL COMMANDING FORCES
OF UNITED STATES,
San Juan River:

SIR: I have the honor to reply to your communication of to-day, written at 8.30 A.M., and received at 4 P.M., demanding the surrender of this city; on the contrary case announcing to me that I advise the foreign women and children that they must leave the city before 10 o'clock to-morrow morning. It is my duty to say to you that this city will not surrender; that I will inform the foreign consuls and inhabitants of your message.

Very respectfully,

José Toral,

Commander-in-Chief 4th Corps.

Immediately following this flag of truce I was visited at my headquarters by the British, Portuguese, Chinese, and Norwegian consuls. They came to request that non-combatants be allowed to proceed to and occupy the town of El Caney and other points upon the railroad which connect Santiago with San Luis. They also asked that the Americans feed these refugees, who they said would number between fifteen and twenty thousand. They also asked that the city be not fired upon until 10 o'clock on the 5th. I sent these requests forward to General Shafter, to which he sent me the following reply:

In Camp near Santiago, July 3, 1898.

Major-General Wheeler:

Sir: Notify consuls that their request for delay until 10 a.m. the 5th is acceded to, provided that Spanish forces inside of city remain quiet. I desire some representative of the foreign governments, to be selected by themselves, to come to my lines to-morrow, say, at 9 o'clock, for further conference as to departure of foreign subjects and caring for them while outside of lines.

Very respectfully,

WM. R. SHAFTER.

Order all firing to cease, and not to be resumed unless enemy fires on us.

General Shafter also sent to the Spanish commander the following despatch for the benefit of would-be refugees from the city of Santiago, which I forwarded to General Toral :

HEADQUARTERS 5TH ARMY CORPS,
July 3, 1898.

THE COMMANDING GENERAL, SPANISH FORCES,
        Santiago de Cuba:

SIR : In consideration of the request of the consuls and officers in your city for delay in carrying out my intention to fire on the city, and in the interest of the poor women and children who will suffer very greatly by their hasty and enforced departure from the city, I have the honor to announce that I will delay such action solely in their interest until the noon of the 5th, providing during the interval your forces make no demonstration whatever upon those of my own.

I am, with great respect,
Your obedient servant,

W. R. SHAFTER,
Major-General, U.S.A.

The following despatches from General Shafter of this date (July 3d) and a despatch from Colonel Wagner, of General Miles's staff, who was at General Shafter's headquarters, tell the story of the advance of General Escario, who commanded Pando's column. I also call attention to General Shafter's despatch in which he speaks of "the tremendous fighting qualities shown by the enemy from his almost impregnable position":

HEADQUARTERS 5TH ARMY CORPS, July 3.
SECRETARY OF WAR, Washington:

Did not telegraph, as I was too busy looking after things that had to be attended to at once, and did not wish to send any news that was not fully confirmed. The Spanish fleet left the harbor this morning and is reported practically destroyed. I demanded surrender of the city at 10 o'clock to-day, but at this hour, 4.30 P.M., no reply had been received. Perfect quiet along the line. Situation has been precarious on account of difficulties of supplying the command with food and the tremendous fighting qualities shown by the enemy from his almost impregnable position.

SHAFTER, *Major-General.*

PLAYA DEL ESTE, July 3, 1898, 11.44 A.M.
SECRETARY OF WAR, Washington:

CAMP NEAR SEVILLA, CUBA, July 3. — We have the town well invested on the north and east, but with a very thin line. Upon approaching it, we find it of such a character, and the defences so strong, it will be impossible to carry it by storm with my present force, and I am seriously considering withdrawing about five miles and taking up a new position on the high ground between the San Juan River and Siboney, with our left at Sardinero, so as to get our supplies to a large extent by means of the railroad, which we can now use, having engines and cars at Siboney. Our losses up to date will aggregate a thousand, but list has not yet been made. But little sickness, outside of exhaustion from the intense heat and exertion of the battle of the day before yesterday, and the almost constant fire which is kept up on the trenches. Wagon road to the rear is kept up with some difficulty on account of rains, but I will be able to use it for the present. General Wheeler is seriously ill, and will probably have to go to the rear to-day. General Young is also very ill; confined to his bed. General Hawkins slightly wounded in foot. During the sortie enemy made last night, which was handsomely repulsed, the behavior of the troops was magnificent. I am urging Admiral Sampson to attempt to force the entrance of the harbor, and will have a consultation with him this morning. He is coming to the front to see me. I have been unable to be out during the heat of the day for four days, but am retaining the command. General Garcia reported that he holds the railroad from Santiago to San Luis, and has burned a bridge and removed some rails; also that General Pando has arrived at Palma, and that the French consul, with about four hundred French citizens, came into his lines yesterday from Santiago. Have directed him to treat them with every courtesy possible.

SHAFTER, *Major-General.*

HEADQUARTERS 5TH ARMY CORPS,
NEAR SANTIAGO, July 3.

SECRETARY OF WAR, Washington:

To-night my lines completely surround the town from bay on north of city to point on San Juan River on south. The enemy holds from west bend San Juan River at its mouth up the railroad to the city. General Pando, I find to-night, is some distance away, and will not get into Santiago.

SHAFTER.

HEADQUARTERS 5TH ARMY CORPS,
July 3, 1898.

GENERAL MILES, Washington:

Killed a Spanish general in affair at Commual, and large number of officers and men, who are still unburied. General Linares' arm was broken. My demand for surrender of Santiago still being considered by Spanish authorities. Pando has arrived near break in railroad with his advance. I think he will be stopped.

SHAFTER, *Commanding*.

NEAR SANTIAGO DE CUBA, July 3.

GENERAL MILES, Washington:

Pando six miles north with 5,000. Garcia opposes with 3,000. Lawton can support Garcia and prevent junction.   WAGNER,
Assistant Adjutant-General.

CHAPTER X

MY ILLNESS OVERSTATED — DID NOT LEAVE COMMAND — GENERAL GARCIA'S BATTLE WITH THE PANDO COLUMN — A WARM ATTACK ON THE CITY — DETAILED REPORT OF BOMBARDMENT — GENERAL MILES TAKES COMMAND — THE FIRST OVERTURES FOR PEACE

THREE days subsequently, the commanding general cabled Washington, mainly concerning the health of certain officers, as follows:

HEADQUARTERS 5TH ARMY CORPS, July 6.
SECRETARY OF WAR, Washington:
CAMP NEAR SANTIAGO, July 5. — Captains Alger and Sewell and Mr. Corbin are well. I am feeling better. Had hoped to be up this A.M., but as everything is quiet I will remain still. General Wheeler is feeble,[1] but remains with his command. General Young leaves for Key West to-day. General Hawkins slightly wounded in foot. All others well.

SHAFTER, *Major-General Commanding.*

When the papers of the early part of July reached us I regretted very much to see that General Shafter had telegraphed as he did re-

[1] See also p. 115, General Shafter's telegram three days before.

garding my health. It is true that I had had
an attack of fever, but the same is true of every
other general in the army in Cuba, and of all my
staff officers except an acclimated Cuban who
acted as Volunteer Aid. Immediately after the
battle of Las Guasimas, June 24th, I received
orders from General Shafter to take command of
all the troops on shore and throw them forward
as far as could be done without risking contact
with the enemy. This contemplated selecting
favorable camps for these troops as they came
up, so that they would be supplied with water
and also be in a defensive position. To accomplish this work properly, required a great deal of
riding in the hot sun; and as I had no tent I was
exposed to the heavy dews of the night. After
six days of this character of exposure I was
taken with the fever; but, by placing myself
under the charge of a doctor and taking all the
prescribed medicine, I was up and ready for duty
on the morning of July 1st, the day of the Battle
of San Juan. I was engaged during all this
day; and even after dark I remained on the
advanced line, to get up intrenching-tools and
to encourage the construction of breastworks.

I was up at 4 o'clock on the morning of
the 2d; was engaged during the entire day;
and at dark, by direction of General Shafter,
I went back to his quarters, and remained
in the open air until nearly 11 o'clock. The
exertions of these two days were very exhaust-

ing, and on the 3d I felt the effect considerably; but from that time I gathered strength, and soon recovered.   I was not off duty for a single moment during the campaign; and I do not think my sickness materially impaired my usefulness.

It appears from the report of the commander of the Pando column, that on approaching Santiago he was met by General Garcia, commanding some four thousand Cuban troops.   An engagement took place in which the Spaniards lost 27 killed and 67 wounded; but it seems that the Spaniards drove the Cubans back and cleared the way to Santiago, joining there General Toral.

Reinforcements meanwhile had reached Siboney and joined our line.   This enabled us to extend our right until it reached to within a little more than half a mile from the shores of the bay.   On the 5th, in view of the bombardment of the town, some 22,000 inhabitants of Santiago passed through the lines to El Caney, Siboney, and other localities.   On the 9th, another demand for surrender was made, was refused, and a warm attack was made upon the city by our artillery and small-arms.   This continued from 4 o'clock until dark on Sunday, the 10th, — the casualties being very small, and the Cavalry Division only losing two men wounded. On the morning of the 11th, the bombardment was renewed, assisted by the navy.   One of my officers, whom I placed where it could be well observed, noted their shots as follows:

Report of Naval Shots during the Bombardment of Santiago, July 11, 1898.

No.	TIME.	REMARKS.
1.	9.30.	Could not see where it went.
2.	10.03.	Heard no explosion; saw no effects.
3.	10.08.	" " "
4.	10.14.	" " "
5.	10.16.	Heard no explosion; did not see where it struck.
6.	10.20.	Exploded apparently in lower part of city, near the bay.
7.	10.21.	Exploded on south side of city; could not see effects.
8.	10.25.	No explosion.
9.	10.25.	Could not tell where it went.
10.	10.28.	Heard no explosion.
11.	10.30.	" "
12.	10.30.	Exploded; could not see where struck.
13.	10.36.	" " "
14.	10.35.	" " "
15.	10.36.	" " "
16.	10.40.	Heard no explosion.
17.	10.40.	Explosion in town; could not see where.
18.	10.45.	Heard no explosion.
19.	10.45.	Expl'n down near water front, apparently.
20.	10.46.	" " " "
21.	10.50.	Explosion on slope toward water front; out of sight.
22.	10.51.	Exploded on south side of town; could not be seen.
23.	10.54.	Exploded on east side of town; effects not seen.

Report of Naval Shooting, — concluded.

No.	TIME.	REMARKS.
24.	10.55.	No explosion heard.
25.	11.01.	" "
26.	11.01.	" "
27.	11.02.	" "
28.	11.03.	" "
29.	11.05.	Explosion on side towards bay ; effects not seen.
30.	11.10.	No explosion heard.
31.	11.11.	" "
32.	11.15.	Explosion on slope of city towards bay ; not seen.
33.	11.16.	No explosion seen; fire seen in city, but did not last long.
34.	11.21.	Exploded on sloe towards bay.
35.	11.24.	" " "
36.	11.25.	" " "
37.	11.28.	Heard no explosion.
38.	11.30.	Exploded on city slope towards bay.
39.	11.33.	" " "
40.	11.33.	" " "
41.	11.34.	" " "
42.	11.35.	" " "
43.	11.36.	" " "
44.	11.37.	" " "
45.	11.38.	" " "
46.	11.40.	Exploded beyond the city.

All shells explode on slope towards bay; cannot see where they strike.

F. WEST, *Captain, 6th Cavalry.*

During the periods occupied by the various flags of truce I had had numerous conversations with the Spanish officers from Santiago, and found that their condition was by no means satisfactory to them.

On the 13th, General Miles, Commander of the Army, arrived from the United States; and this high official, General Shafter, and myself went out and had a long interview with General Toral. Upon General Miles's return to my camp he sent the following despatch to the Secretary of War:

GENERAL WHEELER'S HEADQUARTERS,
BEFORE SANTIAGO, CUBA, July 13, 1898.
To HON. SECRETARY OF WAR,
Washington, D.C. :

At a meeting between the lines, at which Generals Shafter and Wheeler and Spanish General Toral were present, the latter claims that he is unable to act without authority of his Government, but has received authority to withdraw and surrender harbor, forts, munitions of war, and eastern portion of Cuba. He urgently requests until to-morrow noon to receive answer from his Government regarding offer of our Government to send his forces to Spain, which was granted.

NELSON A. MILES,
Major-General Commanding the Army.

The next day, the 14th, the same officers had a much more extended interview, during which the question of surrender was discussed.

It seems that in the conversation, the interpreters used by General Miles and General Shafter were rather careless in their interpretations; and General Shafter and General Miles were led to understand that General Toral had consented to an absolute capitulation.

I heard the conversations on the 14th; and previous to that time General Toral had repeatedly stated, that under the laws of Spain a general could not surrender without the authority of the home or Madrid Government.

He stated, however, that he had authority from General Blanco to arrange terms of surrender which would become effectual upon the reception of authority of the Madrid Government to capitulate on the basis of the Spanish troops being transported to Spain. General Toral and his Spanish interpreter, Mr. Mason, also stated with great emphasis that the Spanish Government would accede to the terms ; because it was the custom of their Government to comply with the recommendations of their captains-general. Both General Toral and Mr. Mason seemed to think that there was no question on this point, and therefore in their talks with General Miles and General Shafter on the morning of the 14th, they referred to the matter as substantially fixed ; and the interpreters, taking the same view, spoke of it with even more emphasis as an absolute agreement.

After General Miles, General Shafter, and

myself returned to my headquarters, General Lawton, Lieutenant Miley, and myself were appointed commissioners on behalf of the United States to negotiate the terms of capitulation, it having been agreed by General Toral and General Shafter that the commissioners to arrange the terms should meet on neutral ground between the lines at 2 o'clock that day.

I immediately commenced dictating to a stenographer the terms for an immediate capitulation, in form quite similar to those that were finally adopted on the sixteenth. Before I had proceeded far with the document, Mr. Mestre, my own interpreter, told me that he thought General Toral did not mean to be understood as agreeing to an immediate capitulation; but, as many others had taken the contrary view, General Lawton, Lieutenant Miley, and myself completed the paper, which contemplated an absolute surrender. Armed with this document, we proceeded to the neutral ground at the hour appointed, 2 o'clock that afternoon, and met the commissioners who had been appointed by General Toral. We soon found that there was a misunderstandng, and at 4 o'clock the Spanish commissioners returned to Santiago, promising to come back at 6 with further instructions.

They returned at that hour, and stated that it would be necessary to postpone the negotiations until morning. I made serious objection to this. Yellow fever was spreading very rapidly, and I felt it important to have this matter adjusted with as little delay as possible ; and finally they consented to return with General Toral at half-past nine that night. We met at the time appointed, and found General Toral very positive in the assertion that he had no power to capitulate; that the authority he was acting under was received from General Blanco, the extent of which was, that he might open negotiations for the basis of a capitulation, awaiting the action of Spain upon a cablegram which had been sent to their Government at Madrid.

Seeing the situation, I suggested to the other commissioners that we discuss separately each paragraph of the paper we had prepared, modifying it in such a way that the Spanish commissioners would submit it to us as a proposition on their part. With this view we proceeded, taking each paragraph at a time, writing it out in English and then translating it into Spanish; and finally, after various changes, none of which were material, the Spanish commissioners expressed themselves as satisfied. When all had been gone over, we asked them if they would submit that to us as their proposition. This they consented to do; and at twenty minutes after midnight they signed their names to the paper, and agreed to meet us at nine the next morning.

CHAPTER XI

WE met as stipulated, in the meantime having had the agreement typewritten; and after some negotiation the following was adopted and signed by all parties:

PRELIMINARY AGREEMENT for the capitulation of the Spanish forces which constitute the Division of Santiago de Cuba occupying the territory herein set forth, said capitulation authorized by the Commander-in-Chief of the Island of Cuba, agreed to by General Toral, and awaiting the approbation of the Government at Madrid, and subject to the following conditions:

Submitted by the undersigned commissioners, — Brigadier-General Don Federico Escario, Lieut.-Colonel of Staff Don Ventura Frontan, and Mr. Robert Mason, of the city of Santiago de Cuba, — representing General Toral, commanding Spanish forces:

To Maj.-Gen. Joseph Wheeler, U.S.V.; Maj.-Gen. H. W. Lawton, U. S. V., and 1st Lieutenant J. D. Miley, 2d Artillery, A. D. C., — representing General Shafter, commanding American forces. For the capitulation of the Spanish forces comprised in that portion of the Island of Cuba east of a line passing through Aserradero, Dos Palmas, Palma Soriano, Cauto Abajo, Escondida, Tanamo, and Aguilera, — said territory being known as the Eastern District of Santiago, commanded by Gen. José Toral.

1. That pending arrangements for capitulation all hostilities between American and Spanish forces in this District shall absolutely and unequivocally cease.

2. That this capitulation includes all the forces and war material in said territory.

3. That after the signing of the final capitulation, the United States agrees, with little delay as possible, to transport all the Spanish troops in said District to the Kingdom of Spain ; the troops, as near as possible, to embark at the port nearest the garrisons they now occupy.

4. That the officers of the Spanish army be permitted to retain their side-arms, and both officers and enlisted men their personal property.

5. That after final capitulation the Spanish authorities agree without delay to remove, or assist the American navy in removing, all mines or other obstructions to navigation now in the harbor of Santiago and its mouth.

6. That after final capitulation the commander of the Spanish forces deliver, without delay, a complete inventory of all arms and munitions of war of the Spanish forces, and a roster of the Spanish forces.

7. That the commander of the Spanish forces, in leaving said District, is authorized to carry with him all military archives and records pertaining to the Spanish army now in said District.

8. That all that part of the Spanish forces known as volunteers, movilizadoes, and guerillas who wish to remain in the Island of Cuba are permitted to do so under parole not to take up arms against the United States during the continuance of the present war between Spain and the United States, delivering up their arms.

9. That the Spanish forces will march out of Santiago de Cuba with honors of war; depositing their arms thereafter at a point mutually agreed upon, to await their disposition by the United States Government; it being understood that the United States commissioners will recommend that the Spanish soldier return to Spain with the arms he so bravely defended.

ENTERED INTO this fifteenth day of July, eighteen hundred and ninety-eight, by the undersigned commissioners, acting under instructions from their respective commanding generals.

JOSEPH WHEELER,   FEDERICO ESCARIO.
Major-General, U.S. Volunteers.

H. W. LAWTON,   VENTURA FRONTAN.
Major-General, U.S. Volunteers.

J. D. MILEY,   ROBERT MASON.
1st Lieutenant, 2d Artillery, A.D.C.

From the beginning of the negotiations I readily saw that the great desire on the part of General Toral was to maintain his honor and prestige as a soldier. It was very clear to me that he cared less about the arms being returned to his soldiers than he did for the recommendations to that effect on the part of the commis-

sioners, couched as it was in language complimenting him and his soldiers for their courage
and chivalry. I also saw that General Toral
was a man of the keenest pride; sensitive in his
feelings to the highest degree, and with a temper
which if touched would entirely control all his
conservative or reasoning feelings; and it is very
possible that had anything occurred during the
negotiations which he felt intrenched upon his
honor as a soldier, he would have broken off any
further attempts at an agreement; and notwithstanding that he was courteous in the extreme,
he would have allowed his pride and passions to
involve him and his army in a conflict which
would have cost many lives on both sides.

It was evident to me, from his preoccupied
look and manner, that General Toral had constantly looming before him in his mind's eye
the events which would follow when he once
more stood upon Spanish soil with his conquered
troops. It was explained to me by one of the
Spanish commissioners that, as general commanding the Spanish forces, he would be held
accountable for the surrender; and that he would
probably, even though he had received the consent of his Government to capitulate, have to
answer for same before a court-martial at Madrid.
This was doubtless the main reason of his insist-
ing so strongly on allusions to the bravery of the
Spanish soldiers being inserted in the conditions
of surrender. He wished to eliminate from this

document everything that might possibly reflect upon his courage as a soldier, or that might give ground for any charges of a serious character by his superior officers.

The following cablegrams with regard to these negotiations were sent to the War Department by General Miles and General Shafter:

DAIQUIRI, July 15.

SECRETARY WAR, Washington:

Commission on behalf of United States was appointed, consisting of Generals Wheeler and Lawton and Lieutenant Miley, with Spanish commission, to arrange details for carrying into effect the capitulation. I will reach Siboney to-morrow.

MILES.

HEADQUARTERS 5TH ARMY CORPS,
July 15, 1898.

ADJUTANT-GENERAL, Washington:

Sent you several telegrams yesterday, as did General Miles, in regard to the surrender. General Toral agreed yesterday positively to surrender all the forces under his command in eastern Cuba upon a distinct understanding that they were to be sent to Spain by the United States ; that this surrender was authorized by General Blanco, and that its submission to-morrow was merely formal. The commissioners to arrange details were appointed, —Wheeler, Lawton, and Miley on the part of the United States. Points were immediately raised by Spanish commissioners. The discussion lasted until 10 o'clock last night. My commissioners think the matter will be settled to-day, and met at 9.30 o'clock this morning. There are about twelve thousand troops in the city, and about as many more in the surrounding district; twenty-five thousand in all will be transported. General Miles was present, and said the surrender was as absolute and complete as possible. It cannot be possible that there will be a failure in completing arrangements. Water famine in city imminent. Have supply cut; this was told Lieutenant Miley by English commissioner. Will wire frequently when negotiations are progressing.

SHAFTER.

The most punctilious courtesy on the part of the Spanish officers was fully reciprocated by myself and the other commissioners, and every effort possible was made to avoid anything which would in any way wound their feelings of soldierly honor. We most readily consented to change words and phrases, such as inserting the word " capitulation," for " surrender," and other things, immaterial in themselves, but which seemed to be desired on the part of General Toral and the Spanish commissioners. The entire conduct of the Spanish officers was such as to elicit our sympathies and regard. General Toral spoke very feelingly of his sad fate. He said to me: " I would not desire to see my very worst enemy compelled to play the cards I have had to play during the last two weeks. All my generals have been killed or wounded; I have not a single colonel left, and I am surrounded by a powerful army. My men counted sixty-seven ships off the coast, all loaded with troops; and besides all this," he continued, wearily pointing his hand towards the city, " I have secret troubles there, of which I cannot speak."

It may not prove uninteresting to insert here the wording of a cablegram which must have cost in the neighborhood of five thousand dollars, sent by General Linares, commanding the Spanish forces in the Province of Santiago de Cuba, to his Government at Madrid. The difference between the appealing tone of this message and General Toral's confident bearing in the presence of the American commissioners is strikingly significant. The cablegram referred to did not come to my knowledge until some weeks after the capitulation :

SANTIAGO DE CUBA, July 12, 1898.

THE GENERAL-IN-CHIEF, TO THE SECRETARY OF WAR :

Although prostrated in bed from weakness and pain, my mind is troubled by the situation of our suffering troops, and therefore I think it my duty to address myself to you, Mr. Secretary, and describe the true situation. Enemy's position very near city, ours extending 14 kilometres (1,400 yards) : our troops are exhausted and sickly in an alarming proportion, cannot be brought to the hospital, needing them in trenches. Cattle without fodder or hay. Fearful storm of rain, which has been pouring continuously for the last 20 hours. Soldiers without permanent shelter, their only food consisting of rice ; have no way of changing or drying clothes. Our losses very heavy ; many chiefs and officers are among the dead, wounded, and sick; their absence deprives the forces of their leaders in this very critical moment. Under these conditions it is impossible to open a breach on the enemy, because this would take a third of our men, who cannot go out and whom the enemy would decimate; the result would be a terrible disaster, without obtaining, as you desire, the salvation of eleven maimed battalions. To make a sortie protected by the Division of Holguin, it is necessary to attack the enemy's line simultaneously. The forces of Holguin cannot come here except after many long days' marching. Impossible for them to transport rations. Unfortunately the situation is desperate. The surrender is imminent, otherwise we will only gain time to prolong our agony. The sacrifice would be sterile, and the men understand this. With his lines so near us he will annihilate our forces without exposing his; as he did yesterday, cannonading by land from elevations without our being able to discover their batteries; and by sea the fleet has a perfect knowledge of the place, and bombard by elevation with a mathematical accuracy. Santiago is not Gerona, a walled city, part of the metropolis, defended inch by inch by her own people without distinction, — old women and children who helped with their lives, moved by the holy ideas of freedom, and with the hopes of help which they received. Here I am alone. All the people have fled, natives as well as Spaniards, even those holding public offices, with few exceptions. Only the priests remain, and they wish to leave the city to-day headed by their archbishop. These defenders do not start now a campaign full of enthusiasm and energy; but for three years they have been fighting tne climate, privations, and fatigues, and they have to confront now this critical situation when they have no enthusiasm or physical strength. They have no ideals, because they defend the property of people who have deserted them, and of those who are the allies of the American forces. The honor of arms has its limits; and I appeal to the judgment of the Government and the entire Nation, whether these patient troops have not repeatedly saved it since the 18th of May, —

date of the first bombardment.   If it is necessary that I
sacrifice them for reasons unknown to me, or if it is necessary
for some one to take the responsibility for the issue fore-
seen and announced by me before in several telegrams, I
willingly offer myself as a sacrifice to my country, and I will
take charge of the command for the act of surrender; as my
modest reputation is of small value when the interest of the
Nation is at stake.

LINARES.

In referring to the battle of June 24th at Las
Guasimas, General Toral said that less than two
thousand Spanish troops were engaged.   He
said : " You thought we had more men, because
our line was so long." He also said, that up to
the evening of June 24th the entire Spanish loss
was two hundred and sixty-five men, about two
hundred and fifty being the casualties in the
fight at Las Guasimas.   He said he could not
correctly say how many Spaniards were killed
or wounded at El Caney, and in the fight at San
Juan before Santiago on July 1st and 2d; but
with dejected air he said : " It was heavy, heavy ! "

The next morning, the 16th, we received a letter
from General Toral, saying that the Spanish
Government had authorized the proposition for
capitulation.   General Toral's letter was as
follows:

SANTIAGO DE CUBA, July 16.

To HIS EXCELLENCY, COMMANDER-IN-CHIEF AMERI-
CAN FORCES :

EXCELLENT SIR : I am now authorized by my Government to capitulate.   I have the honor to so apprise you,
and requesting that you designate hour and place where

my representatives shall appear to compare with those of your Excellency to effect the articles of capitulation on the basis of what has been agreed upon to this date, in due time. I wish to manifest my desire to know the resolutions of the United States Government repecting the return of the army, so as to note on the capitulations also the great courtesy of your great graces and return for their great generosity and impulse for the Spanish soldiers, and allow them to return to the Peninsula with the honors the American army does them the honor to acknowledge, as dutifully descended.

JOSÉ TORAL,
Commanding General 4th Army Corps.

Together with the other two commissioners I immediately went to the place of meeting, carrying with us writing materials, stationery, and a typewriting machine; also taking with me Mr. Mestre, my interpreter and translator, and Mr. Leonard Wilson, my secretary. After the usual polite salutations, proceeded to our work. Some six hours of discussion followed, which finally resulted in the adoption of the terms of absolute capitulation. They were in these words:

TERMS OF THE MILITARY CONVENTION for the capitulation of the Spanish forces occupying the territory which constitutes the Division of Santiago de Cuba, and described as follows: All that portion of the Island of Cuba east of a line passing through Aserradero, Dos Palmas, Cauto Abajo, Escondida, Tanamo, and Aguilera, said troops being in command of General

José Toral ; agreed upon by the undersigned commissioners, — Brigadier-General Don Federico Escario, Lieutenant-Colonel of Staff Don Ventura Frontan, and, as Interpreter, Mr. Robert Mason, of the city of Santiago de Cuba, — appointed by General Toral, commanding the Spanish forces on behalf of the Kingdom of Spain ; and Major-General Joseph Wheeler, U.S.V., Major-General H. W. Lawton, U.S.V., and 1st Lieutenant J. D. Miley, 2d Artillery, A.D.C., — appointed by General Shafter, commanding the American forces on behalf of the United States.

1. That all hostilities between American and Spanish forces in this District shall absolutely and unequivocally cease.

2. That this capitulation includes all the forces and war material in said territory.

3. That the United States agrees, with as little delay as possible, to transport all the Spanish troops in said District to the Kingdom of Spain, the troops being embarked, as far as possible, at the port nearest the garrisons they now occupy.

4. That the officers of the Spanish army be permitted to retain their side-arms, and both officers and private soldiers their personal property.

5. That the Spanish authorities agree to remove, or assist the American navy in removing, all mines or other obstructions to navigation now in the harbor of Santiago and its mouth.

6. That the commander of the Spanish forces deliver, without delay, a complete inventory of all arms and munitions of war of the Spanish forces in above described District to the commander of the American forces ; also a roster of said forces now in said District.

7. That the commander of the Spanish forces, in leaving said District, is authorized to carry with him all military archives and records pertaining to the Spanish army now in said District.

8. That all of that portion of the Spanish forces known as volunteers, movilizadoes, and guerillas who wish to remain in the island of Cuba are permitted to do so upon condition of delivering up their arms, and taking a parole not to bear arms against the United States during the continuance of the present war between Spain and the United States.

9. That the Spanish forces will march out of Santiago de Cuba with honors of war; depositing their arms thereafter at a point mutually agreed upon, to await their disposition by the United States Government; it being understood that the United States commissioners will recommend that the Spanish soldier return to Spain with the arms he so bravely defended.

10. That the provisions of the foregoing instrument become operative immediately upon its being signed.

ENTERED INTO this sixteenth day of July, eighteen hundred and ninety-eight, by the undersigned commissioners acting under instructions from their respective commanding generals and with the approbation of their respective Governments:

JOSEPH WHEELER,   FEDERICO ESCARIO.
    Major-General, U.S. Volunteers.

H. W. LAWTON,   VENTURA FRONTAN.
    Major-General, U.S. Volunteers.

J. D. MILEY,   ROBERT MASON.
1st Lieut., 2d Art'y, A.D.C.

General Shafter having come forward during this meeting of the commission, thereupon discussed with General Toral and the commissioners the details of the ceremonies to be observed the following day in carrying out the terms of the final capitulation which had just been arranged. In the meantime the secretary in attendance had typewritten copies of the articles prepared both in the Spanish and the English; and this, the final capitulation of the Spanish forces in the Province of Santiago de Cuba, was duly signed by the Spanish and American commissioners at 4 o'clock; General Toral retaining the signed Spanish original, one unsigned Spanish copy, and one unsigned English copy, while General Shafter retained the signed English original, one unsigned Spanish copy, and one unsigned English copy.

After courteous salutations and mutual congratulations, the Spanish-American commission which had been appointed to arrange the details of the capitulation of Santiago de Cuba, having successfully accomplished its mission, adjourned its final meeting at 5 o'clock in the afternoon of July 16, 1898.

The original English copy was delivered to General Shafter, who had the pleasure and honor of sending the following despatch :

CAMP NEAR SANTIAGO, July 16.

ADJUTANT-GENERAL CORBIN :

The surrender has been definitely settled ; and the arms will be turned over to-morrow morning, and the troops will be marched out as prisoners of war. The Spanish colors will be hauled down at 9 o'clock, and the American flag hoisted.

SHAFTER,
Major-General.

HEADQUARTERS 5TH ARMY CORPS,
NEAR SANTIAGO, July 16, 1898.

ADJUTANT-GENERAL,
Washington :

The conditions of capitulation include all forces and war material in described territory. The United States agrees with as little delay as possible to transport all Spanish troops in the District to the Kingdom of Spain, the troops, so far as possible, to embark near the garrison they now occupy. Officers to retain their side-arms, and officers and men to retain their personal property. Spanish commander authorized to take military archives belonging to surrendered District. All Spanish forces known as volunteers, movilizadoes, and guerillas who wish to remain in Cuba may do so under parole during the present war, giving up their arms. Spanish forces march out of Santiago with honors of war, depositing their arms at a point mutually agreed upon, to await the disposition of the United States Government, it being understood the United States commissioners will recommend that the Spanish soldiers return to Spain with arms so bravely defended. This leaves the question of return of arms entirely in the hands of the Government. I invite attention to the fact that several thousand surrendered — said by General Toral to be about twelve thousand — against whom a shot has not been fired. The return to Spain of the troops in this District amounts to above twenty-four thousand according to General Toral.

W. R. Shafter.

CHAPTER XII

A VERY skilful stenographer of the War
Department, Mr. Leonard Wilson, was
present in the capacity of secretary at the various
meetings of the commissioners whose work had
resulted in the surrender of the entire Spanish
forces, some twenty-three thousand strong. The
experience of this gentleman has been very
varied. He was private secretary to Mr. H. M.
Stanley, the African explorer, in Africa and in
Europe; then an attaché at the Belgian court;
and was afterwards appointed special translator
and stenographer of the United States at the
Brussels International Monetary Conference.

I was very fortunate in securing this gentleman's services, and he remained with me during
the entire Cuban campaign. He quietly took
down the greater part of the conversations
which occurred between General Toral and the
Spanish commissioners on the one side, and the

American commissioners on the other. He has written out his notes of these conversations, which are incorporated here as follows:

HEADQUARTERS CAVALRY DIVISION, U.S. ARMY,
BEFORE SANTIAGO DE CUBA, July 14, 1898.

The following commissioners were this day appointed to discuss the terms and conditions of capitulation of the city and province of Santiago de Cuba on behalf of their respective commanding generals:

For the Kingdom of Spain:

BRIG.–GEN. DON FEDERICO ESCARIO.

LIEUT.–COL. OF STAFF DON VENTURA FRONTAN.

MR. ROBERT MASON, OF THE CITY OF SANTIAGO DE CUBA.

For the United States:

MAJ.–GEN. JOSEPH WHEELER, U.S.V.

MAJ.–GEN. H. W. LAWTON, U.S.V.

1ST LIEUT. J. D. MILEY, 2D ARTILLERY, A.D.C.

There were also present at the conferences on the part of the United States, — Lt. Joseph Wheeler, jr., A.D.C.; Mr. Aurelius E. Mestre and Mr. Ramon G. Mendoso, Volunteer Aids, acting as interpreters; and Mr. Leonard Wilson, stenographer U.S. War Department, acting as secretary.

The document roughly drawn up by the American commissioners was read and discussed:

The first request of the Spanish commissioners was that the United States would undertake to repair and re-establish immediately the water system of the city of

Santiago, from material to be furnished in said city, which was agreed to by the American commissioners.

Permission was then requested by the Spaniards to carry away with them to Spain all military documents and records pertaining to the Spanish army which were in the various military offices in the capitulated district. This was also acceded to.

It was also agreed between the commissioners that all that portion of the Spanish forces known as volunteers, movilizados, and guerillas who wished to remain in the Island of Cuba should be permitted to do so, they surrendering their arms and being under parole not to take them up against the United States Government during the continuance of the present war. It was pointed out by the Spanish commissioners that this did not apply to Spanish regular soldiers, as all regulars remaining in said district after its capitulation would be considered deserters by the Spanish Government. They first would have to return to Spain and then they could return to Cuba if they so wished.

The Spanish commissioners here inquired whether it was the intention of the United States Government to disarm the Spanish troops. The American commismissioners assured them that this must necessarily be done, but that, at their request and in view of the bravery displayed by the Spanish soldiers, they would be pleased to recommend that their government gratuitously return to Spain the small arms belonging to the regular Spanish troops. The Spanish commissioners explained that they asked for this concession merely on the ground of sentiment, and thought that it should be conceded as these small arms, if returned to Spain with the Spanish troops, would no longer be engaged against the American forces.

General Lawton remarked that he for one would take

pleasure in making such a recommendation, in which sentiments General Wheeler and Lieut. Miley concurred.

General Lawton, on behalf of his colleagues, said that he appreciated to the highest extent the soldierly qualities of the Spanish combatants, as he had very good reasons for believing in their courage.

When asked as to whether the articles as then drawn up and amended coincided with their views, and whether they were prepared to sign them on behalf of their government, the Spanish commissioners replied that they preferred, before doing so, to return and consult with General Toral. This proposition was agreed to by the American commissioners, who stated that they were most anxious to get this matter completed at the earliest possible moment; and that it was their desire, in order to facilitate matters all they could, for as few disagreeable points to be brought up as possible. The Spanish commissioners stated that they had a high appreciation of the courtesy extended to them by the American commissioners.

After an exchange of compliments the commission adjourned to 6 P.M., same date.

The commission duly met, as arranged, a few minutes after 6 o'clock, and immediately proceeded to the continuance of the negotiations:

After expressing the hope that the conference would terminate satisfactorily to both the Spanish and American commissioners the latter suggested that the Spanish commander immediately withdraw his troops from the trenches in front of the city and from the fortifications.

To this the Spanish commissioners made answer that they were unable to give a promise of such a character without first consulting and obtaining the authorization of General Toral. This point was therefore left open for further discussion.

On being asked whether they gave their consent and would lend their aid to the operation of the railroad and the removal of obstructions to navigation in the harbor, so as to permit of the transportation of supplies and the entrance of the Red Cross ship *State of Texas*, which had stores on board for the sick and needy, the Spaniards replied that they had no objection to trains running into the city, but they did not quite see how it would be possible for the *Texas*, or any other ship, to enter the harbor immediately, owing to the presence of submarine mines; and even if these were removed, as there was only fourteen feet of water at the wharves, the cargo from the ship would have to be transferred to lighters, which, they asserted, had to be done in every case where a large vessel entered the harbor. This point was also, therefore, left open for subsequent discussion.

The Spanish commissioners hereupon stated that there were two or three small points in connection with the capitulation upon which they desired to confer further with General Linares, who was then sick in bed suffering from a wound recently received in an engagement; and they requested, in order to enable them to do this, that the commission adjourn until the following morning.

General Lawton stated that he and his colleagues had full powers, and asked the Spanish commissioners whether they had not full powers also. To this the Spaniards replied that they had not, and that they had to get advice from General Toral, to whom they were to refer questions of importance before binding themselves by making a final decision.

The American commissioners insisted that they

understood that the surrender of the Spanish army had already been conceded, and that the main questions of importance had been settled between Generals Shafter and Toral that morning. It was therefore necessary to arrange the details as speedily as might be, in order to carry the surrender into effect.

The Spanish commissioners contended, on the contrary, that the actual surrender could only take place with the consent of the Spanish Government; and they repeated that they had not absolute power, but said they were instructed to inform the American commissioners that they were willing for all Americans and all the people from El Caney to come into the city of Santiago if they so desired.

General Lawton said he had no desire to unduly press matters, but that he and his colleagues had made up their minds to endeavor to arrive at some understanding and settle the matter that night if possible, even if it necessitated sitting up all night to do it. He wanted to go right on then without stopping. He did not wish to return to his camp until a conclusion had been reached. The matter had been under discussion for several days, and he desired for the negotiations to continue until an agreement was reached, or a decision arrived at one way or the other.

The Spanish commissioners regretted that it was absolutely impossible for them to complete the negotiations at that meeting of the conference, as there were several points in the paper, as then drawn up, to which General Escario and his colleagues would have to object, and on which points a further and more extended conference with General Linares was essential.

Mr. Robert Mason, the British Vice-Consul, who was acting as interpreter to the Spanish commission, on being asked by General Wheeler whether he could give any information as to the points to which objection was made by General Linares, replied that all he could say was that there were several points in connection with the document, as drawn up by the American commissioners and amended at the previous meeting, which General Linares desired to be altered or modified, and which he would like to have more amply explained and discussed. Mr. Mason, however, explained that the points to which exceptions were taken, although unimportant in themselves, were of sufficient moment to warrant further discussion.

General Wheeler replied that everything General Toral had said he wanted at the first meeting had been written down and an agreement arrived at. They then came out to that place as commissioners, and more concessions were demanded of them; these were even granted in every particular, for they were trying to show a liberal spirit, and simply wanted to bring the matter to a speedy and satisfactory termination.

Mr. Mason said in explanation that the Spanish commissioners had not been fully empowered by General Linares, the latter not understanding that this was necessary. Under those circumstances the commissioners would be required to report to General Linares before taking definite action.

General Wheeler expressed it as his opinion that the matter should be proceeded with and settled definitely that night. He said his Government would expect the matter to be settled without delay, and that every effort possible should be made to accomplish such a result.

Lieutenant Miley inquired whether the Spanish commissioners would have any objection to the American commissioners accompanying them into Santiago and holding a consultation there for the purpose of concluding the matter more expeditiously.

The Spanish commissioners, without directly making formal objection to the carrying out of this suggestion, thought it would be better, as they had already proposed, for them to return for a consultation with General Linares and have another meeting of the commission the following morning.

General Wheeler said he could not quite understand why the Spanish commissioners had not been given full powers, as the law is that commissioners must necessarily have absolute power, they being commissioners of the Government.

General Escario, on behalf of the Spanish commissioners, said there was one unimportant point which he would like to mention, and, if possible, have changed, which was that wherever the word "surrender" was used in the wording of the document he would wish it to be expunged and the word "capitulation" inserted in its place. This alteration, at the suggestion of General Wheeler, was immediately agreed to by the American commissioners and the document changed accordingly.

The Spanish commissioners, inviting attention to that paragraph in the document (paragraph 9) one portion of which called for the furnishing of a complete inventory of all public property of the Kingdom of Spain then in above-described District, said they could hardly insert that clause in the agreement, pointing out that after the capitulation had taken effect the property in question would necessarily remain in its then location, and would consequently fall into American hands and be subject to American power and control.

Chief-of-staff Don Ventura Frontan explained that it would be impossible for them to furnish the desired list of public property, inasmuch as the only person who possessed such a list or who had the information, without which it was impossible to make one, was the notary public of the Spanish commander, and this notary public was then at Caney.

General Wheeler stated that the American commissioners were willing to modify the wording of the paragraph in question, as all they required was a list of the " arms and military stores " and not of the " public property." The document was changed accordingly.

The Spanish commissioners, referring to the point agreed upon at a previous meeting, and the promise of the American commissioners to recommend their Government to return the arms of the Spanish soldiers, asked whether they were to understand that their troops were to be disarmed first and the arms returned to them afterwards; to which Lieutenant Miley replied that they would certainly be disarmed while they remained in Santiago.

General Wheeler stated that he and his colleagues would certainly ask their Government to return their arms, but they could not on their own responsibility bind themselves to do this.

General Lawton remarked that the American commissioners fully recognized that the Spaniards were brave and courageous soldiers, and consequently they would be delighted to ask their Government to return them their arms. Beyond this, however, they were not authorized to go.

Lieutenant Miley pointed out that the capitulation necessarily included the giving up of the arms, but he was perfectly willing to join his colleagues in recommending that their arms be returned.

General Wheeler observed that the surrender of the arms had been perfectly understood, and arranged between the Spanish and American generals; he was there, and the whole thing had been written down.

General Escario suggested that he return to Santiago

and come back immediately with General Toral, who, during the sickness of General Linares, had full control. General Toral would speedily and definitely settle the matter.

Lieutenant Miley inquired if there was to be any going back after General Linares when they had gotten through with General Toral. General Escario assured him that General Toral would be able to settle the matter himself. Lieutenant Miley replied that the matter could only be settled one way with them as it had been agreed, and it followed as a matter of course that when they surrendered the arms were to be given up.

General Lawton, interposing, stated that it was not the intention of the American commission to humiliate the Spanish officials in any way possible, but that they were making their best efforts to get this disagreeable business over in as pleasant a way as they could, in which remarks General Wheeler fully coincided.

General Wheeler, continuing, suggested that, with regard to the form and manner of giving up the arms, he would even go so far as to say that the American commission would have no objection to the arms being placed in the Spaniards' own arsenal and under the guard of their own ordnance officer, providing, of course, that there was one American officer present when the arms were counted and stored. They might remain stored there until a reply was received from the American Government to the American commissioners' request to have them given back. They would do this purely as a matter of courtesy and chivalry. His Nation was a chivalrous Nation, and if an affirmative reply was received from his Government they would cause the arms to be returned to the Spaniards, even if they had to place them on a separate ship.

General Escario, while appreciating highly the sentiments expressed, begged that he be permitted to fetch General Toral, so that this question might be decided. He said he had implicit faith in the loyalty of the Americans, but as General Toral had personally spoken of this matter, and as it was an important point, he wished to refer it to him.

This was agreed to, and General Wheeler, as senior of the American commission, assured General Escario that they might fully rely on the honor of the American Nation to protect them thoroughly on all points.

After the customary courteous salutations, the commission adjourned to 9.30 P.M., same date.

CHAPTER XIII

THE CONVERSATIONS (CONTINUED)—ANOTHER MISUNDER-
STANDING — THE RED CROSS SHIP TO ENTER FIRST
WITH PROVISIONS — GENERAL TORAL'S APPEAL ON
BEHALF OF SPANISH HONOR — THE REMOVING OF
HARBOR–MINES — ADJOURNMENT

THE Spanish and American commissioners
resumed deliberations at 9.40 o'clock on
the evening of the same day; General José
Toral accompanying the other commissioners
on behalf of Spain:

General Toral objected very strongly to the heading
of the document, and insisted upon it being changed
from " Terms of the Military Convention for the Capitulation " to, using his Spanish words, " Basis preliminaris
por la Capitulacion," or, as we translated it into English,
" Preliminary Agreement for the Capitulation." This,
he said, would give them time to make all preliminary
arrangements for the capitulation while the Spanish commission awaited receipt of the authority from their Government at Madrid to confirm same. The captain-general
had given him authority to enter upon a preliminary arrangement, which, he had no doubt, the Government
would confirm as soon as the necessary cable advices
could reach him.

Lieutenant Miley said that the attitude of the Spanish commission in this matter was not in accordance with the letter which they had sent to General Shafter. Would the details of the capitulation have to be referred to Madrid ? He understood full powers had been given to General Toral to treat on this matter.

General Wheeler remarked he had gathered that morning that General Toral had received full authority from the captain-general to surrender, and all that the Spanish commission had then to do was to arrange the details and notify the captain-general.

Mr. Mason said he considered it certain that whatever General Toral agreed to would be certainly approved, but that the general had to get confirmation of what he did from Madrid. He had understood General Toral to say that morning that the captain-general had authorized him to enter into this preliminary agreement, but that it would have to be approved afterwards by Madrid.

General Toral replying said he wished it to be perfectly understood that what they were doing now was simply making the preliminary basis for the capitulation, and that nothing further could be done by him until he had received authority from his Government to carry same into effect. That agreement would simplify matters very much, for once authority to confirm same reached him they would only have to make the confirmation of what had been already agreed upon.

General Wheeler remarked that under the circumstances they had better modify the document in the way the Spaniards required, and when they had found out what alterations and changes were demanded of them they could get the Spaniards to sign the paper thus amended *as a proposition*, there being evidently no obligation for the American commissioners to put their names to it. This being agreed to by his colleagues, the document was gone over, each paragraph being discussed by both sides of the commission through the interpreters there present.

On the proposition of the Spanish commissioners the heading or title of the paper was modified so as to read as follows : " Preliminary Agreement for the Capitulation of the Spanish Forces which constitute the Division of Santiago de Cuba and which occupy the Territory of the Eastern Part of the Island of Cuba within the Line herein set forth ; to be carried into effect as soon as the proper authority is received from the Government at Madrid, and subject to the following conditions."

This and the remaining portion of the title of the document, as thus amended, was approved by the joint commission.

Paragraph 1, reading as follows, was also agreed to and adopted by both sides : " That, pending arrangements for capitulation, all hostilities between American and Spanish forces in this district shall absolutely and unequivocally cease."

Discussion was then held between the commissioners on the clause relating to the transfer to the American Government of the public property belonging to the kingdom of Spain in the district about to capitulate, and General Toral explained that there were certain public buildings, such as the arsenal, etc., which were considered as State property and of which they could make no transfer while the Spanish authorities remained in possession of the city. This property could not be by them disposed of as long as the State occupied it, but the moment the Spanish Government ceased to occupy it the property would naturally belong to the new occupant.

That clause of the paragraph referred to reading, " all arms and munitions of war," which had been substituted for the words "all public property" at the previous meeting of the commission, was therefore confirmed.

Paragraph 3, reading as follows, was next discussed: "That the Spanish commander immediately make arrangements for the entrance into the harbor of Santiago of the Red Cross ship *State of Texas*, a vessel sailing under the terms of the Geneva Convention, for the purpose of furnishing provisions to those starving in Santiago, without reference to nationality."

The Spanish commissioners explained that they were compelled to take exception to this paragraph, but they would undertake to comply with its requirements immediately after the capitulation had been confirmed; their harbor being mined, they could not give up this means of defence until the capitulation had taken place as a matter of fact. After some discussion the American commissioners agreed to alter the wording of the paragraph in question so as to make it read as follows: "That the chief of the Spanish forces, immediately after the confirmation of this agreement, make arrangements for the entrance into the harbor of Santiago," etc.

General Wheeler desired to know why a ship could not be permitted which sailed under the terms of the Geneva Convention and under the Red Cross flag, to enter the harbor of Santiago, especially as there were only women aboard, and not a single gun.

General Toral explained that the difficulty consisted in the number of mines and torpedoes which were then in the harbor, which permitted no ship to enter, which could not discriminate between one ship and another, and which formed a necessary defence which they absolutely could not give up until the final capitulation had been signed and become effective.

Dealing then with paragraph 4, regarding the entrance into Santiago of the refugees then at El Caney and other points, Lieutenant Miley observed that permission had already been given them by the Spanish to return, and asked whether the railroad might be used for this purpose, and, if they did return, had the Spanish authorities anything to feed them with?

General Toral replied he had already given orders so that our engineers might examine the line the next day, as well as the bridge and river of Aguadores, in order to enable us to make use of that part of the line to bring in supplies, but on the express condition and understanding that if hostilities recommenced the bridge would be destroyed and replaced in its then condition.

Reverting again to paragraph 3, the Spanish commissioners requested that the word "starving" be omitted and the words "persons in want" be substituted therefor, which was promptly agreed to and the paragraph altered accordingly.

Discussing next paragraph 5, which provided for making use of the railroad for the purpose only of transporting food with which to feed the Spanish and American troops, the Spanish commissioners asked that the words "Spanish and American" be expunged, and this alteration being agreed to, the paragraph was changed accordingly. After some further discussion it was mutually agreed upon by the commissioners to still further amend the reading of this paragraph so as to make it read as follows: "That from the signing of this agreement the Spanish authorities afford every facility for the use, by the American forces, of the railroad running from Siboney to Santiago, for the purpose only of transporting food with which to feed the people in need in Santiago de Cuba," the words "until the obstructions to navigation in the harbor of Santiago have been removed " being expunged.

At the request of the American commissioners the

words, "after the signing of the final capitulation," were inserted after the first word of the first line of paragraph 6, said paragraph, in its amended form, reading as follows : " That, after the signing of the final capitulation, the United States agrees, with as little delay as possible, to transport all the Spanish troops in said District to the kingdom of Spain, the troops, as near as possible, to be embarked at the port nearest the garrison they now occupy."

Paragraph 7, reading, " That the officers of the Spanish army be permitted to retain their side-arms, and both officers and enlisted men their personal property," was confirmed without change.

General Toral said he desired to make an appeal to General Wheeler, as the senior officer of the American commission, on a point which was to him of the highest importance, and which affected the honor of the Spanish soldiers, who had striven so long and so arduously to defend the honor and dignity of their mother country on Cuban soil. He appealed more especially to General Wheeler, because he was the oldest and the senior in rank, and because he knew, from the kindly disposition manifested by him during the progress of those negotiations, that he could sympathize with him in the matter to which he was about to refer. It related to the question of his soldiers being permitted, after the capitulation, to bear away with them, when they left tha city, the arms they had so well striven to defend. He begged to remind General Wheeler and his fellow commissioners that they were as yet an unconquered and unvanquished army ; he granted that they had perhaps been outmatched and outnumbered, but they had not been crushed and compelled absolutely to make an unconditional and abject surrender. His city was still well defended, and if his country had called upon him to have still resisted attack, he and his army would still have endeavored to have done their duty; they were then negotiating to see whether an amicable arrangement could not be arrived at so as to save further bloodshed, and he hoped sincerely that such an arrangement would be consummated. It was, therefore, owing to the conditions which he had enumerated, and principally on the ground of their still being an unconquered army, that he appealed to the feelings of an old soldier (indicating General Wheeler), who he was sure would fully understand the motives by which he was actuated and the feelings with which he was animated in making this, to him, important request.

General Wheeler responded, saying that he and his colleagues understood and appreciated fully the reason of General Toral making this request, and they had done their utmost to show in what a liberal spirit they could act, they even exceeding, to accommodate the Spanish commission, the conditions which General Toral had asked of General Shafter. That they had done, being actuated by that same soldierly spirit demonstrated by General Toral.

General Lawton desired to have a little explanation on this point. General Toral had asked that his soldiers be permitted to march out of Santiago de Cuba with their arms, on the ground that they had not been vanquished. He desired to know whether General Toral meant that his soldiers be permitted to march out of the city with their arms, or whether they be permitted to return to Spain with their arms.

General Toral replied that his only desire in making that request was to save the honor of Spanish arms, and, on the ground that his soldiers had not been conquered, all he asked was that they be permitted to march out of the town like soldiers, bearing their arms, and once out

of the town they could stack them somewhere; and
then, if the United States desired to give them back, or
to send them to the ships on which they were embarked,
they could do so.

General Lawton in reply said this explanation was
quite satisfactory. No one, not even their own people,
had a greater consideration for the soldierly qualities or
brave fighting of the Spanish troops than his colleagues
and himself, for none had better reason than they to
have such an opinion. They were considering how this
disagreeable transaction could be gotten through with
as little friction and unpleasantness as possible, and
they were not only willing but anxious to complete it
in an amicable spirit, they being actuated by none but
the most kindly feelings.

General Toral, replying, said he appreciated very
much the expression of the feelings of the American
commissioners in reference to the conduct of the
Spanish soldiers, and it was for this very reason, viz.,
that his soldiers had acted so bravely, that he wished to
insist on their being permitted to leave the city like
soldiers, bearing their arms. They had fought well and
bravely, as even the American commissioners themselves
had conceded, and he saw no reason why they should be
humiliated and their bravery depreciated by being compelled to march out of the city without carrying those
arms which they had so well and so honorably defended.

General Lawton said he fully appreciated, as he had
already stated, the bravery of the Spanish troops, and
although his Government had declined to permit him
and his colleagues to grant such a concession as the
permanent return of the arms, yet they would join in
making application to the Government at Washington
that their arms be given back to them.

An addition was thereupon made to the agreement,

under the heading of Article 13, which read as follows:
" That the Spanish forces be permitted to march out of
Santiago de Cuba with their arms, depositing them
thereafter at a point mutually agreed upon, to await
their disposition by the United States Government, it
being understood that the United States commissioners
will recommend that they be returned."

Dealing then with paragraph 8, which read, " That
the Spanish authorities agree without delay to remove,
or assist the American navy in removing, all mines or
other obstructions to navigation now in the harbor of
Santiago and its mouth," this was amended so as to
read, " That, after the final capitulation, the Spanish
authorities agree without delay to remove," etc.

Paragraph 9, reading, " That the commander of the
Spanish forces deliver without delay a complete inventory of all arms and munitions of war of the Kingdom of
Spain, and a roster of the Spanish forces now in above-
described District, to the commander of the American
forces," was also amended so as to read, " That, after
the final capitulation, the commander of the Spanish
forces," etc.

Paragraph 10, reading, " That the commander of
the American forces agrees without delay to repair and
reëstablish the water system of the city of Santiago de
Cuba, suitable material being furnished in the city of
Santiago de Cuba," was duly confirmed without change.

Paragraph 11, reading, " That the commander of the
Spanish forces is authorized to carry with him all military archives and records pertaining to the Spanish army
now in said District," was amended so as to read, " That
the commander of the Spanish forces, in leaving said
District, is authorized to carry with him," etc.

Discussing then paragraph 12, which read, " That all
of that portion of the Spanish forces known as volun-

teers, movilizados, and guerillas who wish to remain in
the island of Cuba are permitted to do so under parole
not to take up arms against the United States, and that
they deliver up their arms to the Government of the
United States," this was amended so as to read, " That
all of that portion of the Spanish forces known as volunteers, movilizados, and guerillas who wish to remain
in the island of Cuba are permitted to do so under parole
not to take up arms against the United States during
the continuance of the present war between Spain and
the United States, delivering up their arms."

Some further discussion was then had relative to paragraph 13 as quoted on page 160, to which the Spanish
commissioners still made objection.

Lieutenant Miley said they had come out there the
day before to meet General Toral, and General Shafter
had said he could accept the surrender provided the
Spaniards were willing to return to Spain. General
Toral first insisted on the condition that his troops be
permitted to march out to Holguin, but finally said he
was willing to surrender on the condition of returning
with his troops to Spain if he received the consent of
his Government thereto. General Shafter had come
out there, in the presence of General Wheeler, and the
American commissioners understood that he received
the surrender of the Spanish army in that place.

General Wheeler remarked that some misunderstanding had evidently taken place at the first meeting
between the generals. His interpretor, who was present, had told him General Toral had stated that he was
compelled to notify his Government of his negotiations
before same became binding.

Lieutenant Miley said the day before a demand was
made by the Americans for a surrender by 12 o'clock.
The Spaniards had asked for more time and it had been

refused. General Shafter had come down himself for the answer, which appeared to be satisfactory to him, for he had sent his commissioners there to settle the final details for the surrender.

General Lawton said, as far as he was personally concerned, he was prepared to state that, as one of the commissioners, he could not and would not accept any proposition which did not cover the delivering up of the arms.

Lieutenant Miley observed that the first thing the Spaniards had to do, now that hostilities had been stopped, was to surrender and deliver up their arms.

General Wheeler remarked that they had six batteries in position then.

Lieutenant Miley said that General Shafter had stated that the surrender was absolute and without any conditions whatever, except that the Spanish forces were to be returned to Spain by the United States.

General Toral hastened to explain that he had come there that morning because General Shafter had invited him, and he had, at the same time, offered the proposition of Captain-General Blanco, to enter upon a preliminary agreement for the capitulation while waiting for the confirmation of said proposition from his Government in Madrid. He had also come there at that time on the demand of General Shafter. That morning he had sent to General Shafter a communication from the captain-general, informing him (General Toral) that he could enter upon arrangements for the capitulation with the American general by establishing the preliminary basis of said capitulation pending the receipt of the decision of the Madrid Government. That was why that was only the preliminary basis of the capitulation, as he was compelled to await confirmation from his Government, although he had been authorized to discuss a

preliminary agreement by the commander-in-chief of the
Spanish army in Cuba.

Lieutenant Miley said he thought General Shafter
had some doubts as to whether the Madrid Government would confirm these arrangements, and that when
he suggested this to General Toral the latter answered,
How was it possible for his Government not to approve
and confirm that which the captain-general had authorized him to do and to treat about?

General Toral here expressed himself as very sorry
that the American commissioners should believe he first
said one thing and then said another. It was evident
to him there was a serious misunderstanding.

Lieutenant Miley said the American commissioners
had thought this was to be the final capitulation, but
after General Toral's explanation the exact situation
was made clear to them.

General Lawton remarked that he and his colleagues
had understood that the preliminaries had all been
arranged that morning. General Toral replied that this
was not the case—that they were only prepared to make
a preliminary arrangement, and that as soon as his
Government notified him of its confirmation the Spanish
commissioners would sign the final capitulation.

General Toral further remarked that it seemed to him
the misunderstanding had arisen owing to an imperfect
translation and interpretation of his statements to General Shafter at their first meeting. He had written to
General Shafter. Let his letter be translated properly,
and it would then be evident that he was in the right.

Lieutenant Miley said he thought General Toral was
right in this matter. He had the English translation of
the letter in question with him, but when General
Shafter had met General Toral the former came away
thinking that the latter was authorized to make the

final capitulation, and that the commissioners were appointed simply to arrange the details. Under these circumstances, of course the American commissioners naturally concluded that they were to arrange the details for the final capitulation.

General Lawton desired the first paragraph to be re-read both in the English and in the Spanish, which was accordingly done. He then suggested that the words "pending arrangements for capitulation" be omitted, and the words "pending the confirmation of this preliminary agreement" be substituted therefor. This was immediately agreed to and the document altered accordingly. Attention was then again called by the Spanish commissioners to the heading of the document and they desired that the words "on the part of the Kingdom of Spain" be changed so as to read, "representing General Toral," which was agreed to.

The American commission thereupon desired that the words "on the part of the United States" be changed also so as to read, "representing General Shafter," which was done.

The Spanish commissioners further desired that the words, "of the Kingdom of Spain and the roster" be changed so as to read, "of the Spanish forces and a roster," which was agreed to and the document amended.

At this point, all the articles having been gone through, discussed, and translated, and it being apparent that all the changes then made comprised the extent of the alterations then desired by General Toral and the Spanish commissioners, General Wheeler requested the interpreters to ask the Spanish commissioners if they were willing to sign the document as it then stood in its amended form *as a proposition for a final capitulation,* said document to be submitted to General Shafter for

his consideration and approval. After a few moments'
private consultation the Spanish commissioners intimated
that they were willing to sign it as suggested, which
they thereupon did, handing the proposition to the
American commission, who of course did not attach their
signatures thereto.

An arrangement having been made for the
next meeting to take place at 9.30 o'clock the
following morning, the commission adjourned
at twenty minutes past midnight.

CHAPTER XIV

THE CONVERSATIONS (CONCLUDED) — SPANISH FORCES
TO MARCH OUT UNDER ARMS AND SALUTE THEIR
COLORS — THE MISUNDERSTANDING SATISFACTORILY
SETTLED — WATER SUPPLY OF SANTIAGO — THE
FINAL DETAILS

THE Spanish-American commission again met as agreed, on the morning of July 15th, at 9.40 o'clock, and proceeded as follows:

Lieutenant Miley opened the proceedings by remarking that the proposition prepared and amended yesterday had been submitted to General Shafter, and (handing letter to General Toral) " there is General Shafter's reply to the letter he yesterday received from General Linares." That letter dealt with the question of which General Toral had spoken the preceding day, namely, the return of the arms to the Spanish troops. General Shafter wished the Spanish commissioners to know that he would go as far as they wished in this matter. He was willing for them to march out of the city with their arms and would even salute their colors before they passed out.

General Lawton observed that this was as much as any nation could do.

Lieutenant Miley further stated that General Shafter accepted clause 13 as inserted in the proposition.

General Wheeler remarked that he hoped the Spanish

commissioners would now have no doubt in their minds that the American nation were anxious to accord to the Spanish troops every honor they could, as due to good and brave soldiers.

Lieutenant Miley, continuing, stated that General Shafter had not rightly understood that the Government at Madrid had still to approve the articles of capitulation. He had had the impression that the capitulation was an accomplished fact from the moment that General Toral and he had shaken hands. He thought, the agreement having been authorized by General Blanco and agreed to by General Toral, that this was all that was necessary; that the submitting of it to Madrid was a mere matter of form, and that under no circumstances would it be changed by the home Government, it being simply and entirely a matter of form. General Toral then inquired at what decision General Shafter had arrived.

Lieutenant Miley replied that General Shafter suggested that the title of the document be changed to an agreement authorized by General Blanco and agreed to by General Toral, the agreement to be submitted to Madrid as a mere matter of form and without any possibility of change.

General Toral remarked that he was only authorized to treat on the preliminary conditions of the capitulation, of which the Government at Madrid would approve or disapprove. He was not authorized to do anything more.

Lieutenant Miley said General Shafter had asked General Toral the day before, after the negotiations of the preceding two days, if he was to understand that finally they might possibly have to fight again after all, and General Toral had told him that that was not to be thought of.

General Toral said it was true he had given utterance

to that statement, but he had also explained at the same time that that was only his own opinion and belief, and that he could not think it possible, after he had received authorization from the captain-general, that his Government would repudiate it. He was convinced that this would not be the case, but still, after all, that was only his own personal opinion.

Lieutenant Miley inquired whether General Toral would agree to change the heading of the document in accordance with the wishes of General Shafter, who suggested as an alteration that the heading should be changed so as to make it read : " Preliminary Agreement for the Capitulation of the Spanish Forces which constitute the Division of Santiago de Cuba and occupy the Territory herein set forth, said Capitulation authorized by the Commander-in-chief of the Island of Cuba, agreed to by General Toral, and awaiting notification from the Government at Madrid, subject to the following conditions."

The Spanish commissioners suggested that the words " awaiting notification from the Government at Madrid " be changed so as to read, " awaiting the approval of the Government at Madrid."

General Lawton suggested that the word "approbation " be substituted for the word " approval," which he thought represented the true condition of affairs.

The alteration was agreed to and the document amended accordingly, the word " approbation " being adopted.

The whole of the first page was then re-read and confirmed without change.

Lieutenant Miley observed that they wanted to word this document in such a fashion that the American as well as the Spanish commissioners would be able to sign it, in order that steps might immediately be taken to carry out the details of the agreement.

Lieutenant Miley said General Shafter had had an examination made of the bridge at Aguadores, and he had found that it would take at least a week to get the railroad in proper repair. It was his desire and purpose to feed the needy people in Santiago who would be coming in in large numbers from the surrounding country, and he therefore desired that steps be taken, not after the signing of the capitulation, but immediately, to permit the Red Cross ship *State of Texas* to enter the harbor of Santiago.

General Toral replied that he had consulted with his Commission of Harbor Defences, who reported that if he took up the defences referred to, and then if unfortunately their negotiations for the final capitulation fell through and there was a resumption of hostilities, the port would remain entirely undefended. He was, however, quite willing for the vessel to come close up to the harbor mouth and for the stores to be placed on lighters, which, being of a light draft, could pass over the mines without danger. If this were done, however, there would have to be a committee of Red Cross ladies, or consuls or other suitable persons, to arrange for the distribution of the supplies. He had that morning, after due reflection, decided that it would not be politic to let the refugees enter the city of Santiago immediately.

General Lawton said it appeared to him that to decline to take up the mines so as to permit the entrance of the Red Cross ship was to cast a doubt on the successful termination of their negotiations, and if the Spanish commission had any doubt of the confirmation of the agreement it was useless to proceed further. If they had no doubt they should not hesitate to take up the defences.

General Toral replied that the reason why the Spanish commission were proceeding with the negotiations was because he considered they were saving much valuable time, for, after the final agreement had been reached and the consent of his Government received, all they would have to do would be to affix their signatures to the document, and if his Government declined to authorize the final capitulation he would regret it sincerely and it would be by no means his fault. If once the final capitulation was agreed upon it would be a very small matter to open the port, because they could simply destroy the defences; but in order to admit one ship in the present situation of affairs the mines would have to be removed without destroying them, which would be a long and tedious operation.

General Lawton said he did not know it would be necessary for any mines to be removed in order to admit one ship, as he had understood there was always a channel left open so that the initiated could pass in or out at any time.

General Toral replied that this was not the case, and said that even the foreign ships which came to take off their subjects had had to stop outside the port, it not being possible for them to enter the harbor on account of the submarine defences.

General Lawton remarked that, in view of the amicable settlement of affairs, the end being then practically in sight, there seemed to him to be a little over-caution on the part of the Spanish commissioners sufficient to imply that after all they believed their negotiations might be a failure.

To this General Toral replied that he had already explained his position in this matter and he was bound to act accordingly. Of course, if the Red Cross ship came into or near the mouth of the harbor before the final capitulation was signed he relied upon the loyalty of the Americans to permit no photographing of the defences, etc.

General Lawton said they would promise to prevent anything of the kind. They had, as a matter of fact, all the photographs they wanted. There would be only women and doctors on board.

General Toral expressed his belief that the Americans would act in good faith.

The American commissioners here withdrew for a few moments' consultation, and, returning, Lieutenant Miley stated it was the opinion of his colleagues and himself that the clause relating to the admittance of the *State of Texas* should be stricken out of the agreement, as it did not form part of the essential articles of capitulation. They would depend upon a verbal agreement, and treat as a private agreement between General Toral and General Shafter the arrangements for feeding the people.

General Toral, replying, said this was satisfactory to him, and mentioned that he had only three lighters which were in really good condition, and those he had to use to transport water and provisions, so that he would have to ask the American commissioners to supply the necessary lighters on which to transport the supplies from the ship to the wharf.

Paragraph 3, dealing with this question, was thereupon stricken out.

Discussing then paragraph 4, relating to the entrance into Santiago of the refugees, it was decided to strike this paragraph out also, General Toral remarking that the refugees could return into the city as soon as the water supply had been re-established and there was something to eat, there being no market then in existence and nothing on his ships then in the harbor.

Paragraph 5 was also considered to be one that should be omitted. Lieutenant Miley stated that the Americans would have the railroad examined again that day, and it might be they would change their minds about using it, but if they did so it would be a private arrangement, it not being necessary to refer such a point to Madrid, as it nowise affected the main question of the capitulation. Paragraph 6 was re-read and confirmed. Paragraph 7 was re-read and confirmed. Paragraph 8 was re-read and confirmed. Paragraph 9 was re-read and confirmed. Alluding to paragraph 10, Lieutenant Miley said that General Shafter wished to wait until the final capitulation was signed before he re-established the water supply. The Spanish commissioners desired to retain all their defences, and naturally the Americans wanted to retain theirs. If the people from El Caney and other points, however, were permitted to return to Santiago the American commissioners would empower the municipal authorities of the city to handle the water supply, provided they put in a feed-pipe from which the American troops could obtain water. It would be better in any case to repair the aqueduct before the people came into the city, or they would be short of water. The Spanish commissioners might send out some competent men to make an examination and ascertain what repairs would be needed, and what length of time it would take to carry them out.

General Toral said he would be glad to send and have the examination made as suggested.

Lieutenant Miley replied that he would immediately give General Toral a written order authorizing the persons who went out to make the examination to cross the American lines, which they could do under a flag of truce. A letter, addressed to the commanding officer of the American forces on the Cuevitas Road, was thereupon written and handed to General Toral.

It not being considered necessary for the paragraph (No. 10) to remain as one of the articles of the agreement, it was therefore stricken out, Lieutenant Miley re-marking that General Shafter would not permit any one to come into Santiago from El Caney or any other point until the water supply had been re-established.

Paragraph 11 being next considered, General Toral remarked that, some of his regiments being in Santiago and some in other parts of his district, his military records were naturally in various places, and requested that he be permitted to take them with him to Spain together with those in Santiago.

Lieutenant Miley stated that General Toral could send for them if he wished and have them brought to Santiago.

General Lawton agreed, saying that the authority to carry them to Spain, which had already been given, car-ried with it the authority to collect them.

Paragraph 11 was therefore confirmed without change.

Paragraph 12 was re-read and confirmed.

Referring to paragraph 13, General Toral asked that General Shafter's promise that his flag would be saluted, and the allusion of the commission to the bravery of the Spanish soldiers, be included in the agreement.

This being agreed to by the American commissioners, the paragraph referring to this point was altered so as to read: "That the Spanish forces will march out of Santiago de Cuba with honors of war, depositing their arms thereafter at a point mutually agreed upon, to await their disposition by the United States Government, it being understood that the United States commissioners will recommend that the Spanish soldiers return to Spain with the arms they have so bravely defended."

General Toral said he felt the more grateful to the gentlemen of the American commission in granting this concession because the Americans had shown what they were capable of in fighting and in advancing so gallantly, and he considered they had shown themselves to be, in every respect, worthy opponents of his own forces.

General Lawton then drew up, after consultation with his colleagues, a petition to their Government in which they prayed that the arms given up by the Spanish soldiers be returned to them, on the ground of the chivalrous courage and gallantry of Generals Linares and Toral and the soldiers of Spain who were engaged in the battles recently fought in the Province of Santiago de Cuba. This petition was duly translated and read to the Spanish commissioners, who expressed their high appreciation of same.

The whole document was then carefully re-read, paragraph by paragraph, both in the English and the Spanish; and as supplies of stationery and a typewriting machine had been brought to the place of meeting it was agreed that the commission adjourn for a couple of hours, the American commissioners still remaining between the lines, while the Spaniards returned to Santiago for luncheon.

During this interval typewritten copies of the amended document were prepared both in the English and the Spanish, to await the return of the Spanish commissioners. These reappeared promptly at the time appointed, and after a careful revisal of the articles as amended, and a comparison of the English with the Spanish copies, each Spanish commissioner signed his name thereto, immediately after which the American commissioners signed also.

The work for the day being thus accomplished, after an interchange of compliments and congratulations the commission adjourned at 3.30 P.M.

Early the following morning General Shafter received a letter from General Toral stating that he had received the authorization of his Government to make the final capitulation on the terms and conditions agreed upon, including that of the return of the Spanish troops to Spain by the United States. A meeting of the commission was accordingly arranged to take place on that same morning at 9.30 o'clock, in order to settle the final details of the capitulation, and to sign the final document.

About 8 o'clock that morning, the American commissioners met at General Wheeler's headquarters to consider the alterations which would be necessary in preparing the document to be signed. Promptly at 9.30 A.M., on the 16th inst., the commission met at the place appointed, for the purpose of concluding the arrangements for the final capitulation.

The document as drawn up that morning by the American commissioners was most carefully gone over, each paragraph being translated into the Spanish and carefully weighed and considered by all the commissioners, — the changes desired by the Spaniards being few and unimportant :

At the suggestion of the Spanish commissioners, that portion of the title reading, "and Mr. Robert Mason," was altered so as to read, "and as interpreter Mr. Robert Mason, of the city of Santiago de Cuba."

Article No. 6 was objected to as it then stood, by General Toral, on the ground that the addition at the end of the paragraph was not in the preliminary agreement signed the day before. This was acknowledged by the American commissioners, who said that they would not insist upon its insertion if General Toral had serious objection. [1]

The last paragraph in the agreement, reading, "Entered into this sixteenth day of July, eighteen hundred and ninety-eight, by the undersigned commissioners, acting under instructions from their respective Governments," was altered at the suggestion of General Toral so as to read at its termination, "acting under instructions from their respective commanding generals, and with the approbation of their respective Governments."

[1] The clause referred to, closing sentence, read as follows : "with a view of their being properly paroled not to bear arms against the United States during the present war until duly exchanged." As a matter of fact, the American commissioners had received a private message from General Shafter, just as the conference opened that morning, telling them that he did not think it advisable to have this addition to paragraph 6 inserted; hence the readiness of the American commissioners to concede the point.

CHAPTER XV

THE NEWS SENT HOME — CAPITULATION CEREMONIES — THE ENTRY OF SANTIAGO — RAISING THE AMERICAN FLAG ABOVE THE PALACE — MY VISIT TO THE WRECKS OF CERVERA'S SQUADRON

THE place where these negotiations were held, which must of necessity become historical, was in a gently sloping field covered with luxuriant grass, and under the shade of a very large and beautiful ceiba-tree, the trunk of which was nearly if not quite fifty feet in circumference. The branches of the tree were broadly extended, and filled with exceedingly rich foliage, which gave an excellent shade, covering quite an extensive area of ground. The place was not more than fifty or sixty yards south of the main Santiago road, and was probably a little nearer to our lines than to those of the Spaniards. Some two hundred or three hundred yards to the left and down the slope of a hill was a very fine spring, which had been walled up with high walls of masonry, constructed in a workmanlike manner.

For the earlier negotiations, we had always met without any arms being brought either by the Spaniards or ourselves, except that the Spaniards had sometimes worn their *machetes*. As before mentioned, on the afternoon of the 14th, the Spanish officers urged that all matters be postponed until the next day, while we insisted that they should return that night to continue, and, if possible, complete the negotiations; which resulted in an agreement that we should return to the place at half-past nine that night. It did not occur to me at the time, but since I have thought it possible, that the Spaniards may have regarded this insistance on our part as singular, and possibly as an unwarranted exaction. At all events, when we passed our outposts to go to the place to keep the appointment at 9.30 that night, the sentinels informed us that they had heard quite a body of men not far from the place of rendezvous. When we reached the place there was nobody in that immediate vicinity, but after a little delay the Spanish officers came up accompanied by larger escorts than heretofore, and all armed, the Spanish soldiers bringing their carbines.

I was so interested with the negotiations that I did not myself observe this; and we proceeded with our consultation, which occupied some three hours, when, after the proper adieus, we parted, each returning to our respective lines.

A prompt reply to General Shafter's despatch came from the President in the following words:

GENERAL SHAFTER,

    Commanding Front, near Santiago :

The President of the United States sends to you and your brave army the profound thanks of the American people for the brilliant achievements at Santiago, resulting in the surrender of the city and all of the Spanish troops and territory under General Toral.

Your splendid command has endured not only the hardships and sacrifices incident to campaign and battle, but in stress of heat and weather has triumphed over obstacles which would have overcome men less brave and determined. One and all have displayed the most conspicuous gallantry and earned the gratitude of the nation. The hearts of the people turn with tender sympathy to the sick and wounded. May the Father of Mercies protect and comfort them.

WILLIAM MC KINLEY.

This complimentary message from the Chief Executive was gracefully acknowledged by General Shafter as follows:

CAMP, NEAR SANTIAGO, July 16.

TO THE PRESIDENT :

I thank you and my army thank you for your congratulatory telegram of to-day. I am proud to say every one in it performed his duty gallantly. Your message will be read to every regiment in the army at noon to-morrow.

SHAFTER,
Major-General.

The Secretary of War also expressed his gratitude to the army in these words:

To MAJOR–GENERAL SHAFTER,

Front, near Santiago :

I cannot express in words my gratitude to you and your heroic men. Your work has been well done. God bless you all!

R. A. ALGER,
Secretary of War.

That evening arrangements were completed as to the method of capitulation, which it was agreed should take place at nine next morning.

The army was promptly apprised of the surrender, and for the first time in seventeen days the soldiers lay down for a quiet night's rest. Sunday, the 17th, came in with a bright and beautiful morning. The worn and wearied look of the men, which the fearful hardships and exposure of the preceding seventeen days had impressed upon them, gave place to features changed to smiles of good cheer and satisfaction, and a consciousness of a triumphant termination of their efforts, trials, and sufferings.

Pursuant to the arrangements made the night previous, General Shafter, together with the generals and their staffs, rode to a large field in front of Santiago, accompanied by a troop of cavalry; there they met General Toral, who was also accompanied by a company of one hundred men and his and the other Spanish generals' staffs. The American generals were drawn up in line from right to left according to rank, and their staffs were drawn up in the same manner, forming several successive lines. General Shafter rode up to General Toral and presented him with the sword and spurs of the Spanish General Vara del Rey, who was killed at El Caney. The Spanish troops then presented arms, and the Spanish flag, which for three hundred and eighty-two years had floated over the city, was pulled down and furled forever. The American officers and their cavalry troop also presented arms, after which the Spaniards filed to the left and returned to the city; where they, together with the entire Spanish army, were marched to the arsenal and their arms turned over to the American officials. The American generals then rode into town in column of twos, General Shafter and General Wheeler in front, and the other generals following in order of rank; the staff officers following in the same manner, and the whole being followed by the cavalry troop. When we reached the palace we were met by all the officials, civil governor, archbishop, consuls, etc. At about 11 o'clock we were invited to a lunch, and then marched out to the plaza, where thousands of the populace, Spanish and Cubans, had congregated to witness the ceremony. As the clock in the cathedral opposite commenced striking the hour of noon the United States flag (it was my headquarters flag) was hauled to the masthead by Lieutenant Miley, Captain McKittrick, and Lieut. Joseph Wheeler, jr., who had previously mounted the roof of the palace to accomplish this purpose. At the same moment twenty-one guns were fired and the band of the Sixth Cavalry struck up "Hail Columbia!" The Ninth Infantry, which was drawn up in the plaza, presented arms to the American colors, and the Eastern Province of Santiago, with twenty-three thousand Spanish soldiers, and its forts, batteries, guns, etc., was surrendered to the prowess of American arms.

As we rode for the first time into Santiago we were struck by the excellent manner in which the Spanish lines were intrenched, and more especially by the formidable defences with which they had barricaded the roads. The one in question, on which we were traveling, was barricaded in no fewer than four different places, said defences consisting in an enormous mass of barbed iron-wire stretched across the entire length of the road. They were not merely single lines of wire, but pieces running perpendicularly, diagonally, horizontally, and in every other direction, resembling nothing so much as a huge thick spider's-web with an enormous mass in the center. Behind this some ten or fifteen feet were barrels of an extraordinarily large size, filled with sand, stones, and concrete, on the tops of which sand-bags were placed in such fashion as to leave small holes through which the Spaniards could sight their guns. It would, indeed, have been a hard task for American troops, were they never so brave and courageous, to have taken a city by storm which was protected by such defences as these. Nothing short of artillery could have swept such obstructions out of the way, and even then they would still have been more or less effective, owing to the narrowness of the road and the high banks on either side which would not have permitted getting rid of these obstructions by casting them on one side. Even the streets were intrenched in similar fashion, the people taking refuge in the upper stories of their houses; for the mass of the Spanish soldiery had evidently no idea that their commanders would surrender, and had it come, as was at one time feared, to a hand-to-hand fight, the American troops would have suffered a fearful loss, being necessarily placed at such a disadvantage. It was fortunate, therefore, all things considered, that the surrender came when it did; for otherwise many a brave boy who has returned to resume his avocations of peace, or to do his duty as a soldier in his native land, would have found his last resting-place on Cuban soil.

One hears a good deal about the desolation of war, and I have already mentioned that the houses at Siboney and other points on the coast through which we passed were exceedingly limited in number, and even most of these were in ruins. Some further idea of the desolation of the country may be formed from the fact that during the whole of our march from Siboney on the coast to the outskirts of the city of Santiago not one single house was standing, nor one acre under cultivation. It is true that there was one mud hovel in which some ragged Cubans had taken a temporary refuge, who, to all appearances, divided up their time between eating and sleeping.

The destruction by war on the sea has never had a more comprehensive example than that which strewed the remains of Cevera's warships along the coast outside of Santiago. Shortly after the surrender, my staff, various officers from the different regiments of my command, and myself, went on board one of the Government tugs and made a tour of inspection of the wrecks of the Spanish fleet. Passing down the bay, the first wreck we approached was the *Reina Mercedes*, which was sunk in some thirty feet of water just inside the bay near to Morro Castle. Part of her decks and her smokestacks were out of water, the gaping holes in which, and in her side, spoke eloquently of the skill and marksmanship of American gunners. It is said that, seeing escape to be hopeless, her commander endeavored to accomplish that which our brave Hobson, with all his daring, had evidently failed to do, viz., to block the entrance to the channel; but fortunately, as it subsequently

proved for us, he was also unsuccessful, his ship
evidently drifting some distance after her anchors
had been let go, thus leaving the channel un-
obstructed.

Some four miles up the coast we came upon
the *Maria Theresa* and *Oquendo,* both apparently
total wrecks, to which it was impossible for us
to approach very near, it being considered unsafe
to board them, and a guard-ship having been
placed in the vicinity to keep off all would-be
visitors. We saw enough, however, to show us
the terrible havoc which the American shells
had played on these once fine battleships. Being
overtaken by their determined pursuers, they had
both been run ashore, their crews endeavoring
to save their lives by jumping overboard and
making for the beach, thus abandoning the ships
to their fate.

Continuing our trip some ten miles further up
the coast we came upon what was to us the most
interesting sight of all, viz., the wreck of what
was formerly called "the Pride of the Spanish
Navy," — the *Vizcaya.* Here our tug anchored,
as we were determined to make an effort to
board this latter vessel, in order to examine for
ourselves her internal condition. This was attended by no small difficulty, but at length we
managed to scramble through a porthole and
climb, to the detriment of our clothing, on to
what remained of her decks. Not a particle of
woodwork was to be seen, everything of a com-

bustible nature having been destroyed by the fire caused by American shells. The destruction was utter and complete. The heat had twisted the massive iron beams into all kinds of fantastic shapes, as if they had been so many pieces of string, and her heavily protected sides were perforated by shells as if they had been of the consistency of brown paper. Those portions of her iron decks still remaining were covered deep in debris, composed mostly of exploded small arms ammunition; and her large guns, which still seemed to be in fairly good condition, were the only articles on board which retained a semblance of their original shape. In short, so complete was the state of chaos and confusion in which we found this once fine vessel, which a few brief months before had so proudly anchored in New York harbor, that an adequate description is impossible, and, as we were conscious of a pronounced and very disagreeable odor emanating from the remains of some unfortunate Spanish sailors left on board, and which one of the most enterprising of our party had discovered in the conning-tower standing by the big gun, we beat a hasty retreat and returned, after a repetition of our scrambling experiences, to our tug, which was waiting in the near distance.

The wreck of the *Cristobal Colon* we were unable to visit, she having run some forty miles further up the coast before being overtaken. We returned to Santiago, therefore, only delaying for an hour or so in order that we might examine more closely the defences of the redoubtable Morro Castle, which are dealt with in another portion of this book.

On a second trip, I visited and made a thorough examination of the *Infanta Maria Theresa*. This was probably the least injured of all the Spanish war-ships, and it is estimated that by an expenditure of some three millions of dollars this vessel can be made into a valuable man-of-war. At the same time I also visited and thoroughly examined the fortifications of the Punta Gorda and Socapa Batteries, both of which exhibited most skilful engineering.

———

It was but natural that with most justifiable pride and satisfaction General Shafter turned from the glorious scene of triumph that had followed the hardships of this campaign, and dictated the following detailed information to his Government:

SANTIAGO DE CUBA, July 17, 1898.

ADJUTANT-GENERAL, U.S.A.,
            Washington :

I have the honor to announce that the American flag has been this instant, 12 o'clock noon, hoisted over the house of the civil government in the city of Santiago. An immense concourse of people present, a squadron of cavalry and a regiment of infantry presenting arms, and band playing national airs. Light battery fired

salute twenty-one guns.   Perfect order is being maintained by municipal government.   Distress is very
great, but little sickness in town.   Scarcely any yellow
fever.   A small gunboat and about 200 seamen left by
Cervera have surrendered to me.   Obstructions are
being removed from mouth of harbor.   Upon coming
into the city I discovered a perfect entanglement of
defences.   Fighting as the Spaniards did the first day,
it would have cost five thousand lives to have taken it.
Battalions of Spanish troops have been depositing arms
since daylight in armory, over which I have guard.
General Toral formally surrendered the plaza and all
stores at 9 A.M.

W. R. SHAFTER,
Major-General.

Later in the day, after returning to camp,
General Shafter informed Washington as follows
with regard to the Spanish arms and ammunition
captured :

HEADQUARTERS 5TH ARMY CORPS,
July 17, 1898.

ADJUTANT-GENERAL,
            Washington :
My ordnance officers report about seven thousand
rifles turned in to-day, and six hundred thousand
cartridges.   At the mouth of the harbor there are quite
a number of fine modern guns, about six-inch ; also
two batteries of mountain guns, together with a salut-
ing battery of fifteen old bronze guns.   Disarming and
turning in will go on to-morrow.   List of prisoners
not yet taken.

W. R. SHAFTER,
Major-General.

The gathering of the Spanish armament occupied about two days, and on the nineteenth General Shafter cabled further information to the War Department as to the Spanish arms turned in, and garrisons surrendered :

HEADQUARTERS 5TH ARMY CORPS,
July 19, 1898.

ADJUTANT-GENERAL, Washington :

My ordnance officer reports over ten thousand rifles sent in, and about ten million rounds of ammunition. Send officers and troops to-morrow to receive surrender of interior garrisons; about two thousand at these places. Will send officers to receive surrender at coast garrison at Guantanamo, Boicbon (Baracoa), and Saguci Pancinia (Sagua de Tanamo).

W. R. SHAFTER,
Major-General.

CHAPTER XVI

DESCRIPTION OF THE NEIGHBORING COUNTRY — THE
TOWNS: DAIQUIRI, SIBONEY, SEVILLA, AND EL CANEY
— SUFFERINGS OF THE REFUGEES — THE CITY OF
SANTIAGO — CAPTAIN FRY'S FATE RECALLED — SPANISH
ABUSE OF THE RED CROSS FLAG

I PRESUME I should say a word regarding so
much of Cuba as we have seen. It is a rolling
country, exceedingly fertile, and in some respects
quite attractive. It appears to be very free from
such animals as rabbits, foxes, or squirrels;
snakes also are scarce — I have seen only one
since I came on the island, and that of a harmless
species.

The most abundant product that I have
seen is the cocoanut; we passed through
extensive groves, where I should say millions
upon millions of cocoanuts could be gathered
every year. General Castillo, who owns
largely this character of land, told me that he
sold his cocoanuts in Santiago, the price he
got for them ranging from ten to fourteen dollars a thousand. Limes, which make a delicious
beverage, grow very freely; and guavas, which
are very palatable, also are found growing
wild, and mangos grow in great abundance.

Pineapples grow well; coffee is a staple product of the province; tobacco does very well, but
is grown more abundantly in other provinces of
the island.

I also saw wild cotton, the stalks being fully
twelve feet in height. Corn and melons of all
kinds mature very rapidly. Fences are very
cheaply made; small twigs of trees are planted
along the side of the road and in eight months
they have grown strong enough to nail a wire
upon them, and it is by this means that most of
the fences are constructed. The rich magnetic
iron-ore is very abundant in Santiago Province,
and is largely carried to New York, Baltimore,
and Philadelphia.

The small towns were a great disappointment.
Daiquiri has only about some twenty ordinary
frame houses; Siboney probably had a somewhat
larger population. Sevilla, which is put on the
map as a town, has now but the remains of one
building, and of that there is left but little more
than the framework. El Caney is a very ordinary town of some three or four hundred people.
It has a very fine church. The eastern side of the
town is occupied by people well to do who have
servants, while the western side is inhabited by a
squalid set of miserable creatures. When the
commanding-general of Santiago notified the
residents that the place would be bombarded,
twenty-two thousand people left the city, eighteen
thousand of them congregating in this town and

vicinity, while the others scattered around in neighboring fields. Their sufferings were fearful. Notwithstanding the great efforts on the part of the Government and the Red Cross to feed them, there was so little organization that many of them were traveling to and fro to various places in the hope of bettering themselves, and many suffered seriously from want of food. It was a pitiful sight to see men, women, and children, some of them bearing evidences of having enjoyed the comforts and probably even the luxuries of life, tramping through the mud and begging for something to eat.

The city of Santiago had a population variously reported at from 50,000 to 71,000. It is one of the oldest cities in America, being founded in 1516. Like most Spanish or Mexican cities, the streets are narrow; there appears to be no sewerage, and the houses are old and poorly built; they have the large Spanish window enclosed with an iron grating and, as you pass, the females of the family are generally standing in the window looking out through the bars.

The principal streets are about twenty-three feet in width, having sidewalks of about thirty inches and a roadway of about eighteen feet. A few of the best streets are paved, the center being depressed, along which the sewerage from the houses is almost constantly running. Most of the streets are without pavements, and by far the greater part of the city is composed of squalid houses, where the people live with none of the comforts and few of the decencies of life. I noticed a number of stores which were attractive and neat. Dry-goods, Panama hats, and other domestic merchandise was tastefully arranged and had a fresh and inviting appearance. The best drug-stores also presented an appearance which compared well with stores of a like character in our country. The principal plaza is small, but very prettily arranged with walks, plants, and fountains. The plaza is bounded by the palace of the civil governor, a large and well-constructed building with marble and tiled floors. Opposite is the archbishop's cathedral, with a convent and nunnery attached; the whole structure comparing favorably with similar architectural buildings in the United States, making due allowance for the age of the city.

On the side to the left of the palace is the San Carlos Club; a building with a very large and high veranda, marble and tiled floors, used as a first-class hotel, which is much frequented by Spanish officers and officials. The principal banking, commission, and shipping houses are located on the street immediately on the bay. This is a broad and well-constructed roadway, or rather two parallel roadways divided by a parking some twenty feet in width. From in front of this roadway project the piers, a prominent feature among which is a boat-club house built some hundred feet out in the bay, and connected with the land by a tasteful wooden bridge. The club-house is now used as a hospital, and is one of the largest in Santiago. It was organized by Miss Clara Barton and Miss Annie E. Wheeler, the latter having been its superintendent from its inception.

I have visited the bull-fighting ring. It is a large, roughly made wooden amphitheater, constructed in the same temporary manner as that in which we construct our fair ground and exhibition stands, except that the building is enclosed all round in an exact circle, as nearly as I could observe. I also made two visits to the place where the victims of the *Virginius* — Captain Fry, formerly of the United States navy, and his followers — were executed.

I employed two different guides to point out to me the exact spots they occupied, and the manner of their execution. They were made to kneel with their faces to the wall of a large butcher pen. Captain Fry was the center of a group of sixteen on the right hand of the gate as you face the wall, while Lieutenant Ryan was the center of a like group to the left of the gate. These guides pointed out to me the spot, as they said, where Captain Fry knelt. I knelt myself upon the point indicated, with my face towards the wall, and asked them if that was the position occupied by Captain Fry; to which they replied in the affirmative. The reader will recollect that one of his last acts was to write a letter to

General Grant, an old friend of his (the General was then President), asking him to secure for his wife some pay which was due to him when he resigned from the navy of the United States.

Only a portion of the crew were shot. A British naval officer, hearing of the proceedings, sailed into the bay; and the British consul was obeyed when he demanded that the slaughter stop.

_____

After our successful assault of the numerous works of the enemy on July 1st, and after we had occupied the heights of San Juan Ridge, the city of Santiago was spread out before us, some two miles distant, like a panorama. We could plainly discern the huge amphitheater, the barracks, the cathedral, and many other buildings ; and we were struck by the fact that nearly every building of any size or importance was protected by the Red Cross flag. There was no doubt that the Spaniards had abused their privilege in this respect; and later inspection showed this to be correct. In front of the barracks, for instance, which had been converted into a large hospital, the Red Cross flag was in evidence in various parts of the building, and just in front of this hospital they had placed some guns, evidently with the idea of being able to fire at us from that locality, and prevent us from replying, owing to the Red Cross flag and hospital immediately in their rear.

CHAPTER XVII

OUR GENERALS IN THE CAMPAIGN — THE SPANISH
GENERALS AND CIVIL OFFICERS — "SOCIETY OF THE
ARMY OF SANTIAGO" — GETTING THE TROOPS NORTH
— PLACED IN COMMAND AT MONTAUK POINT

I HAVE already spoken of General Shafter, our commander. He is a man of more than ordinary intellect and force of character. The great success of the expedition, resulting in the capture of twenty-four thousand prisoners by an army of about two-thirds of that strength, is a full answer to the criticisms which were made by some of the papers regarding his conduct of the campaign. The most marked criticism that I have heard of him was that he spent too much time in attending to details; but the more I have thought of it the more I could see the evident necessity of this. He gave special orders about the management of his pack-trains, and had special supervision of the bringing forward of rations and ammunition. These were the indispensable questions. Mismanagement in these departments would have caused great suffering. The failure of one or two days' rations for the whole army would have caused great suffering and would have been very serious, and it required all General Shafter's energy and administratability to prevent such a disaster. He was without a harbor, and was compelled to unload his ships on an open coast, often baffled by the waves and surf. The roads, especially after rains, became very bad and sometimes almost impassable, and yet from first to last General Shafter overcame these difficulties, and if any regiment failed to get sufficient rations for every day of the campaign it was probably owing to their own neglect or carelessness.

His plan of the battle of July 1st was for General Lawton and General Bates to attack El Caney, which was defended by four hundred and sixty Spaniards. He expected this place to be taken in an hour, and Lawton and Bates were ordered then to move on toward Santiago by the Caney and Santiago road, where their left would join the right of our cavalry. Unfortunately, Lawton was occupied till nearly 4 o'clock with this undertaking, and by that time the fight at San Juan was practically over. Lawton then started to join the rest of the army; but, being met by fire from the Spaniards early in the night, he turned and made a circuit, so that he did not reach his destination until the next day. Bates had started earlier and his brigade reached the foot of San Juan Hill at daylight on the morning of the 2d.

General Lawton and the commander of his 1st Brigade, General Chaffee, are both superb soldiers. They have spent their lives in military service and are thoroughly familiar with military business. General Ludlow — another of Lawton's brigade commanders — is a very superior officer, though he is younger and has had less experience than either Lawton or Chaffee. General Bates is also a very superior soldier, and in a long military life has built up a most enviable reputation.

General Kent was a schoolmate of mine at West Point. He has always stood very high in the army as an officer of the most excellent qualities. He commanded the 1st Division of Infantry, which went into the battle on the left of the cavalry. As I was directed to give instructions to him, as well as to my cavalry command, his conduct was under my own personal observation. This was rather necessary, as my cavalry and his division were the only troops that attacked San Juan, and as General Shafter was responsible for the entire army, he very properly took a position where he could observe the troops at Caney, as well as those at San Juan. The distance between the two places being some six miles, it really made two separate battles which it became General Shafter's duty to direct. As will be seen, the orders that I received since the 25th had virtually placed me in command of the troops on shore, and this character of delegated control to me was continued to a certain degree until some time after General Shafter had come ashore. I always had had a high opinion of General Kent, but his management of his division in this engagement increased my admiration for him.

Gen. Hamilton S. Hawkins, who commanded his 1st Brigade, was also at West Point with me. He was greatly distinguished in the battle, exhibiting courage and determination. He was wounded on the evening of July 2d; and very properly he and General Kent, General Lawton, General Chaffee, and eventually General Sumner, were all of them promoted to the rank of major-general. General Young, who was absent sick, had been distinguished in the Battle of Las Guasimas, and I recommended him very strongly to the Government for promotion, and I am very glad that he received promotion also. He is an officer of large experience, and in all respects possesses the very highest qualifications. General Ludlow had only been in command for a few days; he was raised as an officer of engineers, but his management as a commander of soldiers, while brief, has been most creditable.

I saw a good deal of the Spanish Commander of Division, Don José Toral, and also of General Don Federico Escario. Both of these officers stand high in their army, and they impressed me very favorably. General Escario won his brigadier-generalship by the rapid and skilful march by which he reinforced General Toral. He marched some two thousand five hundred men a distance of some fifty miles, and on his approach to the city was opposed by General Garcia; he, however, drove back that officer and reached the city without difficulty.

General Linares, who commanded the troops at Las Guasimas on the 24th, and at San Juan on the 1st, was severely wounded towards the close of that action. I had some correspondence with him, and had quite a talk with him one morning. He was lying in bed, his arm bandaged up and resting upon a pillow. It had given him much pain, and had caused him to have an almost constant fever. This officer impressed me very favorably; he is a lieutenant-general in the Spanish army, and evidently a man highly regarded by his countrymen.

When I went to the palace at the time of the capitulation I met the archbishop, the civil governor, the judges, and other public functionaries. Of course I could not judge much of them in a short interview, but they did not impress me at all as well as the ordinary American official.

The attention of the country has been attracted by the number of people of wealth who enlisted in the army as privates or went into the Santiago campaign with subordinate commissions. Prominent among these was John Jacob Astor, a man said to be worth some hundred million dollars, who went to the front and incurred the dangers and underwent the hardships incident to the campaign. Among others I might mention were his cousins, William Astor Chanler and Mr. Woodbury Kane. These three members of the Astor family left their luxurious homes and went with the army to Cuba. I think the first is the only instance on record of a man with the wealth of Colonel Astor voluntarily incurring the hardships and risks which were involved in so arduous and dangerous a campaign. Many other similar instances could be mentioned, among them young Lieutenant Tiffany,[1] Major Creighton Webb, Henry Bull, Craig Wadsworth, Joseph Stevens, Captain Brice — son of Senator Brice, and young Sergeant Hamilton Fish, who fell while bravely fighting at Las Guasimas — the first battle on Cuban soil.

On Sunday, August 1st, officers from the various organizations which had participated in the campaign met at the palace in Santiago. The meeting was called to order by General Lawton, who explained that the object of the meeting was to establish the "Society of the Army of Santiago," and upon his motion General Wheeler was unanimously elected chairman.

[1] From exhaustion following the voyage north in a transport, weakened by fever, Lieutenant Tiffany died in Boston, soon after landing, and before he could be removed thence to his home in New York.

Upon taking the chair, General Wheeler addressed his fellow-officers as follows:

GENTLEMEN: I thank you for the honor of being called as the temporary chairman of this gathering of my fellow-officers, who have met to consider the advisability of organizing a Society of the Army of Santiago. The rapidly occurring events of the campaign of the past five or six weeks have been of a character which will ever bring together the hearts of those who have participated.

This army by its endurance and courage has already won the admiration of the civilized world, and it is most natural and appropriate that men who have stood shoulder to shoulder in such a struggle, crowned as it has been with glorious victory, should desire to cherish and perpetuate such memories.

[General Wheeler adverted to the historic character and value of similar societies, which had been organized at the close of the several wars in which our country has been engaged; enumerating the Order of the Cincinnati, organized by Washington's officers at the close of the American Revolution, the Society of the War of 1812, the Aztec Society, which grew out of the war with Mexico, and the various societies growing out of the War of 1861-'65.]

The campaign in which we have been engaged, though brief in duration, has probably been more fruitful in results than those of any of the wars I have mentioned, and will certainly be classed as one of the most remarkable in military history; and, in closing, I repeat, has made this army famous throughout the world.

Upon the motion of General Ludlow, the chairman appointed the following officers to draw up a constitution and by-laws:

General LUDLOW,	General BATES,
General LAWTON,	Capt. WOODBURY KANE,
General KENT,	Lieut. J. D. MILEY.

The meeting then adjourned, to assemble at the same place at 3 o'clock, Sunday, August 7th. At the adjourned meeting, the committee on by-laws and the constitution were unable to make a further report than to recommend that the society proceed to elect a president, vice-president, and secretary. General Wheeler requested General Lawton to take the chair; and, after speaking in complimentary terms of General Shafter, he nominated him as the permanent president of the society. General Wheeler's motion was unanimously adopted. General Wheeler was elected vice-president; and Major F. D. Sharpe, secretary. The chair appointed a committee, who notified General Shafter of his unanimous election as president; after which the society adjourned, to meet at the call of the president.

After the surrender on the 17th, the only duty left for the army to perform was to guard the unarmed Spanish prisoners; but the hardships and exposures to which our troops had been subjected had so seriously affected the health of the entire command, that the army surgeons made a unanimous report that a change in locality was absolutely essential to restore the command to health.

It must be remembered that this army was composed of two regiments from Massachusetts, one from New York, two from Michigan, one from Ohio, one from Illinois, one from the District of Columbia, and the "Rough Riders" Regiment, about one-half of which came from the North and most of the rest from the healthy plains of New Mexico and Texas. These organizations, together with the regular army, most of which was from the North and nearly all of which had for years been stationed in the extreme North, were the composition of the army in Cuba. It would have been difficult to have found a body of men so ill-adapted to maintain its health in the tropical and malarious climate of this part of Cuba in the sickly season.

To make matters worse, this army had left the ships without carrying with it any tents; and had slept upon the ground for more than three weeks, with no protection whatever from the severe dews of night and the alternations of the heavy rain and the torrid sun of the day. On the morning of the Battle of San Juan the army was compelled to wade the San Juan River, many of the officers and soldiers becoming soaked to their waists; and, as they were without a change of clothes or shoes, they were wet for days.

The necessary consequence was, that after the capitulation of July 17th, the naturally strong men who composed this army had become so weak that a march of five miles was almost an impossibility. By August 1st, this condition, instead of becoming improved, as was hoped, had grown steadily worse. By that time the immune regiments had arrived in Santiago, and orders were received for the embarkation of General Shafter's army.

From the day of the capitulation on the 17th, I had urged most strenuously that the Cavalry Division be sent to Porto Rico, as I felt that the five days' voyage, together with the change of climate and diet, would put them in good campaigning condition; and I am still impressed that such a movement would have resulted in the favorable way that I anticipated. Unfortunately, my repeated applications for my command to go to Porto Rico were not acted upon, and on August 6th I was directed to embark my command upon the *Gate City*, *Matteawan*, and *Miami*. I therefore directed General Sumner to go in advance on the *Gate City*, and, after the *Matteawan* had pulled out into the bay, I, in compliance with orders, went on board the *Miami* with seven hundred of my men and sailed out of the harbor on Monday, August 8th.

On Monday night we sailed through the Windward Channel, passing Cape Maisa at 3.10 A.M. Tuesday. We passed Castle Island

Light-house at 4.40 Tuesday afternoon. We passed Wattling's Island at 5 o'clock on Wednesday morning, August 10th. Upon this island Columbus landed, four hundred and six years ago. Very few houses except those occupied by light-house keepers could be seen on Castle Island. It is a low island rising but a little above the water. The chief occupation of the inhabitants is fishing and catching sea-turtles.

Our ship then took a direct line for Montauk Point, which threw us some four hundred miles east of the Florida coast, and quite out of range of the usual line of travel. Our voyage was therefore without moment, our efforts being specially directed to taking care of the sick. On Thursday night we lost by death Sergeant George Walsh, a soldier of Troop A, 1st United States Volunteer Cavalry ; and on Friday morning he was buried with the usual soldierly and Christian services.

We sailed into the harbor at Montauk Point on Sunday, August 14th, and disembarked next day. I was at once summoned to Washington by the President; who, together with the Secretary of War, gave me a very pleasant interview, and ordered me to return to Montauk Point and take command of the troops at that place. This involved the supervision of the disembarkation of troops, the locating of camps, the erection of tents, and the caring for the numerous sick, with which important work I am still engaged.

CHAPTER XVIII

CAMP WIKOFF, MONTAUK POINT — SANITARY CARE OF
THE SOLDIERS — GIFTS FROM THE AMERICAN PEO-
PLE, OF MONEY, GOODS, AND PERSONAL SERVICE —
A STATEMENT TO THE ASSOCIATED PRESS — VISITS
OF THE SECRETARY OF WAR, PRESIDENT MCKINLEY,
AND SURGEON-GENERAL STERNBERG

IN the space of less than three weeks, twenty
thousand soldiers, fully half of whom were
suffering from diseases contracted in Cuba, were
landed upon the barren fields of Montauk Point,
Long Island. Hospitals, storehouses, and tents
for the soldiers were erected. Nurses, physicians,
and medicines for three thousand sick were
brought from the various localities where they
could be found, and shelters provided for them,
and they were installed in the various wards of
the mammoth hospitals. To be brief, a city of
twenty-two thousand people (the actual number
which landed at this place from Cuba being
21,221), half of them invalids, was erected in
this brief space of time; and medicines, provisions, transportation, sanitary contrivances, and
all else necessary to such a city were provided.
So perfectly was this done that, on September

5th, Dr. Sands, the eminent Chicago physician, stated that the fever patients at the camp at Montauk Point were better taken care of, both medically and in nursing, than in any other hospital he had ever seen ; and that, in fact, the convalescents were living luxuriously.

The Pennsylvania and New York Central railroad companies notified me of their decision to issue, to the officers and men of the various commands who were going home on furlough and paying their own transportation, tickets at half rate; no letter of authority being necessary, the tickets being freely issued to any one wearing the uniform õf a soldier.

It is pleasant to report that no sooner had this camp been thoroughly established, than offers of money, help, and supplies came in in such quantities from all parts of the United States as to speak well for the liberality of the American people.

One gentleman who does not wish his name mentioned telegraphed me that he had placed to my personal credit the sum of $5,000 to be expended by me in such a way as I thought best, to increase the comfort of the soldiers. I preferred, however, not to expend this money myself, and so notified my generous correspondent ; who afterwards spent it in sending a barge of ice to Montauk Point for the use of the command.

Mr. Stuyvesant Fish, President of the Illinois Central Railroad, telegraphed me, offering $1,000.

The Messrs. Kane, Van Cortland & Co., of
New York, offered also a large sum of money;
and Mrs. Ireland sent her steamboat " Kelpie,"
loaded with delicacies.

The Hon. Sherman Hoar,[1] on behalf of the
Massachusetts Volunteer Aid Association, do-
nated cargoes of very valuable supplies; as did
also The Merchants' Association of New York;
the War Relief Committee of Philadelphia; the
Hon. George F. Hoar, of Worcester, Mass.; the
Hon. Melville Bull; Mrs. S. E. Winthrop, and
Mr. C. Dorcher, and others, of Newport, R.I.

We were similarly indebted to Mr. D. W.
Lord and a committee from Illinois; to Commander Gerry, who in person donated stores
for the sick, bringing them to Montauk Point
in his own yacht; to Commissioner Powers of
the United States Fish Commission, who sent
one thousand pounds of fresh fish for distribution
to the soldiers ; to Mrs. K. M. Bostwick of the
Woman's Veteran Auxiliary Corps of Brooklyn,
Mrs. R. B. Cooley of the Soldiers' Relief Committee, Poughkeepsie, N.Y., and to R. S. How-
land, esq., editor of the Providence " Journal."

The Murray Hill Hotel, New York, gratuitously furnished our hospital with forty quarts
consommé daily; and Mr. George H. Cassidy,
New York, offered to receive into his home,

[1] Mr. Hoar died at his home, Concord, Mass., Oct. 7, 1898, of
typhoid-pneumonia, caused by his overwork in twice visiting the
several camps in which were Massachusetts volunteers, and providing
for their comfort through the Massachusetts Volunteer Aid Association.

furnishing medical attendance and nurses free of charge, a number of our soldiers who needed such care.

Mr. Charles Pullman of Watch Hill, R.I., and his colleagues, did most excellent work in donating supplies and superintending their distribution at the Detention Hospital; while the kindly interest manifested in the welfare of the soldiers by Mrs. S. N. McMaster, then staying at Watch Hill, and by my numerous other correspondents in all parts of the United States, was much appreciated.

A complete list of the generous-hearted people who gave freely of their substance for the benefit of the soldiers is impossible; but mention cannot be omitted of the help given by the officials of the "Red Cross" and other kindred societies; or of the liberality of Miss Helen M. Gould, whose donations probably far exceeded any like gifts ever made before for such a purpose, and who personally devoted her time and efforts to relieve the sufferings of the soldiers.

Almost every mail brought me sums of money from one to one thousand dollars to be expended in like manner, but I felt it my duty to decline to accept all such remittances, feeling that it would not be right for the Commanding General to have sums of money placed to his personal credit for this purpose. I made it a rule, however, to suggest that those who wished to provide comforts for the soldiers should send an agent here who could use his discretion and order whatever supplies he thought were most needed; and, in nearly every case, this suggestion was acted upon, and the money expended in purchasing desirable supplies.

Shortly after taking command it was deemed advisable to establish more hospitals and increase the hospital supplies; and complete outfits for this purpose were telegraphed for to New York and promptly installed.

When the pleasing duty of commanding this large army of 20,000 men, many of whom were very sick, was intrusted to me, the President particularly instructed me to spare no expense in providing for the comfort of the soldiers and in endeavoring to restore the sick to health. Accordingly, I took upon myself the responsibility of ordering large amounts of extra supplies and the nourishing articles of diet which I judged necessary, and some little hitch at first occurred in the Commissary Department at Washington with regard to this additional expenditure; yet in a very short time these luxuries were at the disposal of every soldier. Permission was also obtained from the War Department for the expenditure by surgeons of money, not to exceed sixty cents per day per man, in purchasing unusual and extra supplies for the sick under their care.

Some hundred trained nurses were brought

here, and authority given to employ extra physicians, cooks, hospital stewards, and all other
persons whose services were necessary to a command of this size and importance. Special
attention was given to the abundant supply of
medicines, and to the construction of the necessary hospital accommodation, until in the last
days of August I telegraphed the authorities in
Washington that I had just been through the
hospitals, that the health of the command was
improving very much, that every possible care
was taken of the men, and that all the sick to
whom I spoke assured me that the pure air at
this place was bracing them up and rapidly re-
storing them to health.

A doubt being cast upon the continuance of
the purity of the water supply, a mammoth fil-
tering-plant was purchased and erected at a cost
of some seven thousand dollars.

Within a few days a steam laundry was erected
for the sole purpose of laundering clothing and
linen for the sick, its capacity being sufficient to
do all this work for five or sick thousand invalids. A disinfecting machine was also erected
by which all the clothing and linen of the hospitals was thoroughly disinfected.

Five hundred chairs were sent for the use of
the convalescents who were able to get off their
cots, and so far did the solicitude of the government go for the soldiers who had been in Santiago that men who were not acquainted in New

York were not permitted to leave on the evening train for that city, the authorities fearing they would arrive there too weak, and, being in a strange city, would not know where to go.

The convalescents that were put on the trains had attendants, so that they should not suffer en route. A competent officer and men were detailed at Long Island City to meet all trains and provide comfortable lodgings for them, and to see that they were fully instructed as to how to go to take their trains. On the New York side, also, there were ambulances for those who were not able to walk or to hire carriages to convey them to their places of destination. The Red Cross Society joined nobly in this work. In connection with the officers and soldiers detailed from the army, they arranged to meet all trains from Montauk Point, assisted in collecting the furloughed men, to the number of seventy-five or one hundred each day, and to give them food and shelter for the night after they arrived in Long Island City. Money was also donated for the same purpose by the Merchants' Association of New York and the New York Board of Trade, who heartily co-operated in the work.

Large numbers of letters reached me every day from anxious relatives asking of the whereabouts and well-being of their relations; and special arrangements were made to investigate promptly and telegraph immediate replies; the Government even authorizing, in case information was desired concerning any certain soldier of whom no trace could be found in camp, and who it was thought had probably been left behind in Santiago, to cable directly to that point, at the expense of the Government, in order to furnish information to his friends.

Notwithstanding that doctors, nurses, hospital stewards, and all necessary supplies were in abundance, and that a small army of civilian laborers, carpenters, teamsters, and other workmen were busily engaged in their respective departments; that there were unlimited supplies of delicacies for the sick; and that everything was done which hand could do and brain devise for the well-being of the soldiers, yet so numerous had become the newspaper articles concerning what they were pleased to call the maladministration and mismanagement at our military camps, and which according to them had entailed untold hardships and privations upon our brave soldiers, and so many private letters were received by me from relatives of soldiers regarding the latter's well-being, that, on September 2d, I determined to make a full statement to the Associated Press on this subject, — which statement was in these words:

The following is a sample of the letters we are constantly receiving regarding the soldiers in the camp:

In regard to my stepson, we feel very uneasy about him on account of the newspaper reports of the privation and suffering inflicted on the private soldiers. Although he has never uttered a complaint since he has been in the army, we hear from other sources of the cruel and horrible treatment inflicted on our own soldiers under the pretence of humanity for our neighbors, and the whole country is in a state of terrible excitement. I should not be surprised if the feeling should lead to a revolution of some kind, for I assure you I hear on all sides the most violent and bitter denunciations of the War Department and the Administration. It is, indeed, a great pity that the glory of our triumph should be dimmed by such a shameful thing as the ill-treatment and starvation of our own brave soldiers, while the Spanish prisoners have the best treatment that the country can afford.

It will be seen that this letter says that not a word of complaint has been received from this soldier, and, so far as my investigation goes, no complaint has been made by any of the brave soldiers that have added glory to our arms in the Cuban campaign. A great many anxious fathers, mothers, brothers, or sisters arrive here from all parts of the United States to look after their relatives, who, they say, the papers tell them are suffering, and many of them have heard that their relatives are in a condition of starvation. Most of these people are little able to expend the money for such a journey, and they are surprised when they come here to find their relatives surrounded with everything to eat which can be procured by money, and, if sick, in hospital. They are gratified and surprised to find that they receive every possible care.

In reply to a direct request that I give the exact facts as I see them, I will state that every officer and soldier who went to Cuba regarded that he received a great and special privilege in being permitted to engage in that campaign. They knew they were to encounter yellow fever and other diseases as well as the torrid heat of the country, and they were proud and glad to do so. They knew that it was impossible for them to have the advantage of wagon transportation, which usually accompanies armies, and yet officers and men were glad to go, to carry their blankets and their rations on their backs, and to be subjected without any shelter to the sun and rains by day and the heavy dew by night. They certainly knew that the Spaniards had spent years in erecting defences, and it was their pleasure to assault and their duty to capture the Spanish works. They were more than glad to incur these hardships and these dangers. They went there and did their duty; each man seeming to feel that American honor and prestige were to be measured by his conduct.

The brave men who won the victories did not complain of the neglect of the government, but, on the contrary, they seemed grateful to the President and the Secretary of War for giving them the opportunity to incur these dangers and hardships. They realized that in the hurried organization of an expedition by a government which had no one with any experience in such matters it was impossible to have everything arranged to perfection; and they will testify that under the circumstances the conditions were much more perfect than any one could have reason to expect, and that the President and the Secretary of War and others who planned and despatched this expedition deserve high commendation.

One reason why our army was lacking in some respects in equipment was that a telegram was received from Admiral Sampson stating that if the army reached there immediately they could take the city at once, but if there was delay the fortifications of the Spaniards would be so perfected that there might be great difficulty in taking it. On receiving this despatch from Admiral Sampson the War Department directed the army to move at once, and, as all connected with the army will recall, the orders were received after dark, and the army was in motion, had travelled nine miles, and was on the ships at daylight. When the expedition sailed for Cuba it went there escorted by a large fleet of warships.

At that time it was regarded as impossible for a merchant ship to sail on the ocean safely from any American port to Santiago, but as soon as the Spanish fleet was destroyed, so that it was possible for unarmed ships to sail safely to Santiago, the generous people of the United States subscribed money without limit and despatched ship after ship, loaded with luxuries and delicacies for the Santiago army, and everything that could be accomplished for their comfort was done by the President and Secretary of War. After the surrender had been completed and arrangements perfected for transporting the Spanish army to Spain the President and Secretary of War sent ships into Santiago and transported our army to one of the most healthful localities in the United States. The point selected by the Secretary of War was so situated that thorough protection was given to the people of the United States from the danger of yellow fever contagion. The soldiers upon their arrival at this place received every care and bounty which could be procured by money. The President and the Secretary of War directed that their health and comfort should be cared for without reference to expense, and in addition the people within a circuit of three hundred miles vied with each other in shipping to them carloads and steamboat loads of luxuries of all kinds.

I have just finished my daily inspection of the hospitals. With rare exceptions the sick are cheerful and improving. I have nurses and doctors to care for them and in all my many tours I have not seen a single patient who made the slightest complaint. It is true that there has been suffering, and great suffering. The climate of Cuba was very severe upon all our soldiers, and with rare exceptions they were stricken by severe illness; but instead of complaining, the hearts of these brave men are filled with gratitude to the people for the bounteous generosity which have been extended to them.

There is no doubt that there have been individual cases of suffering and possibly neglect among the soldiers, not only in Cuba, but since their arrival at this place. Nearly 20,000 men were brought from a yellow fever district to the United States. It would have been criminal to have landed them and allowed them to go promiscuously among the people. It has been stated by physicians that if it had been done yellow fever would have spread through many of our States. To avoid such a catastrophe, a point which is more thoroughly isolated from the people than any other locality which could be found was selected. By these wise means the country has been saved from a scourge of this fearful disease.

Every one will realize that to land 18,000 men and put them on bare fields without any buildings whatever could not be done without some hardships. Over 5,000 very sick men have been received in the general hospital and as many more sick have been cared for in the camps, and yet only about sixty deaths have occurred in these hospitals. Tents had to be erected and hospitals constructed and preparations made to supply these 18,000 with wholesome water, food, medicines, physicians, nurses, cooks, hospital furniture, wagons, ambulances, and the other numerous needs essential to caring for 18,000 men, fully half of whom are very sick or in a feeble physical condition.   In addition to this, most of the bedding and much of the clothing was left in Santiago to prevent yellow fever infection. All of these deficiencies have had to be supplied.   We had but one line of railroad to bring these supplies and sometimes there have been delays.

On August 24th, the Secretary of War paid a visit to Montauk Point.   He made a thorough investigation of all parts of the camp, and was much pleased with what he saw.   He stayed here two days, and slept under canvas one night. His visit was productive of much good and attended by very beneficial results.   On August 28th, after his departure, I telegraphed the Secretary of War in these words:

The orders which you issued when here are still having a beneficial effect, and are causing a constant improvement.   Things are better than when you left, except that the fever is developing in a great many who came off the ships, which makes our list look large.

WHEELER,
Commanding.

It was a gratification for me to learn from Secretary Alger that the President also purposed visiting the camp within the next few days, and I accordingly, on August 26th, telegraphed the Chief Executive as follows:

AUGUST 26, 1898.

PRESIDENT: I was very glad to hear that you would visit Montauk Point very soon. The visit of the Secretary of War has accomplished more than I can express. He has promptly corrected evils and made valuable suggestions, and given directions regarding administration. In addition, his personal visit to 1,500 sick soldiers in the hospital has cheered them up, and it is difficult to adequately convey to you the change for the better since the Secretary's arrival. The announcement that you were to visit the soldiers has already added to this improvement; and your presence here for even a single day will accomplish good, the great extent of which you can only realize after you make your visit.

WHEELER,
Maj.-Gen., Commanding.

Following is a letter I wrote the President

HEADQUARTERS U.S. FORCES,
CAMP WIKOFF, L.I., August 31, 1898.

HON. WILLIAM MCKINLEY,
President U.S.A., Meadville, Pa. :

DEAR MR. PRESIDENT: I am very glad indeed to hear that you will be at Montauk on Saturday. The Secretary states that you wish the visit to be very informal, but I know you will not object to the preparations that have been made. We have arranged to fire the President's salute, and a regiment .of cavalry with the band will meet you at the depot. Will you please telegraph me the hour at which you will arrive?

I hope you will stay over at least one night and sleep in camp. I have a tent all fixed for you, and nothing would please the soldiers more than to know that the President of the United States had slept in a camp which contains nearly all the regular army, and that his accommodations were precisely the same as those they enjoyed. The Secretary of War slept in camp one night and was very much pleased with his night's rest.

Very respectfully,

Jos. Wheeler,

Major-General Commanding.

Early on the morning of September 3d, the President and party arrived to make his visit of inspection, with the details of which the country is familiar.

September 6th, General Sternberg, Surgeon-General of the Army, also paid a visit to the camp, and after a rigid inspection of all its departments expressed himself as highly gratified at the result of his investigation.

The " New York World " on September 7th, in reporting this visit, quotes the Surgeon-General as saying: " It is the finest place in the United States, and the water is all right. Lieutenant-Colonel Smart's present investigation is the second on his part. The first analysis of the water was made before the camp was opened, and we are having another analysis made, largely to reassure the public."

CHAPTER XIX

MUSTERING OUT THE REGIMENTS — FAREWELLS

ON August 27th orders were received from Washington to prepare the 71st New York Volunteer Infantry to be sent on furlough, at the expiration of which time they were to be mustered out. I thereupon addressed to them the following letter :

HEADQUARTERS U.S. FORCES,
CAMP WIKOFF, L.I., Aug. 27, 1898.

TO THE OFFICERS AND SOLDIERS OF THE 71ST REGIMENT, NEW YORK VOL. INFANTRY:

Pursuant to the directions of the President, you will proceed to your homes and friends to receive the welcome which Americans love to accord returning heroes who have fought, endured, and suffered for the sake of country, its honor and its prestige.

This short but severe campaign has made ours the leading among the great countries of the earth, and you have done your full part in this great accomplishment. Your comrades who fell in battle, and those who became victims of disease in a tropical clime, will be revered and honored, not only by the people of your Empire State, but by the seventy millions of this great republic.

In bidding you adieu, I shall always remember each
and all of you as honored comrades of the Santiago
Campaign, the effect of which, in importance and far-
reaching benefits to our Republic, can hardly be estimated.

Jos. WHEELER,
Major-General Commanding.

I here insert my farewell letter to the officers
and soldiers of the 33d and 34th Michigan Volunteers, when they left camp on furlough, prior
to being mustered out :

HEADQUARTERS U.S. FORCES,
CAMP WIKOFF, L.I., Sept. 1, 1898.

To THE OFFICERS AND SOLDIERS OF THE 33d AND
34TH MICHIGAN VOLUNTEER INFANTRY :

When your country called upon the brave men of the
West to rally to the standard which waves as the em-
blem of American liberty, you were among the first to
respond. You made no request but to be given the
post of danger and honor. You gladly faced the torrid
sun and the disease of a tropical climate. You bravely
hastened to the firing line in front of Santiago, and
nobly did your duty as heroic soldiers.

During this short but sharp campaign, in which you
well performed your part, our country was elevated to
a leading position among the greatest nations of the
earth. Your work having been accomplished, the Secretary of War directs that you proceed to your homes,
where the people of your great commonwealth await
your coming, eager to shower plaudits and honors upon
you.

To those of your comrades whose lives became a

sacrifice to the cause you so bravely upheld, we reverently bow our heads; and it will be the delight of a grateful country to cherish and perpetuate their memories.

You take with you to your homes my best wishes for your prosperity and happiness, and in bidding you adieu, with my whole heart I say, may God give you His best blessing!

JOSEPH WHEELER,
Major-General U.S.V., Commanding.

Shortly after the Michigan regiments had left, the 8th Ohio, the 1st District of Columbia, and the 1st Volunteer Cavalry were also ordered to prepare for departure, and the following are the letters of farewell to these regiments, respectively:

TO THE OFFICERS AND SOLDIERS OF THE 8TH OHIO VOLUNTEER INFANTRY:

By direction of the Secretary of War you are to proceed to your homes, where you will receive the heartfelt welcome and generous plaudits of the people of the great State of Ohio.

You were prompt to answer the call of your country. You eagerly sought to meet your country's foes upon far distant foreign soil. You braved deadly disease in a tropical land. You did your full duty in a war which has won for us the highest place among the nations of the earth.

In bidding you adieu, I wish you Godspeed, and may health, prosperity, and honor be showered upon you.

JOSEPH WHEELER,
Major-General Commanding.

HEADQUARTERS U.S. FORCES,
CAMP WIKOFF, L.I., Sept. 6, 1898.

TO THE 1ST DISTRICT OF COLUMBIA VOLUNTEER
INFANTRY:

The purpose for which you so promptly gave your
services to your country has been accomplished. You
were among the first to respond to the nation's call to
arms. In the face of tropical suns you hastened to the
scene of conflict, and with eager steps marched to the
front of our line of battle at Santiago, and together
with your brave comrades engaged your country's foes
until you saw them surrender their strongholds and lay
down their arms at the feet of the valorous American
army.

The results of this campaign, in which you did your
full duty, have been so momentous and beneficial as to
win for you and your fellow soldiers the applause and
gratitude of your countrymen.

In bidding you adieu, I beg to express my personal
admiration for the fortitude, endurance, and soldierly
qualities which you displayed, and to wish for you every
possible blessing and the best prosperity and happiness.

JOS. WHEELER,
Major-General U.S.V.

HEADQUARTERS CAVALRY DIVISION,
CAMP WIKOFF, L.I., Sept. 7, 1898.

TO THE OFFICERS AND SOLDIERS OF THE CAVALRY
DIVISION, ARMY OF SANTIAGO:

The duties for which the troops comprising the Cavalry Division were brought together have been accomplished.

On June 14th we sailed from Tampa, Florida, to
encounter in the sickly season the diseases of the

tropical Island of Cuba, and to face and attack the historic legions of Spain in positions chosen by them and which for years they had been strengthening by every contrivance and art known to the skilful military engineers of Europe.

On the 23d one squadron each of the 1st and 10th Regular Cavalry, and two squadrons of the 1st Volunteer Cavalry, in all 964 officers and men, landed on Cuban soil. These troops marched on foot fourteen miles, and, early in the morning of the 24th, attacked and defeated double their number of regular Spanish soldiers under the command of Lieutenant-General Linares. Eagerly and cheerfully you pushed onward, and on July 1st the entire Division, consisting of the 1st, 3d, 6th, 9th, and 10th Cavalry and 1st Volunteer Cavalry, forded San Juan River and gallantly swept over San Juan Hill, driving the enemy from its crest. Without a moment's halt you formed, aligning the Division upon the First Infantry Division under General Kent, and, together with these troops, you bravely charged and carried the formidable entrenchments of Fort San Juan. The entire force which fought and won this great victory was less than seven thousand men.

The astonished enemy, though still protected by the strong works to which he had made his retreat, was so stunned by your determined valor that his only thought was to devise the quickest means of saving himself from further battle. The great Spanish fleet hastily sought escape from the harbor and was destroyed by our matchless navy.

After seizing the fortifications of San Juan ridge, you, in the darkness of night, strongly intrenched the position your valor had won. Reinforced by Bates'

Brigade on your left and Lawton's Division on your right, you continued the combat until the Spanish Army of Santiago Province succumbed to the superb prowess and courage of American arms. Peace promptly followed, and you return to receive the plaudits of seventy millions of people.

The valor displayed by you was not without sacrifice. Eighteen per cent., or nearly one in five, of the Cavalry Division fell on the field either killed or wounded. We mourn the loss of these heroic dead, and a grateful country will always revere their memory.

Whatever may be my fate, wherever my steps may lead, my heart will always burn with increasing admiration for your courage in action, your fortitude under privation, and your constant devotion to duty in its highest sense, whether in battle, in bivouac, or upon the march.

JOSEPH WHEELER,
Major-Gen'l U.S.V., Commanding.

NOTE. — The Cavalry Division lost eighteen per cent., or nearly one in five; Kent's Division lost thirteen and three-quarters per cent., or nearly one in seven; while Lawton's Division lost seven per cent., or one in fourteen. In the Cavalry Division the proportionate losses were twice as great as those in many great battles of Europe. At Waterloo the English lost but about ten per cent., and the average loss in Napoleon's great battles did not exceed eight per cent.

ADDENDA.

A. — Officers of the Cavalry Division who participated in the Battle of Las Guasimas, June 24, 1898.

Maj.-Gen. JOSEPH WHEELER, Commanding.
Maj. WILLIAM D. BEACH, Chief Engineer.
AURELIUS E. MESTRE, Volunteer Aid.
Brig.-Gen. S. B. M. YOUNG, U.S.V.
Capt. A. L. MILLS, A.A.G., U.S.V.
1st Lieut. T. R. RIVERS, 3d Cavalry, Aid.
2d Lieut. W. R. SMEDBERG, JR., 4th Cavalry, Aid.
1st Lieut. L. A. FULLER, Ass't Surgeon.

FIRST U.S. REGULAR CAVALRY.

Maj. JAMES M. BELL, Commanding Squadron; wounded.
Capt. THOMAS T. KNOX, Commanding Troop K; wounded.
Capt. R. P. PAGE WAINWRIGHT, Commanding Troop G.
Capt. JACOB G. GALBRAITH, Commanding Troop B.
1st Lieut. EDMUND S. WRIGHT, Commanding Troop A.
1st Lieut. GEORGE L. BYRAM, Squadron Adjutant; wounded.
1st Lieut. PETER E. TRAUB, duty with Troop G.
2d Lieut. WALTER M. WHITMAN, duty with Troop G.
2d Lieut. CHARLES McK. SALTZMAN, duty with Troop B.
2d Lieut. HENRY C. SMITHER, duty with Troop A.

TENTH U.S. REGULAR CAVALRY.

Maj. S. T. Norvell.
Capt. W. H. Beck.
Capt. J. B. Watson.
Capt. C. G. Ayres.
Lieut. R. J. Fleming.

Lieut. G. Vidmer.
Lieut. H. O. Williard.
Lieut. A. M. Miller, jr.
Lieut. F. R. McCoy.
Lieut. R. L. Livermore.

FIRST U.S. VOLUNTEER CAVALRY.

Col. Leonard Wood.
Lieuten't-Colonel Theodore
    Roosevelt.
Maj. Alexander O. Brodie.
Capt. Micah J. Jenkins.
Capt. Frederick Muller.
Capt. Maximilian Luna.
Capt. R. B. Huston.
Lieut. Woodbury Kane.
1st Lieut. Frank Frantz.
2d Lieut. R. C. Day.
Capt. W. H. H. Llewellyn.
Capt. Wm. O. O'Neill.
1st Lieutenant and Adjutant
    John Hall.
2d Lieut. Maxwell Keyes.
2d Lieut. J. C. Greenway.

2d Lieut. D. M. Goodrich.
1st Lieut. J. A. Carr.
1st Lieut. J. B. Wilcox.
1st Lieut. J. R. Thomas, jr.
2d Lieut. Thomas Rhyning.
2d Lieut. J. D. Carter.
2d Lieut. D. J. Leahey.
2d Lieut. H. K. Devereux.
Major and Assist'nt Surgeon
    Henry La Motte.
1st Lieutenant and Surgeon
    J. R. Church.
Captain L. S. McCormack,
    7th U.S. Cavalry.
U.S. Military Cadet Ernest
    Haskell.
Capt. J. C. McClintock.

B. — Officers of the Cavalry Division who participated in the Battle of San Juan, July 1, 2, and 3, 1898.

Maj.-Gen. JOSEPH WHEELER, Commanding.

Lieut.-Col. J. H. DORST, Adjutant-General.

Maj. E. A. GARLINGTON, Inspector-General.

Maj. WILLIAM D. BEACH, Chief Engineer.

Capt. JOSEPH T. DICKMAN, 8th Cavalry.

Capt. WILLIAM ASTOR CHANLER.

1st Lieut. MATTHEW F. STEELE, 8th Cavalry, Aid.

2d Lieut. JAMES H. REEVES, 6th Cavalry, Aid.

2d Lieut. JOSEPH WHEELER, JR., 4th Artillery, Aid.

Maj. VALERY HAVARD, Chief Surgeon.

AURELIUS E. MESTRE, Volunteer Aid.

LEONARD WILSON.

Brig.-Gen. S. S. SUMNER, U.S.V.

Capt. ROBERT L. HOWZE, A.A.G., U.S.V.

Capt. R. H. BECKMAN, C.S., U.S.V.

1st Lieut. J. A. HARMAN, 6th Cavalry, Aid.

2d Lieut. L. C. ANDREWS, 3d Cavalry, Aid.

THIRD U.S. REGULAR CAVALRY.

Maj. H. W. WESSELLS, JR. ; wounded.

Maj. HENRY JACKSON.

Capt. CHAS. MORTON ; w'nded.

Capt. GEO. A. DODD.

Capt. F. H. HARDIE.

Capt. G. K. HUNTER ; w'nded.

Capt. HENRY L. RIPLEY.

Capt. GEORGE H. MORGAN.

Capt. DANIEL H. BOUGHTON.

Capt. F. O. JOHNSON.

1st Lieut. THOMAS B. DUGAN.

1st Lieut. ARTHUR THAYER ; wounded.

1st Lieutenant FRANCIS J. KOESTER.

1st Lieut. ALFRED C. MERRILLAT ; wounded.

1st Lieutenant O. B. MEYER ; wounded.

THIRD U.S. REGULAR CAVALRY, — *concluded.*

2d Lieut. J. T. CONRAD.
2d Lieut. A. E. WILLIAMS.
2d Lt. HARRY H. PATTISON.
2d Lt. JOHN MORRISON, JR.

2d Lieut. WM. D. CHITTY.
2d Lieut. E. A. SIRMYER.
Additional 2d Lieut. JOHN C. RAYMOND.

SIXTH U.S. REGULAR CAVALRY.

Lieut.-Col. HENRY CARROLL ; wounded July 1.
Maj. THOS. C. LEBO ; com'd'g.
Capt. JOHN B. KERR ; w'nded July 1.
Capt. WILLIAM STANTON.
Capt. HENRY P. KINGSBURY.
Capt. F. WEST.
Capt. GEORGE H. SANDS.
Cpt. A. P. BLOCKSON ; w'nded.
1st Lieut. JAMES A. COLE.

1st Lt. RICHARD B. PADDOCK.
1st Lt. EDW.C.BROOKS,Adj't.
2d Lieutenant W. C. SHORT ; wounded July 1.
2d Lieutenant GEORGE C. BARNHARDT.
2d Lieut. HENRY H. STOUT.
2d Lieut. A. C. NISSEN.
2d Lt. A. VAN P. ANDERSON.
2d Lieuten't N. K. AVERILL, 7th Cavalry, attached.

NINTH U.S. REGULAR CAVALRY.

Lieutenant-Colonel JOHN M. HAMILTON ; killed.
Capt. C. A. STEDMAN.
Capt. CHARLES W. TAYLOR ; wounded.
Capt. JOHN F. McBLAIN.
1st Lt. CHARLES J. STEVENS.

1st Lieut. HENRY A. BARBER.
1st Lieutenant MICHAEL M. McNAMEE.
1st Lieutenant W. S. WOOD, Adjutant ; wounded.
2d Lieut. K. W. WALKER.
2d Lieut. E. E. HARTWICK.

MEDICAL DEPARTMENT.

Maj. GEO. McCREERY, Surg.
Maj. HENRY S. T. HARRIS, Surgeon, U.S.V.
Capt. GEO. J. NEWGARDEN, Assistant Surgeon.

DR. MENOCAL, Acting Assistant Surgeon.
DR. H. W. DANFORTH, Acting Assistant Surgeon ; killed.

SECOND CAVALRY BRIGADE.

Col. LEONARD WOOD, 1st U.S.V. Cavalry, Com'd'g Brigade.
Capt. A. L. MILLS, A.A.G., U.S.V.; wounded.
Capt. ROBERT SEWELL, A.A.G., U.S.V.
Capt. MORTON J. HENRY, C.S., U.S.V.
1st Lt. W. E. SHIPP, 10th Cav., Brigade Q'termaster; killed.
Major WEBB HAYES, 1st Ohio Vol. Cav., attached; wounded.
Capt. L. S. McCormick, 7th U.S. Cavalry, attached.

FIRST U.S. REGULAR CAVALRY.

Lieut.-Col. CHARLES D. VIELE, Commanding Regiment.
Maj. ALBERT G. FORSE, Com'd'g 1st Squadron; killed July 1st.
1st Lieut. and Adjutant PETER E. TRAUB.
Capt. R. T. PAGE WAINWRIGHT, Commanding Troop G.
Capt. HERBERT E. TUTHERLY, Commanding 2d squadron.
Capt. JACOB G. GALBRAITH, Commanding Troop B.
Capt. WILLIAM C. BROWN, Commanding Troop E.
1st Lieut. J. F. REYNOLDS LANDIS, Act'g Reg'l Quartermaster.
1st Lieut. GEORGE W. GOODE, Commanding Troop I.
1st Lieut. EDMUND S. WRIGHT, Commanding Troop A.
1st Lieut. JOHN A. L. HARTMAN, Commanding Troop K.
1st Lieut. CLOUGH OVERTON, Commanding Troop D.
1st Lieut. MILTON F. DAVIS, Commanding Troop C.
2d Lieut. WILLIAM H. OSBORNE, duty with Troop E.
2d Lieut. ROBERT C. WILLIAMS, duty with Troop C.
2d Lieut. WALTER M. WHITMAN, duty with Troop G.
2d Lieut. HUGH D. BERKLEY, duty with Troop D.
2d Lieut. NEWTON D. KIRKPATRICK,[1] duty with Troop I.
2d Lieut. CHARLES McK. SALTZMAN, duty with Troop B; sent to hospital sick, July 2d.
2d Lieut. HENRY C. SMITHER, duty with Troop A.

[1] On the afternoon of September 7th, Lieutenant Kirkpatrick and Naval Cadet Thomas H. Wheeler, General Wheeler's younger son, both Aids on General Wheeler's staff, were drowned while surf-bathing

TENTH U.S. REGULAR CAVALRY.

Lieut.-Col. T. A. Baldwin.
Major S. T. Norvell.
Major L. J. Wint ; wounded.
Adjutant M. H. Barnum ;
  wounded.
Capt. W. H. Beck.
Capt. John Bigelow, jr. ;
  wounded.
Capt. T. W. Jones.
Capt. C. G. Ayres.
Capt. J. W. Watson.
1st Lieutenant W. H. Smith ;
  killed.
1st Lieut. J. J. Pershing,
  Quartermaster.
1st Lieut. J. B. Hughes.

1st Lieut. E. D. Anderson ;
  wounded.
1st Lieut. R. L. Livermore ;
  wounded.
1st Lieut. R. J. Fleming.
2d Lieut. G. Vidmer.
2d Lieut. H. O. Williard ;
  wounded.
2d Lieut. A. M. Miller.
2d Lieut. A. E. Kennington.
2d Lieut. H. C. Whitehead ;
  wounded.
2d Lieuten't F. A. Roberts ;
  wounded.
2d Lieutenant T. R. McCoy ;
  wounded.

FIRST U.S. VOLUNTEER CAVALRY.

Lieuten't-Colonel Theodore
  Roosevelt, commanding
  Regiment.
Major and Surgeon Henry
  La Motte ; wounded.
1st Lieut. and Ass't Surgeon,
  J. R. Church.
Maj. Micah J. Jenkins.
Capt. Frederick Muller.
Capt. Maximilian Luna.
Capt. R. B. Huston.

Capt. Henry ; wounded.
Capt. Frank Frantz.
Capt. R. C. Day ; wounded
  July 1st.
Capt. W. H. H. Llewellyn.
Capt. Wm. O. O'Neill ; killed
  July 1st.
Lieut. Woodbury Kane.
1st Lieutenant and Adjutant
  Maxwell Keyes.
1st Lieut. J. C. Greenway.

at Montauk Point. Cadet Wheeler, seventeen years old, entered Annapolis in '97, and had spent his first vacation on board the *Columbia* in Cuban and Porto Rican waters. His name has been confused by the press with his elder brother, Joseph Wheeler, who graduated at West Point in '95, and who served as Aid on General Wheeler's staff in Cuba during the entire campaign.

FIRST U.S. VOLUNTEER CAVALRY, — *concluded.*

1st Lieut. D. M. GOODRICH.
1st Lieut. J. B. WILCOX.
1st Lieutenant J. A. CARR;
  wounded July 2d.
2d Lieut. SHENARD COLEMAN.
2d Lieut. THOMAS RHYNING.
2d Lieuten't D. J. LEAHEY;
  wounded July 1st.

2d Lieut. J. D. CARTER.
2d Lieut. H. K. DEVEREUX;
  wounded.
Captain L. S. MCCORMACK;
  7th U.S. Cavalry.
U. S. Military Cadet ERNEST
  HASKELL; w'nded July 1.

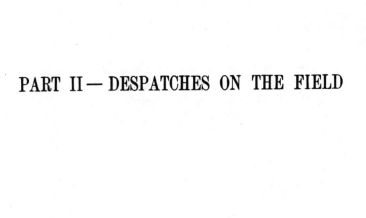

PART II— DESPATCHES ON THE FIELD

NOTE. — *Several important Despatches are not placed in their order here, because they have been incorporated with the text in Part I.*

THE DESPATCHES

CHAPTER I

ADVANCE FROM THE COAST — CUBANS' SKIRMISH WITH
THE SPANIARDS — IN SIGHT OF SANTIAGO — EXAMIN-
ING SPANISH PRISONERS — DIRECTIONS FOR THE LINE
OF BATTLE FROM GENERAL SHAFTER, ON BOARD
S.S. SEGURANÇA — RATIONS FOR CASTILLO'S TROOPS

THE despatches in the Santiago Campaign
form by themselves a continuous official
story. As such, their interest and importance
will be apparent; and I give many of them here,
practically *verbatim et literatim*, in their order as
issued on the field, with one or two descriptive
personal letters. Important statements made
in the original portions of this book may for the
most part be substantiated by reference to these
official despatches. Reports of operations not
referred to here will be found incorporated with
the text in Part I.:

> On Board S.S. Segurança,
> Off Daiquiri, Cuba, June 22, 1898.
>
> Secretary of War,
>   Washington, D.C.:
> Landing at Daiquiri this morning successful. Very
> little, if any, resistance.   Shafter.

DAIQUIRI, NEAR SANTIAGO, CUBA,

June 23, 1898.

To *   *   *

*   *   *

MY DEAR FRIEND: We commenced going ashore yesterday. I rode about 8 miles, penetrating the country about four miles from the sea. The road to Santiago is a very good military road. Bananas and cocoanuts abound, the growth of all kinds so luxuriant it is difficult to leave the road at all except in certain elevated places which are quite open or only have a scrubby growth. The Spaniards have block houses at various points along the road; the nearest one now occupied is 3 or 4 miles beyond the point occupied by our advanced troops. I think they will abandon these places as we approach. I don't think there are more than 18 or 20 thousand Spanish troops in the Province and probably less than 10,000 in the city of Santiago.

Cuba is not so entirely different from other countries as people make out. Our horses are so weakened by the trip that we cannot get them off the ships and make a general forward movement to Santiago for about two days. I suppose you know that our cavalry are dismounted, having come without their horses as we could only bring animals for transportation. Gen. Miles will send our horses as soon as possible. If I had them I could sweep through the Island. The shores are lined with coral rocks. I enclose a little fragment. Soon after getting ashore I sent the flag of the 1st Volunteer Cavalry and had it waved on a high eminence. All the ships answered by blowing their whistles.

With respect, your friend,

JOSEPH WHEELER.

HEADQUARTERS CAVALRY DIVISION,
June 23, 1898.

COL. WOOD,
    Commanding 1st Vol. Cavalry, Daiquiri :

SIR : The Major-General com'd'g directs that you send forward without delay the dynamite gun and development.

    Very res'p'y,
      M. F. STEELE,
    1st Lieut., 8th Cav., Aid.

HEADQUARTERS CAVALRY DIVISION,
JURAGUACITO, CUBA, June 23, 1898.

ADJT–GENL 5TH CORPS,
    On the Steamer Segurança :

SIR : I have the honor to report that Genl Lawton was at this place when I arrived here. He informed me that he has reported to you in full.

The people here report that Genl Linares was here yesterday and left on the train at 4 A.M. to-day.

Genl Castillo reports that the men of his command that followed the Spaniards to-day are now at Sevilla — about 6 miles from here and nine miles this side of Santiago. He reports that 120 insurgents under Lt.-Col. Aguierre (of Genl D. Castillo's command) began fighting the Spaniards about 2 miles west of here, and continued the fight as far as Sevilla.

I have seen the 7 Cubans wounded in the fight; one is wounded severely, the others slightly. Two Cubans were killed.

It is reported that about 1000 or 1200 Spaniards were at this place; they left early this morning.

I directed Col. Wood to come to this place in com-

pliance with your instructions.   He will bring his
dynamite gun.

Genl Lawton and the Cubans have accomplished all
that can be done at present.   I think Genl Lawton has
shown energy and good judgment.

Very respectfully,

Jos. Wheeler,

Maj. Genl U.S. Vol.

P.S. — Genl Castillo reports that one dead Spaniard
was left in the hands of the Cubans.

I understand that Genl Lawton reported the locomo-
tives and coal at this place.

Headquarters Cavalry Division,

Juraguacito, June 24, 1898.

Adjutant-Gen. 5th Army Corps:

Dear Sir: Yesterday afternoon I went out three
miles towards Santiago.   The road is very good, and
there are several good camping places.   At dark the
Spanish rear guard was this side of Sevilla.   The insurgents think the enemy has artillery.   I go out this
morning with Wood's Regiment and will press on to
Sevilla.

Respectfully yours,

Jos. Wheeler.

Siboney, June 24, 1898.

Major–General Joseph Wheeler:

Sir: Colonel Gonzales and Lieut.-Col. Aguierre
have orders to proceed with their commands and join
Major Duany's forces which occupy positions in advance.
Being the Senior Cuban officer in this district my

duties keep me at this place; but as soon as General
Garcia gets here, whom I expect at any moment, I will
have the pleasure of presenting my respects to you.

Respectfully yours,

D. CASTILLO.

HEADQUARTERS 5TH ARMY CORPS,
S.S. SEGURANÇA, June 24, 1898, 1 P.M.

MAJOR GENERAL WHEELER, U.S.V.,
Commanding Cavalry Division:

SIR: The Comd'g Gen'l directs me to say he is glad
to hear such good news and that you are occupying the enemy's ground. A battery will be sent to
you as soon as it can be unloaded and horses are off.
Will also send you some saddle horses from the
Artillery. The Mounted Cavalry will be dispatched as
fast as possible. Kent's Division now disembarked at
Siboney and ordered to hold themselves in readiness to
support you if needed.

The Navy are firing at the point probably where the
railroad crosses the river (San Juan); it was likely the
enemy was sending reinforcements by rail. Rations will
be in Juraguacito to-night and we will have pack trains
out for you during the night, one for each division.

McCLERNAND,

A.A.G.

HEADQUARTERS CAVALRY DIVISION,
½ MILE BEYOND SEVILLA, June 24, 1898, 5 P.M.

ADJUTANT GENERAL 5TH CORPS:

SIR: I have the honor to report we can see Santiago
very plainly from this point, about 7 or 8 miles distant. The country appears level for six miles this side

the city except for heights on the south which extend to within 3 miles of Santiago and from which the city can be shelled. These hills now appear deserted. The country is fairly open, a good tract for campaigning over, and is said to be well watered. The road from this point to Santiago is said to be very good. An engineer force ought to be put to work immediately to repair the road between Juraguacito and Sevilla, as considerable work must be done to it to make it passable for guns and wagons. Sevilla is abandoned, and Genl. Chaffee will occupy it to-morrow.

Very resp.,

Jos. Wheeler,
Major Genl Vol.

Headquarters Cavalry Division,

Sevilla, June 25, 1898.

Adjutant General 5th Corps :

Sir: Col. Dorst having informed me that the Commanding General directs I take general charge of the troops, I have therefore directed the various commanders to commence repairing the road in their vicinity and the officer at Juraguacito to maintain strict police and order at that place. I think it would be a good plan for a Cavalry Engineer Officer and party to come forward and have general superintendence of the work.

Very respectfully,

Jos. Wheeler,
Major General Volunteers.

HEADQUARTERS CAVALRY DIVISION,
IN FRONT OF SEVILLA, ON SANTIAGO ROAD,
June 25, 1898.

To GENERAL SHAFTER : I have just seen two negro boys who left Santiago this morning (Saturday). They report that the soldiers and citizens are very short of food. The soldiers and officers have seized all the food in the shops. They are killing young horses for food, and in the hospitals are subsisting on bread made of rice flour. Three Spanish generals took part in the fight at Sevilla yesterday. Five wagon-loads of wounded were carried into Santiago, and many other wounded got there on horses or afoot. We can see Morro Castle and the flag very distinctly from our position. The Cubans confirm the reports as to the fine character of the fortifications around the city. Seven lines of barbed wire are stretched around the trenches. The Spaniards have recently dug deep trenches around the entire city, connecting a series of small forts.

WHEELER.

HEADQUARTERS 5TH ARMY CORPS,
June 25, 1898.

GEN. WHEELER : I wish you to very carefully examine the valley to the right of the road you are now on. Maps indicate running water there, also a short distance down into the valley in front, and on the left into the hills. If the enemy is developed in the hills to the left, we will work on them when we get ready, with artillery. Should you find the country unoccupied by the enemy, and you find plenty of water there, occupy it with Lawton's Division and bring up Kent, leaving Bates where he now is. Three batteries are now on land. One of them has already gone to you and the others will go in the morning. Four troops of cavalry should also join you to-day. Be very careful of them as they are tired and I want them ready when we need them. Gatling battery is also already on the way. Four escort wagons have been sent out this afternoon to Siboney to Bates, and four ambulances go in the morning. These are all for sick and wounded if needed. Have sent a pack train to each division for the purpose of taking rations and forage (for officers' private horses) of each division. These pack trains must not be diverted to any other purpose, and will be under the charge of the respective Division Quartermasters. Lt. Brooks will have a pack train for the supply of ammunition to the entire command. If you can get up a supply by any means to-morrow it would be a good idea.

Two reserve pack trains will be used to forage and ration Bates' command, the Light Artillery and the Cavalry.

Very respectfully,

WM. R. SHAFTER,
Major-General Commanding.

HEADQUARTERS 5TH ARMY CORPS,
June 25, 1898.

GENERAL WHEELER : Yours in reference to issuing rations received, and all right. Also your report from the negroes in town. Have no doubt it is as they say, but with the single exception of making a little recon- ; naissance, as I have explained to your Aide as well as written you, there must be no forward movement until

I get the troops all up, which I hope will be to-morrow. If you do find water in abundance, advance Lawton's Division, using your dismounted cavalry for the flanks, and bring Kent up and put him where Lawton now is.

Very truly yours,

WM. R. SHAFTER,

Maj. Gen. Comdg.

HEADQUARTERS CAVALRY DIVISION,

June 25, 1898.

ORDERS : By direction of the Commanding General U.S. forces in Cuba, the following officers are detailed as topographical officers and will report without delay to Major W. D. Beach, Acting Engineer Officer Cav. Division, viz. :

1st Lt. E. D. Anderson, 10th Cav.

2nd Lt. M. Batson, 9th Cav.

By command Maj. Gen. Wheeler,

J. H. DORST,

Lt. Col. & Asst Adj. Gen. Vols.

HEADQUARTERS 5TH ARMY CORPS,

ON BOARD S.S. SEGURANÇA, OFF DAIQUIRI, CUBA,

June 25, 1898, 5.50 A.M.

MAJOR GEN. J. WHEELER, U.S.V.,

Commanding Cavalry Division,

Near Sevilla, Cuba :

SIR : Despatch of 5 P.M. just received. Your news is excellent. Have ordered Bates to repair road to Sevilla at once. One battery of Artillery is on way to you, and will have another battery before night. Four troops 2d Cavalry will be gotten to you just as early to-day as possible. Will send them in detachments as ready ; also three pack trains, one for each division, to carry rations to you. The Ordnance Officer with an-other pack train will get ammunition to you. General Kent with two transports could not be found up to last night. The most of his division is at Juraguacito under General Hawkins. Order it to join you, if you can place it in good position ; they are not required where they are, and should be with you. Expect General Garcia's command up to-day, and it will dis-embark at Juraguacito. Keep your front thoroughly picketed and also your right flank, and well in advance ; but *do not try* any *forward movement* until *further* or-ders. From where you are now, or approximately there, I wish to advance in force, and will not move until all the troops are well in hand. I will see you to-day there.

Very respectfully,

WM. R. SHAFTER,
Major General U.S.V., Commanding.

HEADQUARTERS CAVALRY DIVISION,
SEVILLA, June 25, 1898.

ADJUTANT GENERAL 5TH CORPS :

SIR : I send Maj. W. D. Beach, who will give you full information about the condition of the troops and the country. I am doing what I can with scouts to get information about the enemy. I think it important that we send spies into Santiago and to do this effi-ciently we should have funds to pay them. Maj. Beach is an excellent officer to have charge of this fund and I request that he be furnished $100 or $200 for this purpose.

> Very respectfully,
>
> Jos. Wheeler,
>
> *Maj. Genl Vols.*

HEADQUARTERS CAVALRY DIVISION,
SEVILLA, June 25, 1898.

Col. McClernand,
> *Adjutant General 5th Corps:*

Dear Colonel : Several of the communications that I have forwarded have been addressed to *General Shafter direct* for the reason that I have had to send them by Cubans or such couriers as I could find, and by the use of the General's name, I thought it would make the letters more sure of safe delivery.

> Respectfully,
>
> Joseph Wheeler,
>
> *Maj. Gen. Vols.*

HEADQUARTERS CAVALRY DIVISION,
June 25, 1898.

Genl Castillo,
> Juraguacito :

Dear Sir : Will you be kind enough to send one of your officers to report to the Commanding Officer of troops of General Kent's command now out along the water pipe line, with a view of guarding against accidental conflict between your men and his.

General Kent will give your officer directions where to go.

Very respectfully,

Jos. Wheeler,
Maj. Genl Vol.

Headquarters Cavalry Division,
In Front of Sevilla, June 25, 1898.

Adjutant General U.S. Army in Cuba,
S.S. Segurança:

Sir: Gen. Castillo has 600 men at this place and at the picket in front of it, who are without rations. I have told their officers that I would have rations furnished them if they would remain here on duty under our orders, and they have promised to do so. I respectfully request that 1800 rations be turned over to them at Juraguacito. They will send a detail to receive the rations with the bearer of this note.

Very respectfully,
Your obedient servant,

Jos. Wheeler,
Maj. Gen. Vols., Comdg.

Headquarters Cavalry Division,
Camp near Sevilla, June 25, 1898, 3 p.m.

Asst Adjt.-Genl U.S. Army in Cuba,
S.S. Segurança:

Sir: I am investigating the matter of cutting off the water supply of Santiago and would suggest that it would be a very good thing to do. If you will order me to do it I should be very glad to undertake it. It would also be an excellent thing for the Chief Signal

Officer to put the telegraph line from here to Juraguacito in order and to establish a series of signal stations
on the high ground to the front and overlooking the
right of this portion of the Army.   These stations
would also overlook the ground in front.

Very respectfully,
Your obedient servant,
Jos. Wheeler,
Maj. Gen. Vols., Comdg.

In compliance with your instructions I will not make
any forward movement until further orders from you.

Headquarters Cavalry Division,
Sevilla, Cuba, June 26, 1898.

Adjutant General 5th Corps :

Sir : Before receiving your last order, Capt. Dickman of my Staff and Lt. Rivers of General Young's
had already reconnoitered to the front of our forces,
Capt. Dickman going 3½ beyond Sevilla, and I had
ordered General Young to a point 2 miles beyond
Sevilla, and had ordered the 4 troops, 2d Cavalry, to
the same point.   General Lawton will go out with me
this morning and select his camp, and I will arrange
the troops as nearly as possible as directed by you,
taking into consideration water and conformation of
the country.   I have directed General Kent to bring
his command to the front as soon it is supplied and
ready to move, — unless he is otherwise ordered by the
Commanding General.

Very respectfully,
Jos. Wheeler,
Maj. Gen. V., Comdg.

P.S. — Before receiving your instructions to move to the front, there was no room for General Kent's Division — that difficulty is now removed — I do not think there is any possibility of the arrangement I am making bringing on an engagement. Will carefully comply with directions and take great pains to avoid it.

HEADQUARTERS CAVALRY DIVISION,
June 26, 1898.

MAJ. HUGH GALLAGHER, U.S.V.,
Chief Commissary, Cavalry Division,
Aboard S.S. Alleghany:

SIR: The Commanding Officer directs that you supply Brigadier General Demetrio Castillo, commanding Cuban forces at Siboney, with the necessary blanks upon which to make requisitions for rations; explain to him the way to make them out and draw his supplies, and that you issue subsistence supplies to his troops the same as to our own troops.

It is understood that you have been placed in charge of the subsistence stores at Siboney. In case you should be relieved of this duty, please refer this matter to the proper officer.

Information is received that General Garcia has arrived at Siboney. Gen. Castillo's forces are a part of his command, and he may already have drawn rations for Castillo's forces. Please inform yourself upon this point, with a view of not issuing twice to Castillo's forces for the same time.

Very respectfully,

J. H. DORST,
Lt. Col. and Asst Adj. Gen.

CHAPTER II

REINFORCEMENTS EXPECTED — CUBAN REGIMENT RE-
PORTS FOR DUTY — DELAY FOR REINFORCEMENTS —
A REFUGEE'S STATEMENT OF THE FOOD, POPULA-
TION, AND DEFENCES OF SANTIAGO — PANDO COMING
FROM MANZANILLO TO ITS AID WITH 5,000 TROOPS

HEADQUARTERS 5TH ARMY CORPS,
ON BOARD S.S. SEGURANÇA,
OFF SIBONEY, CUBA, June 26, 1898.

MAJOR–GENERAL JOSEPH WHEELER, U.S.V. :

SIR : The Commanding General directs me to say he
expects four thousand reinforcements to-morrow.
This additional force will probably postpone the
advance a little. Get your men well in hand, but
make no forward movement.

Very respectfully,

E. J. McCLERNAND,
Assistant Adjutant General.

SIBONEY, CUBA, June 26, 1898, 7 P.M.

MAJOR GENERAL WHEELER :

SIR : Colonel Pearson, Commanding 2d Brigade,
took 20th Infantry out to reconnoiter along the beach
road on receipt of your order. He had not yet returned and may not to-night. When I hear the results

I will forward report if the matter is of importance, otherwise will see you in the morning.

My division will start from here for General Law-ton's old camp at 5 A.M. to-morrow. Would like an officer sent to meet the head of the column on arrival near your old headquarters.

Very respectfully,

J. FORD KENT,

Brigadier General U.S. Vols.

Comdg 1st Div. 5th Army Corps.

HEADQUARTERS CAVALRY DIVISION,

June 26, 1898.

GENERAL CHAFFEE,
  Commanding Advance:

SIR: By direction of General Castillo, Colonel Gonzales, the bearer, reports to me with 509 men — 413 armed. I have directed him to report to you for duty in your advance guard. Col. Gonzales under-stands that he is subject to your orders.

Very respectfully,

Jos. WHEELER, *Maj. Gen. Vols., Comdg.*

HEADQUARTERS 5TH ARMY CORPS,

ON BOARD S.S. SEGURANÇA,

OFF DAIQUIRI, CUBA, June 26, 1898.

MY DEAR GENERAL WHEELER: I had expected to join you to-day, but there have been so many things that needed special attention, that I could not do it. I mean to come to-morrow. *Do not advance, but have the country, to the right and left of the road, carefully reconnoitered.* I especially desire to know if there is a short cut to the right to Caney, as I believe it will be a good plan to put a division in there and assault the town on that road.

Very respectfully,

Wm. R. Shafter,

Major General U.S.V., Commanding.

Major General Joseph Wheeler, U.S.V.

Headquarters 5th Army Corps,

On Board S.S. Segurança,

Off Daiquiri, Cuba, June 27, 1898.

My dear General Wheeler : I had intended to make an advance to-morrow, with the troops that I have, but, in view of telegrams received yesterday, that a large number of reinforcements (about 4,000) are on the way, and the further fact that one of the ships has arrived this morning, I will not feel justified in advancing until I get them on shore. The Government seems to be very solicitous about us, and it is possible they have information of which we know nothing. I hope your scheme of sending spies into Santiago has worked. I also understand that a large number of poor people came out yesterday and are within the lines. Of course they will be received, as we can't drive starving people back, at least not at the present time. Question them carefully and get as good an idea as you can of the condition of affairs there and of the location of the forces that are said to be on the road to oppose us. I am shipping out stores as fast as possible : ammunition, forage and rations, and will direct it all sent to you, to avoid confusion. Will you have your Quartermaster take charge of it and pile it where we can get at it conveniently ? The forage please issue to the artillery horses and cavalry, as well as horses of officers; and issue subsistence stores to any troops that require it, but not more than three days' at a time for any command.

Best should have reached you yesterday morning, but I found late yesterday afternoon that he had been lying in Juraguacito all day waiting for forage to be sent to him. * * * * * * * *

I hope you will look out the subject of finding if there is any means of moving a division off to your right, bringing it out at El Caney, a good point from which I do not believe we will be expected, which is only about four and a half miles from the city. My Engineer Officer tells me there is a large road leading off to the left on the high ground generally in the direction of the mouth of the San Juan River, and which will be on Kent's left. From the fact that I hear Spanish troops are evidently working down towards the Morro, it is possible they may try or be thinking of attempting to flank us on our left flank; so send at least a regiment of Kent's out that road, a couple of miles I should say, to pretty near opposite the left of where Lawton is to be placed this morning, and establsih a picket line connection with him, if practicable. I am going to have Garcia keep men well to the front on our left. I am coming out to see you this afternoon.

I hope the mounted cavalry are doing well. I had them bring four days' forage on their horses, instead of riding them.

Very truly yours,

Wm. R. Shafter,

Major General U.S. Volunteers, Commanding.

To Major General Joseph Wheeler, U.S.V.

HEADQUARTERS 5TH ARMY CORPS,
OFF SIBONEY, CUBA, June 27, 1898, 9 P.M.

ADJUTANT GENERAL,
    Washington:

All is progressing well. We occupied to-day an advance position abandoned by the enemy yesterday on the Sevilla and Santiago road west of the San Juan River, within three miles of Santiago, and from which it can be plainly seen.

SHAFTER,
Major General Commanding.

HEADQUARTERS CAVALRY DIVISION,
CAMP, ¾ MILE BEYOND SEVILLA, CUBA,
June 28, 1898.

ADJUTANT GENERAL 5TH ARMY CORPS:

SIR: I have to-day examined a young man of fair intelligence who left Santiago yesterday to join the Cubans.

According to what he tells me many of the Spanish troops are sick of malarial fevers and other diseases, (*not* yellow fever), and that they have of late been trying to find extra hospital attendants. The food in the hospitals is sardines and rice bread, as previously advised.

He says there is still a little meat to be had which sells at a dollar a pound to those who are allowed to buy it. Eight days ago it was said by Officers that meat would only last for 12 days. Chief food is rice, of which a large shipment was brought in by a German steamer that failed to get into Havana on account of the blockade, and came here.

There are still a number of Cubans who would like

to come out to join the Insurgents, perhaps five or six hundred, but they fear being arrested on attempting to leave the city. There are but few young Cubans in the city, the population being chiefly composed of women, Spaniards and some few Cubans who are more or less in sympathy with the Spaniards. My informant was unable to say whether, in case we notified the Spanish authorities of the bombardment of the city, they would allow the families to leave ; but considers that, as General Linares and other influential Spaniards have their families there, they would avail themselves of this warning and others might then do the same. Their line of exit would probably be to the N.W. of Santiago, along the bay towards Cobre.

The Spanish soldiers and lower classes speak enthusiastically of their coming victories over us, as they are kept deceived by the ruling classes, but these do not seem to be enthusiastic and appear to be preoccupied.

One of the newspapers of the day before yesterday stated that our numbers were about 16,000, but the people generally believe that we have 25 to 30 thousand. The Spaniards state to the people in Santiago that their forces are 20,000, but my informant does not believe they can have over 12,000. When asked what practice he had in calculating large numbers like that, he said he formed his opinion from what he had previously seen of garrisons in Santiago. Part of the troops in Santiago he says have gone towards the Morro.

This man tells me that the armored cruisers *Vizcaya*, *Oquendo*, *Maria Teresa* and *Colon* are in the harbor, as also the torpedo boats *Pluton* and *Furor*. He was quite familiar with the names and description of the boats.

He says that they have been repairing the upper work of the *Reina Mercedes* (damaged by our shells) but cannot say whether they really expect to make the ship again serviceable.

He has explained to me more clearly what the defences of the city consist of. It appears that instead of the 7 lines of barbed wire fence, there are but two lines of fences running parallel to each other and about 3 yards apart. Each fence has from 7 to 9 lines of barbed wire, and then there are numerous threads running criss-cross in every direction between the two lines of fences. These fences run around the city with only six entrances left open. As to the trenches about the city, he tells me they are not continuous, and are not made with the idea of opposing Cavalry, but are simply made at intervals on rising ground where they can be used for rifle fire. The block houses on the northern side of city do not have any cannon as no attack is expected from that side, my informant telling me that the war ships are supposed to be able to prevent any attack there. On the eastern and southern sides some cannons are mounted in the larger block houses. They are all old-fashioned muzzle loaders, my informant not knowing of any modern gun having been put up there.

He tells me that, according to what the Spaniards themselves say, they had 2,500 men in Las Guasimas. He did not himself see the army re-enter Santiago, but a friend of his did, having seen Lieut.-General Linares, Div. General Toral and Brig.-General Vara del Rey. There were from 4 to 6 carts with sick and wounded, besides stretchers and others on horseback.

He says that Lieut. Hobson and his companions are held in a part of the Hospital Mercedes, and are said to be well cared for.

The forces of San Juan seem to be larger than at first, having been reinforced the night before last. Light mountain Artillery was sent out there, and my informant thinks there must be about a thousand men, although he was not able to take note on passing through. He thinks the Ducrot house is now abandoned, so that it might be occupied, and also thinks that the intrenchments they are making about San Juan will not be quite finished this week. The two hills at San Juan command the road perfectly well, being one on each side of the road. Other heights around Santiago are also being occupied by the Spaniards, but there are only small block houses on them, without cannon. To the south of Santiago there is a commanding height which overlooks the bay and which we can clearly see from the heights we occupy. At this place there is a very old fort made of masonry and a couple of wooden block houses. My informant thinks some small cannon have been set up there.

At Aguadores there is another old stone fort which is a splendid position in every way, commanding all the country up to Santiago. This fort has only very old-fashioned brass guns, and could readily be destroyed from the sea, according to this man's opinion.

The Spaniards are supposed to be very scant of larger ammunition, and what they have is thought to be old.

I am told that 1,000 Marines have been landed from the Spanish war ships, and are now posted in the Santa Ursula battery, in the southeastern part of the city.

My informant tells me that almost every day wounded men are brought into Santiago from the Morro, but that every effort is made to keep the people from ascertaining their numbers.

According to popular report, General Pando is expected from Manzanillo with 5,000 men.

I have been unable to learn the strength of the Spanish forces in Caney from this man, but he does not think they can be very large, nor does he think the Spaniards have any cannon there.

This man fears that, in case we notified the Spanish Authorities of an intended bombardment, they might purposely fail to notify the Cuban families, and that it would be advisable to notify them independently so that they might leave in time.

Yours respectfully,

JOSEPH WHEELER,

Major General Volunteers, Commanding.

CHAPTER III

HEADQUARTERS 5TH ARMY CORPS,
ON BOARD S.S. SEGURANÇA,
OFF DAIQUIRI, CUBA, June 28, 1898.

MAJOR GENERAL WHEELER, U.S.V. :

SIR: Some matters have come up this morning
that I may not be able to get out to see you to-day,
but, under no circumstances, unless you are attacked,
must any fight be precipitated. I have a very strong
telegram from the Secretary, saying some more reinforcements will be here to-morrow, and that a division
is also being forwarded, and that I must not be hasty. I
feel the same way about it, as we are growing stronger
every day and the enemy weaker, so that a waiting
policy is one that we can afford, at least for a few days,
to carry out strictly.

I wish you would select some good officer and have
him take charge of the wagon loads of rations, that I
shall send out now, in establishing a depot. I want to
get three or four days' rations out to the front just as
soon as possible, in addition to the three days' rations
in the men's hands.

See that from the forage that comes out the artillery are supplied; also that the artillery and cavalry are supplied with rations, as they have no transportation set aside for them.

I also wish you would have the road widened at short intervals, so that trains can pass, and to further insure that there is no blockade of the road by trains meeting in narrow places; order all guards along the road not to permit any train of wagons to leave the front to come this way after 9 o'clock in the morning. I will order that trains do not leave here going out until after 11 o'clock. This will give time for the wagons coming in to get down to Siboney before those going up leave.

Very respectfully,

WM. R. SHAFTER,
Major General U.S. Volunteers, Commanding.

HEADQUARTERS CAVALRY DIVISION,
June 29, 1898.

ADJT GENL 5TH CORPS,

S.S. Segurança:

SIR: Colonel Viele, 1st Cavalry, reports that the wire nippers pertaining to his regiment were left aboard the Leona. These nippers are very necessary in our work here and I request that the bearer be furnished a launch to transport him to the Leona for the purpose of getting the nippers.

Very respectfully,

JOS. WHEELER,
Maj. Genl Vols., Comdg.

HEADQUARTERS CAVALRY DIVISION,
June 29, 1898.

ADJUTANT GENERAL 5TH CORPS,
S.S. Segurança:

SIR: Two men and 3 boys have come in from Caney this morning and I learn from them, as follows:

The garrison of Caney consists of 500 regulars under General Vara del Rey, who was in the engagement at Las Guasimas and 70 local guerrilla. The latter man the six forts that defend Caney — 1 masonry and 5 wooden. About 3 days ago the garrison received from Santiago a pack train of munitions and provisions. The provisions will probably last 8 or 10 days. The informant does not believe this garrison can offer serious resistance and believes it will evacuate promptly if attacked. There are no cannon in the forts at Caney. The population of Caney is estimated at about 500, which, with the garrison, amounts to about 1,070 persons. The people are all poor and have very little to live on — the only article of food that can be bought in town being rice and a little oil.

Col. Gonzales informs me to-day that his reconnoiterers report that they examined the Ducrot house and found it abandoned, as also the forts in Marianeja. He has at present parties out examining the block-houses on the heights north of us, with a view to seeing if they are occupied.

The work on the San Juan forts seems to be progressing.

I still believe that the garrison at Caney can be driven out or captured.

Very respectfully,

JOS. WHEELER,
Major Genl Vols., Comdg.

[By the Associated Press.]

AT THE FRONT ON THE RIO GUAMA,
June 27, 1898.

Gen. Lawton, Gen. Chaffee and Gen. Wheeler have thoroughly reconnoitered the Spanish position, and with the aid of information furnished by the Cubans have very good maps of the roads and defenses of the city.

Much information has also been obtained from Spanish pacificos who have slipped out of the city.

The sick in the hospitals — the pacificos say — are suffering from lack of food, and they also report that seventy-seven Spaniards were killed and that eighty-nine were wounded as the result of the engagement on Friday last.

NEW YORK, June 28, 1898.

A despatch to the "Journal" says that on Sunday night Gens. Shafter, Garcia, Wheeler, Kent, Lawton and Demetrio Castillo held a council of war at Siboney and decided to move upon Santiago Tuesday morning.

The water-supply of the city of Santiago, the despatch adds, was cut off Sunday night, and nothing but cistern water is now available to the Spaniards.

A bulletin issued to the fleet by Rear-Admiral Sampson yesterday said:

From a report made by one of the wounded, a nephew of Surgeon Berryhill of the flagship New York, a considerable part of the damage to our troops on Friday last was done by seven-millimeter machine guns manned by seamen, so that there would seem to be some probability in the report of the use ashore of the crews of Admiral Cervera's squadron.

[Special Cable to the "Sun."]

SIBONEY, June 29, 1898.

Another conference was held this morning between Generals Shafter, Garcia and Wheeler. The meeting was arranged by General Shafter and is still in progress as this despatch is written. — *New York Sun, July 2.*

[Special Cable to the "Sun."]

WASHINGTON, July 1, 1898.

According to the latest information received by the War Department, there are now in Santiago city thirteen battalions of infantry of 800 men each, four squadrons of cavalry of 75 men each, one battery of artillery, three companies of sappers and miners of 100 men each, two transport companies of 100 men each, a telegraph company of 100 men, one telegraph section, and 750 other men besides, making in all 11,450 men, exclusive of volunteers. In the province altogether there are 37,825 men, of which the Manzanillo Division and 4,000 men from the Holquin Division are hurrying toward Santiago city. Shafter has at present 16,000 men, and with the second expedition will have 24,000 men to attack the city. — *New York Sun, July 2.*

HEADQUARTERS 5TH ARMY CORPS,
IN THE FIELD,
CAMP NEAR SAN JUAN RIVER, CUBA, June 30, 1898.

THE COMMANDING GENERAL CAVALRY DIVISION,
In Camp near Sevilla, Cuba:

SIR: In addition to rationing the four batteries of light artillery and four troops of mounted cavalry, as you have already been directed to do, the Commanding General directs that you also furnish them with forage.

Very respectfully,
E. J. McCLERNAND,
Asst Adjutant-General.

HEADQUARTERS CAVALRY DIVISION,
June 29, 1898.

OUTPOSTS.

Each Division will furnish the outposts for its own front.

An Officer shall be detailed to command the entire outposts; he shall make his headquarters with the reserve (support), which should be posted as centrally as practicable. The Outpost Commander receives from the Commander of the Forces (Commander of the Division) instructions as to the general front to be occupied by the outposts, their object, and the amount of resistance they are expected to make. He is also informed about the trails and roads of approach from the direction of the enemy, and is made acquainted with everything known in regard to the position and probable intention of the enemy. He will also be informed of the location and orders under which the Cuban forces are operating. If in existence, a topo-

graphical sketch of the position selected for the camp
and the surrounding country should be furnished the
Commander of the Outposts. The Outpost Commander
sends to the Commander of the Forces (Division Commander), all information received, first testing its
accuracy as far as practicable.

He instructs his subordinate Commanders as follows :
1.   General front of outpost line.
2.   The ground to be occupied by each.
3.   The position of neighboring supports and
     pickets.
4.   The night position of pickets and supports.
5.   What is known of enemy.
6.   Trails by which enemy might advance.
7.   Direction and method of patrolling.
8.   What is to be done in case of attack.
9.   How flags of truce and deserters are to be
     received.
10. Kind of reports required.
11. Where he is to be found.
12. Countersign and parole. (The countersign and
     parole of Cuban forces should be identical
     cal with those of U.S. forces.)

The outpost should strengthen the position by
intrenching ; the pickets and supports should intrench
and the sentinels should shelter themselves in pits about
$2\frac{1}{2}$ feet deep, the earth being thrown up towards the
enemy and covered with grass, twigs, etc., in order
that they may not attract attention.

Part of the picket should be constantly under arms
at night, separated from others who sleep close at hand.

The pickets should be under arms an hour before
daybreak and remain in ranks until it is full daylight,

and word has come from the line of observation that all is clear and no enemy in sight.

Sentinels should be posted so as to have a good view to the front and the flanks, and be concealed as much as possible.

Each sentinel should clearly understand :

1. The countersign.
2. The number of his own post.
3. The number and position of his own picket and the name of its Commander.
4. The position of the neighboring sentinels.
5. The direction of the enemy and probable line of his advance.
6. The points to which all roads, trails, or paths in sight lead.
7. The name of villages, hamlets, and rivers in view.
8. The signals by which he should communicate with the pickets or detached posts.

Only persons in the performance of duty with the outposts or having authority over, and Cuban soldiers having an Officer in command are allowed to cross the line of sentinels. All other people, except deserters and bearers of flags of truce, are halted, and, after examination, are conducted by one of the sentinels to the picket. If they refuse to halt or attempt to escape they must be shot down.

Deserters should be halted some distance from the post and required to lay down their arms. The Commander for the picket is at once notified and he sends out a patrol to bring them in and sends them, under proper guard, to the Officer commanding the forces (Division Commander). No conversation should be had with deserters. The bearer of a flag of truce and his escort (if he has one) are halted in front of the line of sentinels and ordered to face in the direction in which they came. Word is sent at once to Commander of the picket. The sentinel must not converse with the bearer of a flag of truce or his escort nor allow them to reconnoiter while they remain halted. The Commander of the picket will receive any communications the bearer of the flag of truce may have and send them at once to the Commander of the forces.

When immediate alarm is not necessary, firing should be avoided. Everything observed by the sentinel in regard to the enemy should be communicated at once to the pickets. If the sentinel is satisfied that the enemy is advancing to attack he gives the alarm at once by firing. The same men should be kept on same posts. The more intelligent men should be selected for the most important posts. When sentinel's post is not in plain view of picket, a connecting sentinel should be posted.

JOSEPH WHEELER,
Maj.-Gen. U.S.V.

CHAPTER IV

THE STATUS, MORNING OF JULY FIRST — GENERAL
SHAFTER TAKES COMMAND ON SHORE — DESPATCHES
DURING FIRST DAY, BATTLE OF SAN JUAN — INTER-
VIEWING SPANISH PRISONERS —WASHINGTON NOTIFIED
OF THE ENGAGEMENT

HEADQUARTERS CAVALRY DIVISION,
SAN JUAN, July 1, 1898.

GENERAL SHAFTER :

GENERAL : I am at the foot of the hill, and will endeavor to carry out your directions.

Very respectfully,

JOS. WHEELER,
Maj. Genl Vols.

P.S. — I hope reinforcements will arrive soon.

HEADQUARTERS CAVALRY DIVISION,
SAN JUAN, July 1, 1898.

LT. MILEY :

SIR : The crest of the hill and houses are occupied
by our troops and the reserves are just in rear below
the crest. I hear reinforcements are coming up ; they
should get up as soon as possible to support the artillery which has now gone to the crest of the hill. The
Gatling gun reached the crest some time ago and has
done good work.

Please ascertain from General Shafter if I shall continue commanding and supervising as I am, and commanding the Cavalry Division through General Sumner, or shall I resume command of the Cavalry Division and displace Sumner, or shall I wait till to-morrow before doing this?

I have just sent the ammunition up to the Gatling gun.

Very respectfully,
Jos. Wheeler,
Maj. Genl Vols.

Headquarters 5th Army Corps,
July 1, 1898.

General Wheeler:

Resume command of your Division. Conform your movements to those who join you on the right and left. I have ordered Lawton an hour ago to join on your right. From my position in the center I can supervise the battle better than from anywhere else, as I have it in full view.

Shafter.

Headquarters Cavalry Division,
July 1, 1898.

Brig. Gen. Sumner, U.S.V.:

Pursuant to direction of the Commanding General I hereby resume immediate command of the Cavalry Division; you will resume command of the 1st Cavalry Brigade.

Very respectfully,
Jos. Wheeler,
Major General U.S.V., Comdg Cav. Div.

HEADQUARTERS 5TH ARMY CORPS,
July 1, 1898.

GENERAL WHEELER: Just received your note. Have urged Second Battery and reinforcements to be sent to top of hill. Your note has gone back to General Shafter.

J. D. MILEY,
A.D.C.

HEADQUARTERS CAVALRY DIVISION,
SAN JUAN, July 1, 1898.

GENERAL SHAFTER,
Comdg:

GENERAL: Our skirmish line is on top of the crest, and reserves this side the crest to avoid Spanish fire.

The Gatling guns reached the crest of the hill and did good work. Capt. Best's field battery is also now on the hill. I think that position should be supported by more infantry.

Very respectfully,

JOS. WHEELER,
Maj. Gen. Vols.

HEADQUARTERS 5TH ARMY CORPS,
EL POZO, July 1, 1898, 2.05 P.M.

TO GENERAL WHEELER,
Commanding Dismounted Cavalry Division:

SIR: The Commanding General directs me to say your message about Generals Sumner and Kent are received. We understand all are over the San Juan now, and that all is going well at the front.

A battery has just been ordered over the San Juan to give what assistance it can. Do you think another

can be used to advantage? I send two extra letters.
Please send to Generals Sumner and Kent by two of
the mounted orderlies you have.

                    Very respectfully,
                        E. J. McCLERNAND,
                            A.A.G.

                HEADQUARTERS 5TH ARMY CORPS,
                            July 1, 1898.

GENERAL WHEELER : Hold the ground where you are
until night, keeping under the hill where entrenching
tools will be sent to the front as soon as it is dark.
Rations and artillery will be sent also.   Lawton's Division and Bates' Brigade which have practically been out
of the main fight trying to capture the town of Caney
were ordered an hour and a half ago to close in on
Sumner's right.

                            SHAFTER.

                HEADQUARTERS 5TH ARMY CORPS,
                            July 1, 1898.
GENERAL WHEELER,
        Cavalry Division:

SIR : Commanding General directs me to say he has
just heard from General Lawton.   He will move and
join on your right to-night.   General Kent says he is
short of ammunition.   Can you not spare him some
from the train you received?

                    Very respectfully,
                        E. J. McCLERNAND,
                            A.A.G.

HEADQUARTERS CAVALRY DIVISION,
SAN JUAN, July 1, 1898, 5.45 P.M.

GENERAL SHAFTER:

SIR: I think the important question now is to fortify this ridge. To do this effectively we should have Col. Derby and the Engineers to lay out the lines, and the Generals should be here to superintend the work and press it forward. We will probably have to make some traverses. If we get this work well forward to-night we can continue it to-morrow and the men can have comparative security.

The left flank is our weakest point. I have called Gen. Kent's attention to this and asked him to do all he can.

I cannot hear of Gen. Lawton's approach. Please express your wishes to me for to-night.

Very respectfully,

JOS. WHEELER,
Maj. Gen. Vols.

HEADQUARTERS 5TH ARMY CORPS,
July 1, 1898.

MAJOR GEN. WHEELER,
Cavalry Division:

SIR: Commanding General directs me to say ammunition, rations and intrenching-tools (all that we have of the latter) will go forward. General Lawton has captured Caney and will join the right of our line before daybreak, bringing his battery with him. All artillery are ordered to open at daylight.

McCLERNAND,
A.A.G.

HEADQUARTERS CAVALRY DIVISION,
SAN JUAN, July 1, 1898, 6.40 P. M.
GENERAL SHAFTER :

SIR : It is now approaching dark, and the situation remains unchanged. Our right is weak, as so many men have been wounded and drifted away. I am now trying to strengthen it, but wish very much for Lawton to make connection on my right. Capt. Galbraith, on the extreme right, fears a return attack by the Spaniards to-night, but I do not think this is probable. I have just seen Gen. Hawkins ; he says he will commence intrenching and his line is all right for to-night. I have given him part of the intrenching tools. The three commanding officers of Sumner's Brigade are wounded. We need more intrenching-tools.

Very respectfully,

JOS. WHEELER, *Maj. Gen. Vols.*

P.S. —Have just seen Col. Wood, and he will commence intrenching at once. Will give him what tools I can.   J. W.

Will you send Col. Derby to me at once?

Maj. Beach and I are making a preliminary reconnaissance now.   J. W.

HEADQUARTERS CAVALRY DIVISION,
SAN JUAN, July 1, 1898, 8.20 P.M.
GENERAL SHAFTER :

SIR : I examined the line in front of Wood's Brigade and gave the men shovels and picks and insisted on their going right to work. I also sent word to General Kent to come and get intrenching-tools, and saw General Hawkins in person and told him the same thing. They all promise to do their best, but say the earth is very difficult, as a great part of it is rocky.

The positions our men carried were very strong and the intrenchments were very strong.

A number of officers have appealed to me to have the line withdrawn and take up a strong position farther back, and I expect they will appeal to you. I have positively discountenanced this, as it would cost us much prestige.

The lines are now very thin, as so many men have gone to the rear with wounded, and so many are exhausted; but I hope these men can be got up to-night, and with our line intrenched and Lawton on our right we ought to hold to-morrow, but I fear it will be a severe day. If we can get through to-morrow all right, we can make our breastworks very strong the next night. You can hardly realize the exhausted condition of the troops. The 3d and 6th Cavalry and other troops were up marching and halted on the road all last night, and have fought for twelve hours to-day, and those that are not on the line will be digging trenches to-night.

I was on the extreme front line. The men were lying down and reported the Spaniards not more than three hundred yards in their front.

Very respectfully,
Your obedient servant,

JOS. WHEELER, *Major-General Volunteers.*

HEADQUARTERS CAVALRY DIVISION,
SAN JUAN, July 1, 1898, 8.45 P.M.

GENERAL KENT:

DEAR GENERAL: There seems to be a good deal of apprehension about the left of your line. I do not know the situation myself. You understand it better than I do; I know you will protect it. Gen. Shafter writes that Lawton will be up and form on the right of your Cavalry by morning. I also learn that he has taken Caney. If you get some covering for your troops I think we can stand our ground to-morrow.

Very respectfully,

Jos. WHEELER, *Maj. Genl Vols.*

HEADQUARTERS CAVALRY DIVISION,

July 1, 1898.

GENERAL SHAFTER :

My interpreter, Mr. Mestre, has been interviewing some Spanish prisoners captured in the trenches of San Juan, with the following result :

The intrenchments of San Juan, or one of them, appear to have been defended by 2 companies of the Porto Rico Battalion, under the command of Major Lamadrid, numbering proximately 250 to 300 men. At about 11 o'clock in the morning, reinforcements were sent out under Col. Vaquero, including some more regulars of the Porto Rico Battalions and volunteers, to the total number of about 500 men. They brought with them 2 mountain pieces, which were planted in the road between the two heights of San Juan a little to the front. Gen. Linares also came out from the City of Santiago, but did not go to the front. The cannons that were fired at El Pozo in the morning, in answer to our fire, are from batteries in Santiago, from which the fire was kept up during the whole engagement, as also from the mountain pieces set up in the road. From the report of 2 of the soldiers, there appear to be about 6 larger cannons in Santiago and 2 smaller in the different batteries, as follows : In Transeunte fort 1 cannon, in Seuno 2 large and 2 small, in Canadas 1 cannon, probably the one that has done most of the firing at the entrance from Caney, and 1 cannon in front of the barracks and Mercedes hospital where Lt. Hobson is kept.

According to all the prisoners (examined separately), the regular troops in the City are not more than 6000 to 8000 and as many more volunteers and guerrillas.

The troops are all very badly fed, but the soldiers admit that since the blockade they have been a little better, having had some of the American relief provisions. These provisions are gone or only kept now for the hospitals. The Porto Rico Battalion received a little pay some days ago for the first time in 10 months. According to these prisoners, there are numerous heads of cattle in the city, but only the officers eat meat. These men had no idea how large our army is and say their officers have given them no information on this head. The prisoners are all wounded and are being sent down to the hospital.

Yours respectfully,

JOS. WHEELER, Major General Vols.

HEADQUARTERS 5TH ARMY CORPS,

July 1, 1898.

SECRETARY OF WAR,

    Washington :

Had a very heavy engagement to-day, which lasted from 8 A.M. till sundown. We have carried their outworks and are now in possession of them. There is now about three-quarters of a mile of open between my lines and the city. By morning troops will be intrenched, and considerable augmentation of forces will be there. Gen. Lawton's Division and Gen. Bates's Brigade, which have been engaged all day in carrying El Caney, which was accomplished at 4 P. M., will be in line and in front of Santiago during the night. I regret to say that our casualties will be above 400. Of these not many killed.   SHAFTER.

CHAPTER V

THE STATUS, MORNING OF JULY SECOND — DESPATCHES
DURING SECOND DAY, BATTLE OF SAN JUAN — ORDER
FOR LIST OF CASUALTIES

HEADQUARTERS CAVALRY DIVISION,
SAN JUAN, July 2, 1898, 4 A.M.

GENERAL SHAFTER :

SIR : The batteries are in position. Shall they commence bombardment at daylight, though Lawton is not
up? There has already been some firing against our
right, and the Chief of Artillery understands that the
order for Lawton to be on the right was a part of the
order for him to commence firing, and each depended
on the other. Major Dillenback thinks if he com-
mences firing before Lawton gets up he will be subject
to a flank fire from the enemy's infantry.

We certainly expect Lawton up very soon and there
will not be much delay. We still hope he will get up
by daylight. Another reason is, Lawton will have to
go on line under fire if the firing begins before he
gets up.

Very respectfully,

JOS. WHEELER,
Maj. Gen. Vols.

HEADQUARTERS 5TH ARMY CORPS,
July 2, 1898, 4.50 A.M.

To GENERAL WHEELER,
    Commanding Cavalry Division:

SIR : The Commanding General directs you do not commence firing until General Lawton's Division is up.

Very respectfully,

McCLERNAND, *A.A.G.*

General Lawton will probably come via our camp and El Pozo House. Guide was sent him at 1 A.M., but no news from him yet.

E. J. McC.

HEADQUARTERS CAVALRY DIVISION,
July 2, 1898.

GEN. S. S. SUMNER,
    Commanding 2d Brigade, Cavalry Division:

SIR : Col. Wood is making his defenses very strong, and the infantry are also improving theirs very much. I wish you to improve yours and it might be well for you to send an officer to see the work done by Col. Wood.

JOS. WHEELER,
Maj. Gen. Vols.

HEADQUARTERS CAVALRY DIVISION,
July 2, 1898.

COL. WOOD,
    Comdg 2d Brigade:

The Commanding Officer Division directs that you relieve the 13th Infantry, and have it report as soon as practicable to General Kent, on the left of the line.

Please arrange with General Lawton to connect with your right before you withdraw the 13th. You will of course close in the 9th Cavalry to the left on the 3d. If not safe to do this to-day, make the change to-night.

Very respectfully,
M. F. STEELE,
1st Lt. 8 Cav., Aid.

HEADQUARTERS 5TH ARMY CORPS,
EL POZO HOUSE, July 2, 1898, 8 A.M.

TO GENERAL WHEELER,
    Comdg Dismounted Cavalry:

SIR: A message from you announcing the arrival the head of General Lawton's Division is just received. Major Dillenback arrived here a moment ago and reported this as the only place for artillery, and all four batteries will be placed here and shell the town to the left of our line. The balance of General Lawton's Division and General Duffield's Brigade are moving to the front.

By command of Major General Shafter,
McCLERNAND,
A.A.G.

P. S. — If you see General Lawton please say the 1st Infantry will be held, temporarily at least, to guard the batteries.

HEADQUARTERS CAVALRY DIVISION,
SAN JUAN, July 2, 1898, 10.15 A.M.

MAJOR DILLENBACK,
El Pozo Hill :

SIR : In shelling the City from your present position
please bear in mind that we have troops to the left of
the blockhouse on a hillside about 400 yards nearer the
City than the blockhouse is.

Very respectfully,
Jos. WHEELER,
Maj. Gen. Vols.

HEADQUARTERS 5TH ARMY CORPS,
EL POZO HOUSE, JULY 2, 1898, 10.45 A.M.

COMMANDING GENERAL CAVALRY DIVISION :

SIR : The Commanding General desires to be informed
of your position and the general situation in your
front.   The four batteries of artillery will take position near the Pozo House, but will not open fire to-day
unless the enemy provokes it.

Very respectfully,
E. J. McCLERNAND,
Asst Adjt Genl.

HEADQUARTERS CAVALRY DIVISION,
SAN JUAN, July 2, 1898, 11 A.M.

MAJOR GENERAL SHAFTER,
5th Corps:

The situation is the same as it has been all day.

I have reinforced Kent's left with one of Duffield's
regiments.

The Duffield regiment to remain only until I can give Kent back the 13th Infantry.

I regret that we are having some killed and wounded. The Cubans are still at this point.

Very respectfully,

Jos. Wheeler,
Maj. Gen. Vols.

Headquarters Cavalry Division,
July 2, 1898, 12.15 p.m.

General W. R. Shafter,
  Comdg, etc. :

Sir : General Bates is now on our extreme left with his left flank refused or thrown back so as to face southwest and also to face batteries that we feared would infilade us. Kent's Division is on Bates' right; the Cavalry Division is on the right of Kent; Lawton is formed on the right of Cavalry Division. One regiment of Duffield sent over to strengthen Kent's left to remain until I could lend him the 13th Inf., which in the hurry of movement got mixed in with Cavalry yesterday. I asked General Lawton to put one platoon in the San Juan building to N.E. of us for purpose of observation.

The men have made some breastworks and they are endeavoring to keep as quiet to-day as possible so as to secure rest and peace which they need very much.

We are losing a few killed and wounded, but are fighting as little as possible. I suppose Lawton will throw his right forward so as to somewhat encircle the city, but I presume he will await instructions from you on that point and that he has already received such instructions. One regiment of General Duffield is in reserve near my Headquarters.

The Cubans have moved over to our right. We have distributed ammunition and rations so far as I learn there is any need for them.

Very respectfully,

JOSEPH WHEELER,
Major Genl, Commndg Cav. Div.

HEADQUARTERS CAVALRY DIVISION,
July 2, 1898.

GENERAL SHAFTER : General Lawton's Division is now taking position on the right of our Cavalry. I had to let the artillery withdraw to take a better position. They were exposed to so hot infantry fire that they were unable to fire where they were. Maj. Dillenback is sure of being able to effectively bombard Santiago from the position he had withdrawn to.

Very respectfully,

JOS. WHEELER,
Maj. Gen. Vols.

HEADQUARTERS CAVALRY DIVISION,
July 2, 1898.

GENERAL SHAFTER : General Chaffee's Brigade of General Lawton's Division is now in line on the right of Cavalry. General Lawton's other two are on the road coming up. The Cubans under Col. Gonzales have come up and General Lawton is holding them to decide where to put them in. The batteries have been delayed by bad ford and have caused General Lawton's two Brigades some delay, but they are pushing on and hope they will be here soon.

General Ludlow's Brigade is now arriving and General Lawton is putting it in position. The men are firing as little as they can and we are trying to let them rest as much as possible, in order that they may be in condition to work on the intrenchments to-night.

Very respectfully,

Jos. Wheeler,

Maj. Genl Vol.

Headquarters 5th Army Corps,

July 2, 1898.

My dear Gen. Wheeler: What do you think of the idea of sending a division in rear of the left division to clear out the forts along the entrance to the bay so as to let the Navy in and have the business over. Can it be done?

Very respectfully,

Wm. R. Shafter.

Headquarters Cavalry Division,

July 2, 1898.

Major General Shafter,

Comdg U.S. Forces:

Dear General: I regret to say that I do not think Infantry can take the forts along the entrance of the bay. I would like to do it, but the effort would be attended with terrible loss. We can procure artillery ammunition without limit. It seems to me it would be a good plan to place our siege guns and other artillery in position and hammer at Santiago and at all the batteries that interfere with us. Our artillerymen should be studying positions to do this work and I can have no doubt as to the final result. If we hammer at the enemy's batteries they will fire back upon ours, and we all know that there are so few men connected with batteries and they learn to take such care of themselves that losses are comparatively small. Again, if there is a heavy fire at the batteries which can enfilade our line they will be apt to neglect our line and devote themselves to our batteries.

Very respectfully,

Jos. Wheeler,
Major Genl Comdg.

What I mean by infantry not being able to take forts along entrance of bay is that it would take a large force and an enormous loss would be sustained.

Headquarters Cavalry Division,
July 2, 1898.

Major Dillenback,
   Chief Artillery:

Sir: Will you please have an artillery officer reconnoiter the extreme right of General Sumner's line (which may now be occupied by General Lawton) passing around the foot of the hill on top of which Sumner's right is posted? There appears to be a range of low hills near by at right angles to Sumner's right, from which an oblique fire could be had on the Spanish lines of approach from Santiago, and which may be beyond infantry range from the positions the Spanish infantry occupy.

By command of Maj. Genl Wheeler,

Very respectfully,

Your obedient servant,

J. H. DORST,

Lt. Col., A.A.G.

HEADQUARTERS CAVALRY DIVISION,

July 2, 1898, 2 P.M.

GENERAL SHAFTER: Referring to enclosed note from General Kent, it is believed that the position toward which the gun is being taken enfilades our lines and takes part of it in reverse.

Very respectfully,

JOS. WHEELER,

Maj. Gen. Vols., Comndg Cav. Div.

HEADQUARTERS CAVALRY DIVISION,

July 2, 1898.

GENERAL SHAFTER: The enemy's battery near the city, which faces southwest, will I fear be a serious menace. I have told General Kent's Adjt General that they must do the best they can by building traverses until our siege guns can be gotten up to silence it. Could not our field guns silence this battery?

JOS. WHEELER,

Major Gen. Vols.

HEADQUARTERS 5TH ARMY CORPS,
July 2, 1898.

COMMANDING GENERAL CAVALRY DIVISION :

SIR : The Commanding General directs me to call upon you to submit as early as possible a list of the killed and wounded in your command.

Very respectfully,

E. J. McCLERNAND,
Asst Adj. Gen.

HEADQUARTERS CAVALRY DIVISION,
July 2, 1898.

GENERAL SHAFTER : I have received your note directing me to send a list of killed and wounded and I will attend to it at once. Everything is about as it has been all day, but firing has ceased all along the line.

Very respectfully,

JOS. WHEELER,
Maj. Gen. Vols.

CHAPTER VI

THE STATUS, MORNING OF JULY THIRD — NEWS OF
THE DESTRUCTION OF CERVERA'S FLEET — LETTER
FROM GENERAL TORAL — CONSULS NEGOTIATING FOR
REMOVAL OF CIVILIANS DURING PROPOSED BOMBARD-
MENT — A FOURTH OF JULY CELEBRATION

HEADQUARTERS CAVALRY DIVISION,
July 3, 1898.

To COL. MCCLERNAND, In Field :

The Spanish fleet ran out of Santiago harbor about 9
A.M. to-day. Terrific naval battle outside. Three Spanish gunboats and one torpedo boat destroyed. Run on
beach and burned up. One Spanish gunboat still at large
going westward and greater portion of fleet in pursuit.

I saw the three gunboats and one torpedo boat. Signal
fires on hills west of Morro Castle last night. The torpedo
boat on beach about 3 miles, two gunboats about 6 miles
and third gunboat about 20 miles west of Morro Castle.

FRED A. SMITH, *A.A.A.G.*

HEADQUARTERS CAVALRY DIVISION,
July 3, 1898.

GENERAL SHAFTER :

GENERAL : I saw General Miles' telegram asking
what we wanted. Among other things they should
send underclothing and shoes enough to give every

man a change. When we get our line a little stronger, many of the men can rest while a few hold the trenches. This should keep the whole Army sufficiently rested. There is a little fire along the position this morning.

Very respectfully,
Jos. Wheeler,
Maj. Gen. Vols.

Headquarters 5th Army Corps,
El Pozo, July 3, 1898, 1 p.m.

Col. McClernand: Lieut. Allen, 2d Cav., from our extreme right where he overlooked the bay states that Admiral Cervera's fleet steamed out this morning and engaged our fleet. French consul who came into our lines yesterday informed Gen. Garcia, Admiral Cervera said yesterday, it was better to die fighting than to sink his ships. Rush this notification all around our lines to the front.

Shafter, Comdg.

Headquarters 5th Army Corps,
July 3, 1898.

Major Gen. Wheeler:

Sir: Now that the fleet is destroyed I believe the garrison will surrender, and all we have to do is hang on where we are and very soon starve them out. Lawton is with Garcia charged with stopping the reinforcements the advance of which have arrived too near where Garcia tore the railroad up and are there disembarking. I do not believe he can get in. If necessary we can move Bates around to your immediate right and let Lawton's whole Division cut loose on Gen. Pando, whose men will have to come into the open and charge us. I have sent Lawton a battery of Lt. Artillery to play on them. There is but one road which they can come in on which heretofore has been under the guns of the fleet.

Very respectfully,

Wm. R. Shafter.

Headquarters Cavalry Division,
July 3, 1898.

Gen. Wheeler: Have just sent message to you saying that I will accede to the request of the foreigners not to fire on the town if the Spanish will keep quiet.

Shafter.

Headquarters Cavalry Division, U.S. Army,
July 3, 1898.

General Shafter:

General: I have received your communication and will send it forward promptly. The condition here is about the same as last reported.

Very respectfully,

Jos. Wheeler, *Maj. Gen. Vols.*

Army of the Island of Cuba, 4th Army Corps,
Santiago de Cuba, July 3, 1898, at 9 o'clock.

To His Excellency

The General of the Cavalry Division of the Forces
of the United States:

Your Excellency: I am receiving at nine at night through the English Consul your esteemed communication dated this afternoon at 6.45 and referring to the withdrawal, from danger of the bombardment, of foreign subjects and women and children in the city. I do not hesitate to order my troops to remain quiet during that time, if they be not attacked by the Americans; this in aid of the proposals of Your Excellency and believing that the commissioners of the foreign governments will go to-morrow, the fourth, and have a conference with Your Excellency, in accordance with a communication presented by the Dean of the Consuls.

I remain, Your Excellency,
Your most obedient servant,
J. TORAL,
Commander-in-Chief in the Interim, 4th Army Corps, and Military Governor of Santiago de Cuba.

HEADQUARTERS CAVALRY DIVISION,
July 3, 1898.

GENL. SHAFTER: I enclose a copy of the letter which I sent forward with the flag of truce. I wrote it as I did so as to convey the impression to the Spaniards that the line I occupy was only an advance line. Do you send Orders to Lawton to make the move, or do you expect me to send them? If you send the Orders to Lawton please advise me when to move Bates.

Very respectfully,
JOSEPH WHEELER,
Major General Vols.

HEADQUARTERS 5TH ARMY CORPS,
EL POZO, July 3, 2.30 P.M.

GEN. WHEELER,
Comdg Cavalry Division:

SIR: The Commanding General directs me to ask if any reply has been received to our message sent under flag of truce, and for the situation generally.

A good many of our men can be seen straying away from the trenches where they would be at disadvantage if the enemy should attack suddenly.

Very respectfully,

E. J. McClernand,

A.A.G.

Headquarters Cavalry Division,
July 3, 1898.

Gen'l Shafter: Generals Kent and Sumner wrote you this morning concerning the importance of cutting two or more new trails cut through from this point. A great deal could be done very promptly to relieve the situation by widening the main road to the width of two or three roads. The Cubans could do this with their machetes, or if they are not available our men should be put at it with axes.

Very respectfully,

Jos. Wheeler,

Maj.-Gen. Vols.

P.S. — Genl Sumner and Col. Wood are now with me. They report entire loss of Cavalry Division last night one killed and one wounded.

Headquarters Cavalry Division,
July 3, 1898.

Genl Shafter: Col. Dorst has just returned bringing the British, Portuguese, Chinese, Norwegian Pro-Consuls representing the Consular Corps. They wish to know if the old men and all non-combatants may come out and occupy Caney and places on the railway line. They also want a postponement till 10 a.m. the

5th instant. Please answer at once as these gentlemen desire to return before dark.

Very respectfully,

JOS. WHEELER,

Major-General Vols.

They received notice only at 3 o'clock.

There are 15 to 20,000 women and children in the city.

Consuls who called under flag of truce, July 3d, 1898:

FREDERICK W. RAMSDEN, *H.B.M. Consul*, Santiago de Cuba;
ISIDORO P. AGUSTINI, *Swedish and Norwegian V.-Con.;*
MODESTO RAS, *Portuguese Consul;*
ROBERT MASON, *British Pro-Consul and Chinese Consul;*
FREDERICK WM. RAMSDEN *(fils).*

HEADQUARTERS 5TH ARMY CORPS,

EL POZO, July 3, 1898, 4.25 P.M.

TO GENERAL WHEELER,

Commdg Cavalry Division:

SIR: The Commanding General directs me to say it has been reported a truce has been arranged for part of the afternoon, and to ask you to state the details if the rumor be true.

Very respectfully,

E. J. McCLERNAND,

A.A.G.

HEADQUARTERS 5TH ARMY CORPS,
CAMP NEAR SAN JUAN RIVER, CUBA, July 4, 1898.

COMMANDING GENERAL CAVALRY DIVISION:

SIR: I enclose herewith copies of a telegram received last night from General Miles, which I desire to have read at the head of each regiment this morning. At noon have bands play. No salutes will be fired.

Very respectfully,

WM. R. SHAFTER,
Major-General U.S. Vols., Commanding.

WASHINGTON, D.C., July 3, 1898.

GENERAL SHAFTER,
    Siboney:

Accept my hearty congratulations on the record made of magnificent fortitude, gallantry and sacrifice displayed in the desperate fighting of the troops before Santiago.

I realize the hardships, difficulties and suffering, and am proud that amidst it all the troops illustrated such fearless and patriotic devotion to the welfare of our common country and flag. Whatever the result to follow, their unsurpassed deeds of valor is already a gratifying chapter of history. Expect to be with you within one week with strong reinforcements.

MILES,
Major-General Comdg.

CHAPTER VII

GARCIA ALLOWS PANDO WITH REINFORCEMENTS TO SLIP
PAST HIM — GENERAL MILES COMING — A PRISONER'S
INFORMATION ABOUT FORT AGUADORES — WOUNDED
SPANISH OFFICERS — EXCHANGE OF HOBSON AND HIS
MEN — RETURNS OF THE KILLED AND WOUNDED

HEADQUARTERS CAVALRY DIVISION,
SAN JUAN, July 4, 1898, 7.50 A.M.
GENERAL SUMNER,
    Comdg 1st Cav. Brgde:

SIR: General Wheeler desires that you instruct your
officers to make all reasonable efforts to locate definitely
the position of the enemy's batteries.

Very respectfully,
JAMES H. REEVES, *Aid.*

———————

HEADQUARTERS 5TH ARMY CORPS,
July 4, 1898, 10.20 A.M.

To GENERAL WHEELER: Just received letter from
General Garcia that five thousand men entered the city
last night over the Cobu road. I understood from
Lawton that this road was securely covered by Garcia's
men, nearly 4,000 in number since day before yesterday. Garcia must have withdrawn and given them free
entrance. If this was the case there will probably be
an attack made at any minute. Our lines must be

made as strong as possible. I am expecting 6,000 men every hour and 3,000 from Camp Alger hourly. Telegram from General Miles last night says that he will be here with strong reinforcements within a week. Have just wired above information. Acknowledge receipt.

SHAFTER.

HEADQUARTERS CAVALRY DIVISION,
July 4, 1898, 11.25 A.M.

GENERAL SHAFTER : I have received your message regarding Spanish reinforcements. Will instruct troops to be on strict guard.

JOSEPH WHEELER.

HEADQUARTERS 5TH ARMY CORPS,
July 4, 1898.

To MAJOR GENERAL WHEELER : General Shafter has instructed me to say that he has sent for Major Dillenback in regard to sites selected by his Engineer Officer yesterday.

J. D. MILEY, *Aid.*

HEADQUARTERS 5TH ARMY CORPS,
CAMP NEAR SAN JUAN RIVER, CUBA, July 4, 1898.

COMMANDING GENERAL CAVALRY DIVISION :

SIR : I am directed by the Commanding General to inform you Capt. L. M. Brett, 2d Cavalry, has been appointed Provost Marshal General at these Headquarters, and with his Troop F, 2d Cavalry, will perform the duties pertaining to that position.

Your attention is invited to the fact that a great many stragglers coming to the rear claim to have been sent back by different officers for various kinds of property.

No man will be sent to the rear except in cases of urgent necessity, and will be provided with written passes signed by the proper officer.

Very respectfully,

E. J. McClernand, *A.A.G.*

Headquarters Cavalry Division,

San Juan, July 4, 1898.

Adjutant Gen'l 5th Corps:

Sir: I have your communication with reference to the men straying from the front and have given immediate orders to have it stopped.

Very respectfully,

Jos. Wheeler,

Major-Gen'l Vols.

I am sending this to Lawton also. Is that right?

J. W.

Headquarters U.S. Forces,

San Juan River, July 4, 1898.

General Orders }
   No. 21.   }

I. The General Commanding congratulates the army on the results of its first general engagement with the enemy. The strongly fortified outpost and village of Caney was captured after a most stubborn resistance, nearly its entire garrison being killed, wounded or captured by the 2nd Division, 5th Corps, Brigadier-General Lawton commanding. The heroic valor displayed by those troops adds another brilliant page to the history of American warfare. To Major-General Wheeler of the Cavalry Division was probably given the most difficult task, that of crossing a stream under fire, and deploying under the enemy's rifle-pits. These he almost immediately charged, and carried in the most gallant manner, driving the enemy from his strong positions to the shelter of the stronger works in rear. This was only accomplished by the most persevering and arduous efforts, officers and men exposing themselves to the deadly fire of the Spanish troops. In these efforts he was ably seconded by Brigadier-General Kent with the 1st Division on the extreme left, who also captured the works on his front.

Numerous distinguished acts have been reported, and in due time will be made known to the proper authorities.

By command of Major-General Shafter,

E. J. McClernand,
Assistant Adjutant General.

Headquarters 5th Army Corps,
July 4, 1898.

Maj. Gen. Wheeler,
Com'dg Cavalry Division:

Sir : The Commanding General directs me to say he agrees with you, it would be a mistake to move Bates under the present circumstances. He intended to do it only to stop Pando, but as he got into the city last night with probably five thousand men, through the inefficiency of the Cubans, there is no occasion to move him.

McClernand,
A.A.G.

HEADQUARTERS 5TH ARMY CORPS,
CAMP NEAR SAN JUAN RIVER, CUBA, July 4, 1898.

MAJOR GENERAL WHEELER,
Comdg Dismounted Cavalry Division:

SIR: The Commanding General directs you to send the three accompanying communications to the Spanish Commander, under a flag of truce.

He believes the best results will be obtained by having the same officer attend to such matters, and therefore desires Lieut. Col. Dorst to be sent.

Very respectfully,
E. J. McCLERNAND,
Assistant Adjutant-General.

HEADQUARTERS CAVALRY DIVISION,
July 4, 1898.

ADJUTANT GENERAL 5TH CORPS:

SIR: There are several dead animals lying in the San Juan River above the point where this command obtains its drinking-water. The only way to remedy this is to have a wagon sent up there to haul them out. We have not the facilities for doing this here.

Very respectfully,
JOS. WHEELER,
Major Gen'l Vols.

HEADQUARTERS 5TH ARMY CORPS,
July 4, 1898.

Wagon will be sent you to-morrow forenoon to draw the animals out of the way.

Very respectfully,
McCLERNAND, *A.A.G.*

HEADQUARTERS CAVALRY DIVISION,
SAN JUAN, July 4, 1898.

GENERAL SHAFTER :
Commdg 5th Army Corps:

Your order has been received about General Bates and about letters to be forwarded to the Spanish Commander, and Colonel Dorst is getting ready to start.

Very respectfully,

JOS. WHEELER.

HEADQUARTERS CAVALRY DIVISION,
SAN JUAN, July 4, 1898.

A.-G. 5TH CORPS :

SIR : Please notify me when Lawton is to move so I can move Bates to take his place.

Very resp.,

WHEELER,
Maj.-Gen. Vol.

HEADQUARTERS 5TH ARMY CORPS,
CAMP NEAR SAN JUAN RIVER, CUBA, July 4, 1898.

COMMANDING GENERAL CAVALRY DIVISION :

SIR : The Commanding General directs you send in, to-day, a list, by regiment, of the killed and wounded in your command.

Very respectfully,

E. J. McCLERNAND,
Assistant Adjutant-General.

HEADQUARTERS CAVALRY DIVISION,
July 4, 1898, 6.30 P.M.

MAJOR GENERAL SHAFTER,
     Commanding:

SIR : I send with 2 men from the 9th Massachusetts, a Spanish soldier, whom they captured to the left of our line, with his rifle. He belonged to the garrison of Fort Aguadores, which he says is in command of Major Soler. He says there is only one company of 100 men in the fort, which is of stone and has 3 cannons. Of these cannons, however, only one is serviceable. Its bore seems to be about 6 inches. The men will tell you the circumstances of his capture. The prisoner informs me that the back part of the fort has been somewhat damaged by the guns of our navy.

Yours respectfully,

JOS. WHEELER, *Maj.-Gen.*

[Telephone message.]

HEADQUARTERS CAVALRY DIVISION,
July 4, 1898.

GENERAL SHAFTER : The Artillery Officers ought to be at San Juan examining the ground and forts of the enemy. This is very important.

JOSEPH WHEELER,
Major-General.

HEADQUARTERS 5TH ARMY CORPS,
July 5, 1898, 1 A.M.

GENERAL WHEELER,
     Comd'g Cavalry Division:

SIR : The Commanding General directs me to say you will inform the Spanish officers that our Navy having destroyed the Spanish fleet is probably attacking the forts near the mouth of the harbor with a view of reducing them.

We are pledged here not to open fire until noon to-day, and it will be observed by the Army.   So inform the Spaniards.
Very respectfully,
E. J. McCLERNAND, *A.A.G.*

HEADQUARTERS 5TH ARMY CORPS,
July 5, 1898.

MAJ. GEN. WHEELER: I had intended to come out to see you this morning, but do not feel able to do so. Large reinforcements are expected.   Hoping you are all well,
Very respectfully,
W. R. SHAFTER.

HEADQUARTERS 5TH ARMY CORPS,
July 5, 1898.

To GENERAL WHEELER: Have the ambulances with the wounded Spanish Officers reached your lines yet? Send them on under flag as soon as they do.
SHAFTER.

HEADQUARTERS CAVALRY DIVISION,
July 5, 1898.

MAJOR GENERAL SHAFTER: No wounded Spanish officers have come out this way.   Are they to come out by this road or direct through Caney?   I have just returned from the extreme left of our line.   We have strengthened it very much.
Yours respectfully,
JOS. WHEELER, *Major General.*

[Telephone message.]

HEADQUARTERS CAVALRY DIVISION,
July 5, 1898, 6.25 P.M.

GENERAL SHAFTER:

General Toral sends word by a flag that the wounded have arrived safely and he expresses his thanks for the kindness shown them.

JOS. WHEELER.

HEADQUARTERS 5TH ARMY CORPS,
July 5, 1898.

GENERAL WHEELER: General Toral has just acceeded to my proposition to exchange Hobson and his men, and it will be done to-morrow A. M.

SHAFTER.

HEADQUARTERS 5TH ARMY CORPS,
CAMP NEAR SANTIAGO, July 5, 1898.

ADJUTANT GENERAL,
Washington:

I am just in receipt of a letter from Gen. Toral, agreeing to exchange Hobson and men here. To make exchange in the morning. Yesterday he refused my proposition of exchange.

SHAFTER,
Major General.

HEADQUARTERS 5TH ARMY CORPS,
CAMP NEAR SAN JUAN RIVER, CUBA, July 5, 1898.

COMMANDING GENERAL CAVALRY DIVISION:

SIR: The Commanding General directs me say he desires to get a list by regiments of the killed and wounded in your command during our operations since the 30th ultimo, and hope you will send it in as soon as possible. If you have the necessary blanks, use the "Return of Casualties"; if not, forward the information in the best form you can.

Very respectfully,

E. J. McCLERNAND,
Assistant Adjutant General.

HEADQUARTERS 5TH ARMY CORPS,
IN CAMP NEAR SANTIAGO,
July 5, 1898.

ADJUTANT GENERAL,
Washington :

Impossible to get returns, but there have been treated in the hospital at Siboney, 1,052 wounded and there are still 200 in the hospital here. In Lawton's Division there are killed 4 officers and 74 men; wounded, 14 officers and 317 men; missing, 1 man. In Kent's Division : killed, 12 officers and 87 men; wounded, 36 officers, 562 men; missing, 62 men. In Bates' Brigade : killed, 4 men; wounded, 2 officers and 26 men; missing, (?) men. Signal Corps : killed, 1 man. General Wheeler's report not yet received.

SHAFTER,
Major General.

HEADQUARTERS 5TH ARMY CORPS,
July 5, 1898.

MAJ. GENERAL WHEELER :

General Randolph with 3,000 men and six batteries of Artillery enrouted here. Make it known along the line.

SHAFTER.

CHAPTER VIII

REINFORCEMENTS REPORTED FROM KEY WEST, NEW
YORK, AND CHARLESTON — A SIEGE PREFERRED TO
ANOTHER ASSAULT — EXCHANGE OF HOBSON EFFECTED
— NO FIGHTING ON THE 7TH AND 8TH — THE LINE
SWUNG FORWARD AND STRENGTHENED

HEADQUARTERS 5TH ARMY CORPS,
July 5, 1898.

GENERAL WHEELER: Please communicate the following dispatches, just received, along the whole line:

WASHINGTON, D.C., July 5, 1898.

GENERAL SHAFTER, Siboney: Reinforcements are
being hurried to you. Randolph leaves Key West to-
night with fast convoy; he has about 3500 men, including the six light batteries from Tampa. The St. Paul
will leave New York Wednesday evening with the 8th
Ohio Volunteers. The Yale and Harvard will take all
the troops they can carry, sailing from Charleston; the
day and hour of their departure will be communicated
to you as soon as known, probably the 6th.

By command of Major General Miles,

H. C. CORBIN,
Adjutant General.

HEADQUARTERS 5TH ARMY CORPS,
July 5, 1898.

COMMANDING GENERAL CAVALRY DIVISION :

The Commanding General directs me to say great care must be exercised in arresting men claiming to be Cubans, and that nothing will be done to them until their identity is thoroughly established. Several Cubans have been arrested and mistaken for guerrillas. Please give the necessary orders to prevent these occurrences in your command.

Very respectfully,

E. J. McCLERNAND,
Assistant Adjutant General.

HEADQUARTERS 5TH ARMY CORPS,
CAMP NEAR SAN JUAN RIVER, CUBA, July 6, 1898.

GENERAL WHEELER,
Commanding Cavalry Division:

SIR : Referring to your letter of this date about the general order complimenting the troops, the Commanding General directs me to say he is aware many officers who performed gallant deeds have not been mentioned, but it is his intention to do so to the proper authorities, as soon as possible.

Your request about blindfolding the prisoners going to the front will receive attention. We are waiting for an additional Spanish Officer (prisoner) to come from Siboney.

Very respectfully,

E. J. McCLERNAND,
Assistant Adjutant General.

HEADQUARTERS CAVALRY DIVISION,
July 6, 1898.

GENERAL SHAFTER : A battery has been reported as
being constructed on the ridge near the bay, near the
place where the battery was located that bothered us on
the 1st day.   I should like to have an Artillery Officer
come out and examine it.

Very respectfully,

Jos. WHEELER,
Maj. Gen. Vols.

HEADQUARTERS 5TH ARMY CORPS,
July 6, 1898.

GENERAL WHEELER : There is no Artillery Officer
available just now.   Artillery is being put in position that will cover the whole line.   Call on Derby
when you see him.

Respectfully,

WM. R. SHAFTER.

HEADQUARTERS 5TH ARMY CORPS,
IN CAMP NEAR SANTIAGO, July 5, 1898.

ADJUTANT GENERAL,
Washington :

The Iroquois sailed two days ago with 300 wounded.
Cherokee sails to-day with 325 wounded.

SHAFTER,
Major General Commanding.

HEADQUARTERS 5TH ARMY CORPS,
IN CAMP NEAR SANTIAGO, July 5, 1898.
ADJUTANT GENERAL,
Washington:
Iroquois already sailed for Key West. If Cherokee has not sailed will have her go to Fort Monroe. Hereafter all wounded will be sent to Fort Monroe.

SHAFTER,
Commanding.

HEADQUARTERS 5TH ARMY CORPS,
July 6, 1898.
MY DEAR GEN. WHEELER: Yours in reference to armament received. I dislike very much the thought of working another assault, it would be attended with fearful loss of life. I have hoped to so entrench ourselves that we could hold the position and starve them out. If it was possible to get between the town and the lower bay and try and clear those batteries out and let the Navy in the capture of the city would be easy; but I am at a loss how to accomplish it.

At present the only thing seems to be to hang on. I have told Kent to look out for the gun on his left which you report they are trying to get out.

Very truly yours,
WM. R. SHAFTER.

HEADQUARTERS 5TH ARMY CORPS,
CAMP NEAR SAN JUAN RIVER, CUBA, July 6, 1898.
COMMANDING GENERAL CAVALRY DIVISION:
SIR: The Commanding General directs you will cause to be detailed, immediately, in each brigade of your command, an Acting Engineer Officer, who will

report to Lieut. Col. Derby, Chief Engineer, for instructions, without delay.

Very respectfully,

E. J. McCLERNAND,

A.A.G.

HEADQUARTERS 5TH ARMY CORPS,

July 6, 1898.

To GENERAL WHEELER: Send flag General Toral and inform him that 2nd Lieut. C. T. Emilia Vallez, 29th Regiment and 7 men have arrived at my Headquarters for exchange for Lieut. Hobson and men. Through an error, 2d Lt. Constanzio Germain, of the 29th Regiment, and 1st Lt. Adolfo Ariaz, of the Provisional Battalion of Porto Rico, were not sent, but within the next four hours they will be here, so that General Toral can make his selection of Officers.

WM. R. SHAFTER.

HEADQUARTERS CAVALRY DIVISION,

SAN JUAN, CUBA, July 6, 1898.

To HIS EXCELLENCY LT. GENERAL TORAL,
  Commanding Spanish Forces, Santiago, Cuba:

GENERAL: I am directed by the Commanding General, U.S. Forces, to inform you that 2nd Lieutenant C. F. Emilio Valez, 29th Regiment, and seven men have arrived at my Headquarters for exchange for Lieut. Hobson and men. Through an error 2nd Lieutenant Constanzio Germain, 29th Regiment, and 1st Lieut. Adolfo Arioz, Provisional Battalion, of Porto Rico were not sent. The Commanding General, however, states that within the next four hours these officers will be here, so that you can make your selection of Officers for exchange. Lieut. Hobson should be sent on the San Juan road. Your Officers will be sent on this road.

With great respect,

JOSEPH WHEELER,
Major General, Commdg Advance Line.

HEADQUARTERS CAVALRY DIVISION,
NEAR SANTIAGO DE CUBA, July 6, 1898.

To HIS EXCELLENCY LIEUTENANT GENERAL TORAL,
Commanding Spanish Forces at Santiago de Cuba:

SIR: There has been delay in getting the Spanish prisoners up to this point. They are now en route and we will follow them on immediately to effect their exchange for Lieutenant Hobson and his seven sailors.

With respect,

JOSEPH WHEELER,
Major General Commanding Advance Line.

HEADQUARTERS 5TH ARMY CORPS,
July 6, 1898.

COLONEL McCLERNAND : Will get you ammunition at once. Send this to the front.

WM. R. SHAFTER.

HEADQUARTERS CAVALRY DIVISION,
July 6, 1898.

GENERAL SHAFTER,
Commanding U.S. Forces in Cuba:

SIR : We are short of rations.   Please hurry them up and also please send us some stationery.

Col. Derby promised us sand bags.   They have not come : we need them very much.

Very respectfully,

JOS. WHEELER,
Maj. Gen. Vols.

HEADQUARTERS 5TH ARMY CORPS,
July 6, 1898.

GENERAL WHEELER : I send half of the stationery we have in camp.   I hope to get some more to-day. Rations and sand bags will be sent to the front as soon as possible.

Very respectfully,

E. J. MCCLERNAND, *A.A.G.*

[Circular.]

HEADQUARTERS CAVALRY DIVISION,
BEFORE SANTIAGO, CUBA, July 6, 1898.

Owing to the irregular shape of our line, particularly the forward bend on the extreme right, there is danger of men at one point firing by mistake at our own men. To designate our lines, each regiment will place its national colors on its own works.

By command of Major General Wheeler,

J. H. DORST,
Lieut. Col. U.S. Vols.,
Assistant Adjutant General.

[Circular.]

HEADQUARTERS CAVALRY DIVISION,
July 6, 1898.

The exchange of prisoners will be over in an hour, and we may expect an attack at any moment.

Have your men prepared for it.

By command of Major General Wheeler,

J. H. DORST,
Assistant Adjutant General.

[Circular.]

HEADQUARTERS CAVALRY DIVISION,
BEFORE SANTIAGO, CUBA, July 6, 1898.

The Major General Commanding directs me to inform you that the truce will cease at 5 o'clock P.M. this date.

By command of Major General Wheeler,

J. H. DORST,
Lieut. Col. U.S. Vols.
Assistant Adjutant General.

HEADQUARTERS 5TH ARMY CORPS,
CAMP NEAR SANTIAGO, July 7.

HON. R. A. ALGER,
Secretary of War:

Perfect quiet to-day. At request of Spanish general, employes of the English Cable Company were sent in to him to telegraph his government as to surrendering. Men are in good spirits and are making themselves more secure every hour. Wounds are much less dangerous than similar ones made of caliber 45. Among the large number of wounded there are few amputations.

Perhaps ten will cover it. General health of the command is good. One hundred and fifty cases of fever, which runs its course in four or five days, but is not serious. I am feeling much better.

SHAFTER, *Major General.*

HEADQUARTERS 5TH ARMY CORPS,
July 7, 1898.

MAJOR GENERAL WHEELER,
Commanding Cavalry Division:

SIR: The Commanding General directs me to say he wishes you to forward at once the accompanying communication to the Spanish Commander, using the flag of truce. There is little probability of fighting to-day.

Very respectfully,

E. J. McCLERNAND, *A.A.G.*

HEADQUARTERS CAVALRY DIVISION,
July 7, 1898.

GENERAL WHEELER: Message received. Important communications have passed and others will probably follow. Little danger of any fighting to-day.

By command of General Shafter,

E. J. McCLERNAND, *A.A.G.*

HEADQUARTERS 5TH ARMY CORPS,
July 7, 1898.

COMMANDING GENERAL CAVALRY DIVISION:

SIR: Commanding General directs that whenever an officer or enlisted man leaves your command to go to a hospital at the rear, his blanket, shelter tent, and haversack be sent with him.

E. J. McCLERNAND, *A.A.G.*

HEADQUARTERS CAVALRY DIVISION,
BEFORE SANTIAGO, CUBA, July 8, 1898.

TO MAJOR GENERAL WM. R. SHAFTER,
    Commanding 5th Army Corps:

DEAR GENERAL : I have nothing special to report except that everything is quiet. We are still strengthening our position and advancing our lines in many places. I have most of my staff out reconnoitering and I think everything is perfectly satisfactory. Some of the regiments have more sickness, but, taking all in all, we are in pretty fair health.

I sent in my report this morning.

I am trying digging wells for water and will report to you the result.

With great respect,
    Your obedient servant,

JOS. WHEELER,
Major General U.S. Volunteers.

INDEPENDENT BRIGADE, IN FRONT OF SANTIAGO,
July 8, 1898.

MAJOR GENERAL JOSEPH WHEELER :

MY DEAR GENERAL : Your note just received. I have swung my line forward so that it is now along the bluff next to the city. Am holding the 9th Mass. to cover any turning movement the enemy might make around my left flank. It was my intention, as soon as the truce was over, to feel out on the left to see if more advantageous positions could be secured. I should therefore be sorry to lose the 9th now. While I feel that I can make good use of them, the Regiment

will be returned to you at once if you say so. I wish
to thank you for numerous courtesies.

Most respectfully,

J. C. BATES,.

Brig. Gen. Vols.

WASHINGTON, D.C., July 8, 1898.

GENERAL SHAFTER,

Playa, Cuba:

Telegram which it appears you did not receive read
as follows:

The President directs me to say you have the gratitude and thanks of the Nation for the brilliant and
effective work of your noble Army in the fight of July
1st. The sturdy valor and heroism of officers and
men fill the American people with pride. The country
mourns the brave men who fell in battle. They have
added new names to our roll of heroes.

R. A. ALGER, *Secretary of War.*

CHAPTER IX

ARMY OF THE ISLAND OF CUBA, 4TH ARMY CORPS,
SANTIAGO DE CUBA, July 9, 1898.

To His EXCELLENCY,

Commander-in-Chief of the United States Forces,
In camp at San Juan:

YOUR EXCELLENCY: In acknowledging to your
Excellency the receipt of your communication of this
day, stating that you had notified Washington of my
proposition of evacuation of the territory of Division of
Santiago de Cuba, I have the honor to inform your
Excellency that I repeat the orders for my troops to
preserve the same attitude as the American troops.

By "arms" is to be understood portable weapons,
that is, those that soldiers carry and the field artillery
that is transported on mule back; there being excluded
field guns and fixed siege and coast defence guns, which
cannot be considered as forming an integral part of the

units of the army. I make this explanation in reply
to your note, and beg your Excellency to consider me
Your obedient servant,
JOSÉ TORAL.

*Commander-in-Chief of the 4th Corps of the Army of
the Island of Cuba.*

TO HIS EXCELLENCY
  The Commander-in-Chief of the U.S. Forces,
    In camp at San Juan River.

[Telephone message.]
HEADQUARTERS 5TH ARMY CORPS,
July 9, 1898.

To GENERAL WHEELER,
    Commanding:

The Spanish Commander submits proposition to
march out of Santiago, abandoning all this territory
and not to be molested by our forces until he reaches
Holguin. Have submitted the matter to Washington.
Meanwhile the truce will continue.

J. D. MILEY, *Aid.*

HEADQUARTERS 5TH ARMY CORPS,
July 9, 1898.

GENERAL WHEELER:

The Commanding General directs me to say that the
Spanish Authorities claim our troops with some civilians with them are taking advantage of the truce to pass
to the front of our line. He wishes you to give strin-
gent orders in your Division that no one shall pass from
the rear to the front of our line and to immediately inform other Division Commanders and General Bates in
his name to the same effect.

MCCLERNAND, *A.A.G.*

HEADQUARTERS CAVALRY DIVISION,
BEFORE SANTIAGO, CUBA, July 9, 1898.

SPECIAL ORDER)
No. 22.   )

Pursuant to instructions from the War Department, Captain William E. English, Assistant Quartermaster, U.S. Volunteers, is assigned to duty as Aide to the Major General Commanding, to date June 10, 1898, the day on which he reported for duty.

By command of Major General Wheeler,

J. H. DORST,
Lieut. Col. U.S. Vols.
Assistant Adjutant General.

HEADQUARTERS CAVALRY DIVISION,
IN FRONT OF SANTIAGO, CUBA, July 9, 1898.

TO HON. SECRETARY OF WAR,
Washington, D.C. :

SIR : In my official report I have stated the gallant services of the Officers of my Staff.

I especially request that the following Officers be given a brevet upon their rank in the regular army for their services during this campaign :

Lieutenant Colonel J. H. Dorst.
Major William D. Beach.
Major E. A. Garlington.
Captain Joseph E. Dickman.
1st Lieutenant M. F. Steele.
2nd Lieutenant James H. Reeves.
2nd Lieutenant Joseph Wheeler, junior.

Very respectfully,
JOSEPH WHEELER,
Major General Volunteers.

HEADQUARTERS, CAVALRY DIVISION,
BEFORE SANTIAGO, CUBA, July 9, 1898.

MAJOR GENERAL WM. R. SHAFTER,
Commanding 5th Army Corps:

DEAR GENERAL : Since I saw you this evening I have seen the New York "Times" of July 1st, which has what appears to be an authoritative statement that Major General Brooke is to take troops from Chickamauga Park to Porto Rico and that our troops are to be left here.

One of the reasons I gave in my letter to-day for closing the campaign here promptly was the importance of the troops being carried to Porto Rico, which I regard as a very important movement, and one that should be done quickly.

Now if it is the intention of the Government to carry other troops to Porto Rico and leave us here, this reason for prompt action would cease to exist and it is possible that the Government would think we should occupy ourselves against the Spanish troops until they were captured.

I simply suggest this as I know you desire to carry out the wishes of the Government and I have a special desire to help you in doing so.

With regards,
Truly your friend,
JOS. WHEELER,
Major General Vols.

[By telephone.]

HEADQUARTERS CAVALRY DIVISION,
BEFORE SANTIAGO DE CUBA, July 9, 1898, 8.35 P.M.

To MAJOR GENERAL WM. R. SHAFTER,
    Comdg 5th Army Corps:

There is a movement among the Spaniards to-night.
It looks as though they were preparing to get away.
Of course I cannot be certain about this.

JOS. WHEELER,
Maj.-Genl Vols.

———————

HEADQUARTERS 5TH ARMY CORPS,
CAMP NEAR SANTIAGO, July 10, 9.10 P.M.

GENERAL WHEELER : Information about suspicious
movement of the enemy received.   Have notified Lawton and direct him to notify General Garcia.

By command of General Shafter,

McCLERNAND,
A.A.G.

———————

HEADQUARTERS CAVALRY DIVISION,
BEFORE SANTIAGO DE CUBA,
July 10, 1898, 10 minutes past midnight.

MAJOR GENERAL WM. R. SHAFTER,
    Commanding 5th Army Corps:

SIR : The enclosed letter has just been brought into
our lines from the Spanish.   The man who brought it,
who has been halted at our outpost, said he would wait
for an answer.

Very respectfully,

JOS. WHEELER,
Maj.-Genl Vols.

HEADQUARTERS 5TH ARMY CORPS,
July 10, 1898.

MAJ. GENL JOS. WHEELER:

DEAR GENL: The following promoted to Maj. Genls: Lawton, Chaffee, Hawkins, Bates, Kent, Young; to be Brig. Genls: Col. Wood, Lt. Col. McKibbin, Carroll.

J. C. GILMORE.

HEADQUARTERS 5TH ARMY CORPS,
July 10, 1898.

MAJOR GENERAL WHEELER,
Commanding Cavalry Division:

The Commanding General directs you find 25 or 30 teamsters in your command and send them here at once; they are absolutely necessary to keep wagons going.

McCLERNAND,
A.G.

HEADQUARTERS 5TH ARMY CORPS,
CAMP NEAR SANTIAGO, CUBA, July 10, 1898.

COMMANDING GENERAL CAVALRY DIVISION:

SIR: The Commanding General directs me to say a demand has been made this morning for the unconditional surrender of Santiago, with notification that unless favorable reply is received by 3 P.M., hostilities will be resumed at 4 P.M. In resuming hostilities, it is the intention of the General Commanding to drive the enemy out of his works and into the town by means of artillery and rifle fire. To do this the volume of fire is of importance, but its accuracy is of the utmost importance. The greatest care, therefore, should be exercised to direct your fire wherever men can be seen, firing deliberately and taking good aim and keeping your own men well covered. An advance upon the City is not expected to be made until after the bombardment and until ordered. A shot from the battery with General Lawton's Division will be the signal to authorize firing to be commenced.

Very respectfully,

E. J. McCLERNAND,
Assistant Adjutant General.

HEADQUARTERS 5TH ARMY CORPS,
July 10, 1898, 3.45 P.M.

ALL DIVISION COMMANDERS: The Spanish Commander having declined to surrender, the cessation of hostilities will be regarded as no longer existing after 4 P.M., but there will be no firing until a shot fired from a battery on Gen. Lawton's front.

By command of Gen. Shafter,

McCLERNAND,
A.A.G.

HEADQUARTERS 5TH ARMY CORPS,
July 10, 1898, 12.20 P.M.

TO MAJOR GENERAL WHEELER: The Commanding General wishes that you would please send in to these Headquarters immediately the Spanish prisoners you captured this morning.

J. C. GILMORE,
A.A.G.

HEADQUARTERS 5TH ARMY CORPS,
BEFORE SANTIAGO DE CUBA, July 10, 1898.

TO COMMANDING GENERAL, 1ST & 2D BRIGADES:

SIR: The Commanding General directs that all Officers and men of your Brigade be prohibited from going to the town of Caney or thereabouts or from holding any communication with refugees in that vicinity. This precaution is taken with a view to guarding against infectious and contagious diseases.

Your obedient servant,

M. F. STEELE,

Aid.

HEADQUARTERS CAVALRY DIVISION,
BEFORE SANTIAGO, July 11, 1898.

COMMANDING GENERAL *1st and 2nd Cavalry Brigades:*

The Commanding General desires you to inform him immediately of the position at your front this morning. Everything appears quiet.

JOS. WHEELER, JR.,

Aid.

[By telephone.]

HEADQUARTERS CAVALRY DIVISION,
July 11, 1898, 6 A.M.

MAJOR GENERAL WM. R. SHAFTER,
Commanding 5th Army Corps:

The Spanish lines seem to be very thinly manned; but they had reveille this morning as usual.

JOS. WHEELER,

Maj. Gen. Vols.

HEADQUARTERS CAVALRY DIVISION,
BEFORE SANTIAGO, CUBA, July 11, 1898.

GENERAL WM. R. SHAFTER,
        Commanding 5th Army Corps:

DEAR GENERAL : When I received an intimation yesterday that you desired my lines spread out to the right, I went up and examined the line and arranged to have it done the moment I received your order. This morning when I received the order I went in person to the extreme right of the line, and also over to the line occupied by General Chaffee, taking General Sumner and General Wood with me, and personally made the arrangements for extending the line which was done with all the promptitude possible.

Respectfully,

JOS. WHEELER,
Maj. Gen. Vols. Commdg.

HEADQUARTERS CAVALRY DIVISION,
July 11, 1898.

MAJOR GENERAL WM. R. SHAFTER :

SIR : Your telegram message received. I have just returned from the front, where I have been all morning. Together with General Sumner and General Wood I examined the lines and arranged to communicate with General Lawton's left, as directed. The movement will be made with all celerity possible.

Very respectfully,

JOS. WHEELER,
Maj. Gen. Vols.

HEADQUARTERS 5TH ARMY CORPS,
July 11, 1898.

To GENERAL WHEELER: Navy will begin firing slowly soon. Have an officer on the picket line to note fall of each shot, and report it to me at once.

SHAFTER,
Maj. Gen.

HEADQUARTERS 1ST DIVISION, 5TH ARMY CORPS,
July 11, 1898.

DEAR GENERAL WHEELER: I judge the navy shots to be well placed by smoke of bursting shells. I think you can assure Gen. Shafter more certainly of effect if you could send mounted man to right, where city is in view. I see here only suburbs.

KENT.

HEADQUARTERS 5TH ARMY CORPS,
July 11, 1898.

To GENERAL WHEELER: The Commanding General wishes to know if the Spaniards are making any return fire either with artillery or small arms.

McCLERMAND,
A. A. G.

HEADQUARTERS 1ST DIVISION, 5TH ARMY CORPS,
July 11, 1898, 10.40 A.M.

GENERAL WHEELER: None since navy opened from artillery, but few shots from small arms. I judge they are saving themselves for an attack.

KENT.

HEADQUARTERS 5TH ARMY CORPS, July 11, 1898.
GENERAL WHEELER,
    Commanding Cavalry Division:
It is reported General Chaffee is ready to move to extreme right. Please arrange at once to connect with Gen. Lawton's left as directed this morning.
By command of General Shafter,
McCLERNAND, *A.A.G.*

HEADQUARTERS CAVALRY DIVISION,
BEFORE SANTIAGO, July 11, 1898.
MAJ. GEN. WM. R. SHAFTER,
    Commndg U.S. Forces:
Everything seems quiet. I am investigating and will telephone you shortly.
JOS. WHEELER,
Maj. Gen. Vols., Commndg.

[Telephone message.]
HEADQUARTERS CAVALRY DIVISION,
July 12, 1898.
GENERAL H. W. LAWTON : General Shafter directs me to say that he does not wish you to extend your lines any further.
JOSEPH WHEELER,
Maj. Gen. Vols., Commndg.

HEADQUARTERS 5TH ARMY CORPS,
July 12, 1898.
To GENERALS WHEELER AND KENT : General Shafter desires that you stop all movements of your troops in the direction of the City of Santiago.
J. D. MILEY, *Aid.*

CHAPTER X

HEADQUARTERS 5TH ARMY CORPS,
July 12, 1898.

To GENERAL WHEELER: The Commanding General directs me to inform you that he has two pack
trains which are practically useless on account of sickness. He says he desires you to call for two squads
of 12 men each from the Rough Riders. Send men
who have had some experience in packing, if possible,
for temporary duty with these trains. Have them
report here as soon as possible.

GILMORE,
A.A.G.

———————

HEADQUARTERS CAVALRY DIVISION,
July 12, 1898.

MY DEAR GENERAL WHEELER: All right. Will send
the 24 men, but this most seriously depletes my already
thin line; I have but 340 officers and men fit for duty

all told; I should have some relief for the men in the trenches against a possible attack.

Yours respectfully,

THEODORE ROOSEVELT.

HEADQUARTERS CAVALRY DIVISION,
BEFORE SANTIAGO, CUBA, July 12, 1898.

MAJOR GENERAL WILLIAM R. SHAFTER,
    Commanding United States Forces:

SIR: The Archbishop of Santiago met the Officer who went out with the flag of truce to receive the last message, and said he had come out to speak to this Officer without consulting the Commander-in-Chief of the town.   He wishes to get permission for himself and all his priests — about 30 in number — and for the nuns — some 28 in all — to leave the city and come within our lines before the bombardment recommences.   He said that he made this request without letting the Military Authorities know that he was going to make it. He would like to get the answer in duplicate in two envelopes left unsealed, one addressed to him and one addressed to the Commander-in-Chief, so that there will be no delay in the permission getting to him.   He stated that about a dozen houses were blown down by the shells yesterday but no one was killed.

Respectfully,

JOSEPH WHEELER,
Maj. Gen. U.S. Vols., Commndg.

HEADQUARTERS 5TH ARMY CORPS,
July 12, 1898.

To GENERAL WHEELER: General Shafter inquires if Capt. McKittrick has started back to Headquarters; he also wishes me to say that two letters have just started to you and that they must go in by flag to-night.

J. D. MILEY, *Aid.*

HEADQUARTERS 5TH ARMY CORPS,
July 14, 1898.

MAJOR GENERAL WHEELER:

SIR: The Commanding General desires you to send the two accompanying letters through to the Spaniards, under a flag of truce, as quickly as possible.

Very respectfully,

E. J. McCLERNAND, *A.A.G.*

HEADQUARTERS 5TH ARMY CORPS,
July 12, 1898.

To GENERAL WHEELER: I wish to know if two flags of truce have been received from the Spanish this afternoon and what disposition was made of them.

SHAFTER, *Maj. Gen. Commndg.*

[Telephone message.]
HEADQUARTERS CAVALRY DIVISION,
July 13, 1898.

To GENERAL WM. R. SHAFTER: The enemy is sending in another white flag. I will send the message by mounted courier as soon as received.

JOSEPH WHEELER,
Major General Volunteers.

[By telephone.]

HEADQUARTERS CAVALRY DIVISION,
July 13, 1898.

To MAJOR GENERAL WM. R. SHAFTER,
Commanding U.S. Forces:

There is a quantity of lumber on the "Alleghany" which I had placed on board at Tampa. I respectfully suggest that you give orders for it to be disembarked, as it would be useful for the erection of hospitals, shelters, etc.

JOSEPH WHEELER,
Major General Vols., Commdg.

HEADQUARTERS 5TH ARMY CORPS,
July 13, 1898.

MAJ. GEN. WHEELER: Genl. Lawton reports the enemy is entrenching and throwing up entanglements in his front. The Commanding Genl. directs you to send a message to the Spanish commander that he asks this work stopped.   By command Genl Shafter,

MCCLERNAND,
A.A.G.

HEADQUARTERS CAVALRY DIVISION,
BEFORE SANTIAGO DE CUBA, July 13, 1898.

To HIS EXCELLENCY MAJOR GENERAL TORAL,
Commanding Spanish Forces, Santiago de Cuba:

SIR: Major General Lawton reports that your troops are entrenching and throwing up entanglements in his front.

The Commanding General directs me to write you and ask that this work be stopped. We regard it as a violation of the truce. We are certain that this work is being done without your knowledge.

With very great respect,
Your obedient servant,

JOSEPH WHEELER,

Major General Commanding Cavalry Division and Advance Lines.

ARMY OF THE ISLAND OF CUBA, 4TH ARMY CORPS,
SANTIAGO DE CUBA, July 13, 1898.

To HIS EXCELLENCY
The General Commanding the Cavalry Division of the American Army:

YOUR EXCELLENCY: In reply to your favor of this date I have the honor to inform you that I order the suspension of the works of intrenchments to which your Excellency refers and of which I have no knowledge, begging you on your part to take similar action.

The only thing I have knowledge of is that the rains have washed down some trenches, and perhaps the sediment may have made your officers believe that a new kind of work was being constructed on the first line, which I did not order.

I remain, Your Excellency's
Most obedient servant,

JOSÉ TORAL,
Commander-in-Chief of the 4th Army Corps.

[By telephone.]

HEADQUARTERS CAVALRY DIVISION,
July 14, 1898.

To MAJOR-GENERAL WM. R. SHAFTER:

Everything is quiet.   General Toral states that what we thought was working on trenches was simply baling out water as they had become inundated.   He asks that we abstain from working on our trenches.

JOSEPH WHEELER,
Major-General Vols., Commdg.

HEADQUARTERS CAVALRY DIVISION,
BEFORE SANTIAGO, CUBA, July 13, 1898.

COMMANDING GENERAL CAVALRY BRIGADE:

The truce will continue until twelve o'clock noon to-morrow the 14th instant.

General Shafter directs that not a shot be fired until this time and not then until ordered.

By command Major General Wheeler,

J. H. DORST,
Lieut. Col. U.S. Vols.,
Assistant Adjutant Gen.

HEADQUARTERS, U.S. ARMY,
BEFORE SANTIAGO, CUBA, July 14, 1898.

GENERAL WM. R. SHAFTER,
Commanding 5th Army Corps:

SIR: The Cavalry Division are separated from their horses and have been doing most extraordinary service. If it is possible I desire to have them separated from the rest of the Command, so they can be put on board ship and sent to other fields, as I desire to have them remounted as soon as possible.

Very respectfully,

NELSON A. MILES,

Major General Commdg U.S. Army.

HEADQUARTERS 5TH ARMY CORPS,

July 14, 1898.

GENERAL WHEELER :

Am not particular as to minor details, but General Toral must withdraw from his fortification and trenches and the taking up of torpedoes must begin at once, so as to clear the way for our ships. The navy will probably assist in the moving of obstructions to-morrow.

SHAFTER,

Maj. Gen. Commndg.

NOTES OF CONFERENCE OF GENERALS MILES, SHAFTER, AND WHEELER, WITH GENERAL JOSÉ TORAL, COMMANDING SPANISH FORCES, JULY 14, 1898.

[*Taken by Mr. Aurelius E. Mestre, of General Wheeler's staff.*]

General Toral said he was authorized by the Captain-General of Havana to treat with us on the basis of capitulation and " repatriacion," — that is, sending home of the troops to Spain ; but the agreement reached is to be accepted by the home Government. He thinks this will surely be confirmed, as otherwise the Captain-General would not have authorized it. He wishes to begin treating at once, so as to gain time. Being

Commander-in-Chief of numerous forces, he would like to have the whole of the Division under his command included in the capitulation. These troops are in Guantanamo, Baraçoa, Sagua de Tanamo, along the railway and at different points, and should be embarked from the nearest port to the place where they are. He agreed with General Shafter that there should be a total cessation of hostilities in Santiago and in the other places as soon as information can be brought out to them. All the forces in General Toral's Division are embraced in this capitulation, as above stated; that is, the forces of his own command, but not those of General Linares' command which are by accident now under his orders. The dividing line goes from Aserradero through Palma to Sagua de Tanamo and all the territory lying East of this is comprised. General Toral said that the "City of Texas" could not enter the harbor of Santiago, but that he would study the matter with the Technical Commission. He agreed to let the people of Caney return to Santiago and be provisioned by us. He also agreed to let the Juragua railroad be used by us to bring in food, if assured that it would only be used for that purpose. This assurance was given him. The "Texas" would come under the rules of the Geneva Society for the gratuitous distribution of food and hospital supplies, whereas the railroad would be for rationing the American and Spanish troops and the people in Santiago. General Shafter offered to post troops around the city to prevent the entrance of American or Cuban troops.

HEADQUARTERS 5TH ARMY CORPS,
July 14, 1898.

GENERALS WHEELER AND KENT:

Apparently there is every prospect of a capitulation. I will inform you at the earliest practicable moment.

SHAFTER, *Maj. Gen.*

GENERAL WHEELER'S CAMP,
BEFORE SANTIAGO, CUBA, July 14, 1898.

TO MAJOR GENERAL WILLIAM R. SHAFTER,
Commanding U. S. Forces:

SIR: You are authorized to appoint Commissioners to draw up Articles of Capitulation on the terms upon which the Spanish Division have been surrendered, namely the return of the Spanish troops to Spain at the expense of the United States. The Spanish troops will be supplied at the expense of the United States and assembled at such a place as may be available for their embarkation on the arrival of the necessary transportation.

The attention of the Commissioners should be called to the importance of the return of the people that have fled from the City of Santiago and the supplying them with food.

2. The sending of supplies into the Harbor on the Red Cross ship and other vessels.

3. The removal of all obstructions to the entrance of the Harbor or notification to the fleet that no obstacle will be placed in the way of their removing such obstructions.

Respectfully,

NELSON A. MILES,
Major General Commanding the Army.

HEADQUARTERS 5TH ARMY CORPS,
BEFORE SANTIAGO DE CUBA, July 16, 1898.

TO HIS EXCELLENCY GENERAL JOSÉ TORAL,
Commanding Spanish Forces:

DEAR SIR: Your Excellency's suggestion that the Representatives be here at 4 o'clock to arrange for the final act of capitulation is received and we will wait until that time.

The troops I referred to requesting you to withdraw are those at Aguadores, those along the railroad to the City and those on the bluff in a Southeasterly direction from the City.

Respectfully,

WM. R. SHAFTER,
Major General Commanding U.S. Forces.

HEADQUARTERS 5TH ARMY CORPS,
July 15, 1898.

GENERAL WHEELER: What is the prospect? That surrender yesterday was as positive as it possibly could be made and commissioners were appointed to arrange details. They cannot go back on it now.

SHAFTER,
Maj. Gen.

HEADQUARTERS 5TH ARMY CORPS,
July 15, 1898.

GEN. WHEELER: It is impossible to submit terms of surrender to Madrid. Surrender was, as you know, made yesterday.

SHAFTER,
Maj. Genl.

[By telephone.]

HEADQUARTERS CAVALRY DIVISION,
BEFORE SANTIAGO, CUBA,
July 15, 1898, 3.40 P.M.

To GENERAL WM. R. SHAFTER,
Commanding U.S. Forces:

I received your despatch and am certain that when you know all the facts you will concur that we did the very best possible. To have an agreement which we had drawn up by authority of Generals Blanco and Toral is as complete as surrender can be without being an absolute surrender, and Mr. Mason and General Toral assured us that there could be no doubt about the Madrid Government consenting to it. I know you will appreciate that we used our best efforts to comply as near as possible with your wishes.

JOS. WHEELER,
Maj. Gen. Vols., Commdg.

CHAPTER XI

GENERAL WHEELER'S CAMP,
BEFORE SANTIAGO, CUBA, July 14, 1898.

To HONORABLE SECRETARY OF WAR,
Washington, D.C. :

General Toral formally surrendered the troops of his
Army Corps and Division of Santiago on the terms and
understanding that his troops would be returned to
Spain.

General Shafter will appoint Commissioners to draw
up conditions of arrangement for carrying out the
terms of surrender. This is very gratifying, and
General Shafter and the Officers and men of this
Command are entitled to great credit for their tenacity,
fortitude, and the almost insurmountable obstacles
which have been overcome. A portion of the Army
has been infected with yellow fever, and efforts will be
made to separate those who are infected and those free
from it and keep those that are still on board ship

separated from those on shore. Arrangements will be immediately made for carrying out the further instructions of the President and yourself.

NELSON A. MILES,
Maj.-Gen. Commndg the Army.

———

GENERAL WHEELER'S CAMP,
BEFORE SANTIAGO, CUBA, July 14, 1898.

To MAJOR GENERAL WM. R. SHAFTER,
Commanding U.S. Forces:

SIR: The Spanish Army having surrendered, the terms of capitulation will be carried into effect with as little delay as practicable on the understanding that their troops will be returned to Spain at the expense of the United States.

You will, with as little delay practicable place such troops as are not infected with yellow fever in separate camps and as soon as practicable report the number that will be available for service with another expedition. Those organizations which have been infected with yellow fever, every effort will be made to improve their sanitary condition and to check the spread of the disease by placing them in as healthy camps as possible.

Respectfully,

NELSON A. MILES,
Major General Commanding the Army.

GENERAL WHEELER'S CAMP,
BEFORE SANTIAGO, CUBA, July 14, 1898.
To HONORABLE SECRETARY OF WAR,
Washington, D.C. :
Your second dispatch received. Have already anticipated in part by giving directions for separating the
troops that have been infected and have kept the
troops that came on the " Yale," " Columbia," " Duch-
ess," and part of those on the " Comanche " ready to
disembark at Cabanas, on the West side, where I had
made all arrangements for putting the troops in on that
side of the Harbor and opening the entrance of the bay
in conjunction with Admiral Sampson. I will now keep
these troops away from the infected districts and will
probably let them go ashore at Guantanamo. Other
vessels en route will go into the Harbor at Guantanamo.
Presume that will be a good rendezvous at least for the
troops coming from Tampa. They could come in on
the South side and go into a safe harbor there. Will
consult with the Admiral with regard to rendezvous
our troops at Porto Rico or one of the Islands immediately adjacent thereto. Will keep you fully apprised
of any important information.

NELSON A. MILES,
Major General Commanding the Army.

GENERAL WHEELER'S HEADQUARTERS,
BEFORE SANTIAGO, CUBA, July 14, 1898.
To MAJOR GENERAL WILLIAM R. SHAFTER,
Commanding U.S. Forces:
SIR : For a double reason I think it would be advis-
able to isolate the troops that have just joined your
Command in separate camps on healthful ground to

keep them free if possible from infection by yellow fever, and it will also form a strong force to meet any force that might by any possibility come from Holguin.

Respectfully,

NELSON A. MILES,
Major General Commanding the Army.

HEADQUARTERS CAVALRY DIVISION,
SAN JUAN, July 15, 1898, 8 A.M.

GENERAL SHAFTER:

SIR: The French Consul has gone into Santiago from Caney. Shall other people be allowed to go in?

JOS. WHEELER,
Maj. Gen. Vols.

[By telephone.]

HEADQUARTERS CAVALRY DIVISION,
BEFORE SANTIAGO, CUBA,
July 15, 1898, 6.15 P.M.

TO MAJOR GENERAL WM. R. SHAFTER,
Commanding U.S. Forces:

There is a woman here who says she is the wife of a Spanish Major and another the wife of a Spanish Lieutenant, with their children and mother. They want to go through the lines to Santiago.

JOS. WHEELER,
Maj. Gen. Vols., Commdg.

[Telephone message.]

HEADQUARTERS CAVALRY DIVSION,
July 15, 1898, 7 P.M.

To MAJOR GENERAL WM. R. SHAFTER,
Commanding U.S. Forces:

Mr. Ramsden, British Consul at Santiago, asks that Mr. Barrueco and family (three in number) from Caney be permitted to go into Santiago. He already has the permission of the Spanish General to cross their lines. Two carts have come out from Santiago to get their effects which he desires to cross and recross our lines.

JOS. WHEELER,
Maj. Gen. Vols. Commdg.

HEADQUARTERS 5TH ARMY CORPS,
July 16, 1898.

To GENERAL WHEELER AND GENERAL KENT:

The Commanding General directs you strictly prohibit any of our troops, Cuban Forces or other persons other than those authorized refugees to pass beyond our trenches towards Santiago.

MCCLERNAND.

HEADQUARTERS CAVALRY DIVISION,
BEFORE SANTIAGO, CUBA, July 16, 1898.

GENERAL LEONARD WOOD,
Commanding 2nd Cavalry Brigade:

SIR: You will place an Officer of discretion and one who understands the Spanish language with a guard at both the points where the roads from Caney to Santiago pass your line. The Officers will be instructed to permit the passage through the lines to Santiago of all refugees without arms, but they will be careful to permit no other persons to pass the line.

Respectfully,

Jos. Wheeler,

Maj. Gen. U.S. Vols. Commndg.

Headquarters 5th Army Corps,

Before Santiago de Cuba, July 16, 1898.

Commanding General Cavalry Division :

Sir : The Commanding General directs you report with your staff at these headquarters at 8.45 a.m. to-morrow, to accompany him to receive the surrender of General Toral.

Direct each General Officer in your division to report with his staff also. Have all your regiments drawn up on the lines from 9 to 9.30 a.m. At 11.45 all the troops will again be put in line, and at 12 o'clock precisely a salute of 21 guns will be fired from Captain Capron's Battery which will indicate that the American flag is being hoisted over the Governor's Palace. Bands will play the Star Spangled Banner and other national airs, and the men will cheer.

Acknowledge receipt.

Very respectfully,

E. J. McClernand,

Assistant Adjutant General.

Before Santiago de Cuba, July 16.

To * * *

My dear Sir : We have been very busy and have had some hard fighting and the men have suffered a great deal on account of their exposure, the intense heat, and terrible rains ; and even when it does not rain the dew makes everything as wet as though it had been raining.

Yesterday, after working for many hours, including work in the open air, until half past twelve o'clock the night before, we succeeded in getting an agreement from the Spaniards. The agreement was made by order of General Blanco and General Toral, the Spanish Commander here, General Linares, having been badly wounded. The matter is, however, to be confirmed by the Madrid Government, and if they do not confirm it we will open on them terribly and they will be compelled to surrender soon. General Toral told me yesterday that he would not wish his worst enemy to be in his place ; he said his Generals and Colonels were all killed or wounded, and, pointing to Santiago, he said, " There are other secret things which I cannot tell, which makes things very bad."

I was quite sick on June 30th but nothing was done that day ; my temperature was up to 103½ but it did not prevent me from doing full duty on July 1st, the day of the battle, and ever since that time.

As they have burnt the Post Office at Siboney on account of the yellow fever I understand that a good deal of the mail is lost.

With high regards, truly your friend,

JOSEPH WHEELER.

P.S. — Since writing the above I have received the news that the preliminary agreement made with the Spaniards for the capitulation of Santiago has been confirmed by the Madrid Government.

HEADQUARTERS CAVALRY DIVISION,
BEFORE SANTIAGO, CUBA, July 17, 1898.

To MAJOR GENERAL WM. R. SHAFTER,
Commanding U.S. Forces:

SIR : My son examined the spring which is built up, and found that the water was not depreciated by what was taken out.   The Spanish soldiers are also getting water along the ravine leading from the road to the spring which he supposes is the same spring.   My Aid, Lieutenant Wheeler, asked the Spanish soldiers regarding the quality of the water and they said it was very good.

Respectfully,

JOS. WHEELER,
Maj. Gen. Vols. Commdg.

HEADQUARTERS CAVALRY DIVISION,
BEFORE SANTIAGO DE CUBA, July 17, 1898

To GENERAL COMMANDING CAVALRY BRIGADE :

DEAR GENERAL : General Shafter desires that the Cavalry Division move to-morrow morning over on the right in a favorable location near where the pipe line is, so that the Division can get water from the pipe line. I am sending Major Beach and Captain Chanler over to select a place for my Headquarters, and I wish that you would have your camp selected this afternoon and the troops near by notified where you will locate, so that there will be no danger of their taking up your camps before you get there.   It might be well for you to send an officer over to stay to-night with a few men, so as to notify any one that may come to get your camp that it has been selected for Brigade.   It will be well for the

two Brigade Commanders to send their representatives
together, so that there may be no conflict in selection.

Respectfully your friend,

Jos. WHEELER,

Maj. Gen. U.S. Vols., Commanding.

HEADQUARTERS U.S. TROOPS IN CUBA,
SANTIAGO DE CUBA, July 19, 1898.

GENERAL ORDERS, ⎰
No. 26.   ⎱

The successful accomplishment of the campaign
against Santiago, resulting in its downfall and the surrender of the Spanish Forces, the capture of large
amounts of military stores, together with the destruction of the entire Spanish fleet in the harbor, which,
upon the investment of the city, was forced to leave,
is one of which this army can well be proud.

This had been accomplished through the heroic deeds
of the Army, and to its officers and men the Major
General Commanding offers his sincere thanks for their
endurance of hardships heretofore unknown in the
American Army. The work you have accomplished
may well appeal to the pride of your countrymen, and
has been rivalled upon but few occasions in the World's
history. Landing upon an unknown coast, you found
dangers in disembarking and overcame obstacles that
even in looking back seem insurmountable. Seizing,
with the assistance of the Navy, the towns of Daiquiri
and Siboney, you pushed boldly forth, gallantly driving
back the enemy's outposts in the engagement of Las
Quasimas, and completed the concentration of the Army
near Sevilla, within sight of the Spanish stronghold at
Santiago de Cuba.

The outlook from Sevilla was one that might well have appalled the stoutest heart; behind you ran a narrow road, made well nigh impassable by rains, while to the front you looked out upon high foothills covered with a dense growth, which could only be traversed by bridle-paths, terminating within range of the enemy's guns. Nothing daunted, you responded eagerly to the order to close upon the foe and attacking at Caney and San Juan, drove him from work to work, until he took refuge within his last and strongest entrenchments immediately surrounding the city.

Despite the fierce glare of a southern sun and rains that fell in torrents, you valiantly withstood his attempts to drive you from the position your valor had won. Holding in your vice-like grip the army opposed to you, after seventeen days of battle and siege, you were rewarded by the surrender of nearly 24,000 prisoners — 12,000 being those in your immediate front, the others scattered in the various towns of eastern Cuba — freeing completely the eastern part of the Island from the Spanish troops. This was not done without great sacrificing. The death of 230 gallant soldiers, and the wounding of 1284 others, shows but too plainly the fierce contest in which you were engaged. The few reported missing are undoubtedly among the dead, as no prisoners were lost. For those who have fallen in battle with you, the Commanding General sorrows, and with you will ever cherish their memory. Their devotion to duty sets a high example of courage and patriotism to our fellow-countrymen.

All who have participated in the campaign, battle and siege of Santiago de Cuba will recall with pride the grand deeds accomplished, and will hold one another dear for having shared great sufferings, hardships and triumphs together. All may well feel proud to inscribe on their banners the name of " Santiago de Cuba."

By command of Major General Shafter,

E. J. McCLERNAND,
Assistant Adjutant General.

SANTIAGO DE CUBA, July 19, 1898.

HIS EXCELLENCY GENERAL WHEELER:
Commanding the Cavalry Division:

SIR : General Escario has requested me to send you this letter in view of the readiness you showed during our conferences about the capitulation to permit that the families and baggage of the officers of his column, now in Manzanillo, might be brought to this city so as to share the same fate as the garrison.

As the matter is really of importance, if you consider the unprotected condition in which these families may remain and the lack of baggage on the part of the Officers referred to, who to-day scarcely have uniforms to wear, I appeal to Your Excellency, joining my request to that of General Escario which I trust may be granted, especially as the hazards of war should not be made to bear needlessly on those in misfortune.

General Escario tells me he spoke with you about the manner of carrying this out, for which reason I beg you will inform me when the proper time has arrived for same.

Yours etc.,

JOSÉ TORAL.

HEADQUARTERS CAVALRY DIVISION,
CAMP HAMILTON NEAR SANTIAGO, July 20, 1898.

MAJOR GENERAL WM. R. SHAFTER,
Commanding U.S. Forces:

DEAR GENERAL : The command is improving, but we need cooking utensils so as to re-establish the Company messes. The Red Cross has offered us oatmeal and various delicacies if we can get wagons to transport them. This would give the men a change of diet, and would put them all in fine fix in a very short time. I hope that wagons can be furnished for this work.

Respectfully,
JOSEPH WHEELER,
Maj. General U. S. Vols. Commdg.

HEADQUARTERS CAVALRY DIVISION,
CAMP HAMILTON, NEAR SANTIAGO, July 20, 1898.

GENERAL WM. R. SHAFTER,
Commanding U.S. Forces:

DEAR GENERAL : I received a letter from General Toral yesterday which I have had translated and send you the translation. I presume he has sent the same letter to General Lawton and Lieutenant Miley. I thought this matter had been arranged in the way that the letter of General Toral requests, and I was glad to hear so, because I think in these little matters a great Government like ours ought to be very liberal, and I think being liberal with these people about personal matters will have the effect to encourage other Spanish soldiers in giving the thing up and getting the same terms.

Respectfully,
JOSEPH WHEELER,
Maj. Gen. U.S. Vols. Commdg.

HEADQUARTERS CAVALRY DIVISION,
SANTIAGO, CUBA, July 20, 1898.

To His EXCELLENCY LIEUTENANT GENERAL LINARES :

DEAR GENERAL : It was my desire to have called upon you on July 17th, the same day that I was in the City, but my duties there were of an official character and all my time was occupied and after 12 o'clock we marched out together. It was my special desire to call upon you personally and express my appreciation of the courage and fortitude displayed by yourself and your Army.

Should I be able to visit the city of Santiago again soon, which I trust will be the case, I shall do myself the honor to personally call upon you.

With great respect,

JOSEPH WHEELER.

HEADQUARTERS CAVALRY DIVISION,
SANTIAGO, CUBA, July 20, 1898.

To His EXCELLENCY MAJOR GENERAL JOSÉ TORAL :

DEAR GENERAL : I received your letter last night and had it translated, and sent a copy to General Shafter, together with a letter of my own to the Commanding General, a copy of which I enclose.

I understood that the matter had been attended to as you desired ; if not I hope most earnestly it will be.

I also enclose to you a copy of a communication which General Lawton, Lieutenant Miley and myself sent to our Government.

I hope that you are quite well.

With very high regards,

Yours with respect,

JOSEPH WHEELER, *Major General.*

ARMY OF THE ISLAND OF CUBA, 4TH ARMY CORPS,
July 21, 1898.

HIS EXCELLENCY SENOR GENERAL WHEELER,
Chief of the Cavalry Division
of the American Army:

EXCELLENT SENOR : I answer your esteemed letter of yesterday and take note of your having forwarded to Senor General Shafter the petition of Senor General Escario relative to the shipping of the families and baggage of the officers of his columns. I also take note of Senor General Shafter's answer, of all of which I informed Senor General Escario. I feel deeply grateful for the good opinion which your Excellency, in common with Senors Lawton and Miley, hold of the Spanish soldier, and which has dictated the request you made to your government with reference to the return of the arms to us ; I therefore take pleasure in expressing my gratitude to your Excellency and the two above mentioned generals.

I remain,
Your Excellency's most humble servant,
q. s. m. c. (kissing your hand),
JOSÉ TORAL.

P.S. — The forces defending El Caney on the 1st inst. were composed of three companies of the "Constitution" battalion, one troop of guerillas and local forces, making a total of a scant five hundred men.

HEADQUARTERS CAVALRY DIVISION,
SANTIAGO DE CUBA, July 21, 1898.

MAJOR GENERAL NELSON A. MILES,
Commanding the Army:

SIR: My command is now on high ground and is improving. They were simply worn out by constant service and the rest they are now getting will soon restore them. There is not a particle of infection of yellow fever in the command, and has not been. I think the Cavalry Division would be of great service in Porto Rico.

With great respect,
Your obedient servant,

JOSEPH WHEELER,
Maj. Gen. U.S. Vols., Commdg.

CHAPTER XII

HEADQUARTERS CAVALRY DIVISION,
NEAR SANTIAGO DE CUBA, July 23, 1898.

To COLONEL E. J. McCLERNAND,
Adjutant General 5th Army Corps:

SIR : I received your letter instructing me to consolidate all the recommendations commending Officers for good conduct in the battle of Las Guasimas on June 24th, in the battle of San Juan on July 1st, and in subsequent operations. I therefore transmit herewith the recommendations referred to.

I also respectfully recommend, for the consideration of the Government, the following Officers who served upon my staff:

Major William D. Beach did distinguished service in the battle of Las Guasimas on June 24th and in operation before San Juan.

Lieutenant Colonel Dorst, Adjutant General of the Cavalry Division, Major E. A. Garlington, Captain Joseph P. Dickman, 1st Lieutenant Matthew W. Steele, 2nd Lieutenant James H. Reeves, and 2nd Lieutenant Joseph Wheeler Jr., were all distinguished in the battle of July 1st and in subsequent operations. I recommend them for the consideration of the Government.

In forwarding these recommendations I respectfully request a favorable endorsement from the Commanding General of the Forces in Cuba.

I also desire to commend the good conduct of Captain William Astor Chanler of the Volunteers and of Mr. Aurelius Mestre, Volunteer Aid, in the battle of July 1st and in the operations round San Juan.

I also desire to commend Captain P. W. West, who, although not actually in the engagements, has been efficient in the highest degree in performing the duties of Quartermaster of the Division and in assisting materially as Quartermaster of the Army.

Respectfully,
Jos. Wheeler,
Maj. Gen. U.S. Vols. Commdg Cav. Div.

Headquarters Cavalry Division,
Near Santiago de Cuba, July 24, 1898.
To Major General William R. Shafter,
Commanding U.S. Forces:

Sir : We find that the fresh meat which is sent daily for the use of this command is very much deteriorated owing to its exposure in the sun while en route. I write to ask whether it could not be arranged for the teams bringing these supplies to start very early in the morning, say at three or four oclock, as this would preserve the meat from injury and it would be much easier both on the teams and the men.

Respectfully,
Jos. Wheeler,
Major General U.S. Vols.

HEADQUARTERS CAVALRY DIVISION,
NEAR SANTIAGO DE CUBA, July 24, 1898.

To MAJOR GENERAL WM. R. SHAFTER,
    Commanding U.S. Forces:

SIR: I understand that General Garcia is out with
his whole command on the road to Holguin. I would
like to know where he is; and now that we have a few
horses, would it not be well to send out an Officer with
an escort to see General Garcia and learn the situation?
While I do not think that the troops at Holguin will
venture to come down, they might send a scouting
party to bother us. Anyway we must watch them.

Please give me any information you may have of
Garcia, so that my Officer may find him easily.

    Very respectfully,
        JOS. WHEELER,
        Maj. Gen. U.S. Vols.

HEADQUARTERS CAVALRY DIVISION,
SANTIAGO DE CUBA, July 24, 1898.

MAJOR GENERAL NELSON A. MILES,
    Commanding the Army:

DEAR GENERAL: I am very glad to hear that you
have started with the Porto Rican Expedition and that
you are to command it. We still have some sickness,
but it is a fever which is by no means of the character
of yellow fever and not contagious at all. Our total
sick list was 340 cases yesterday. Our command is
isolated on the hills nearly 5 miles from Santiago, and
there has been but one case sent from the whole Division that was regarded even with suspicion as yellow
fever. We could move to Porto Rico with 2200 or
2300 men entirely free from disease or contagion of

any kind, and they would be very valuable to you. If you do not want to move the Cavalry Division immediately, I am certain that I could be very valuable to you with my staff, and should be very glad to serve you in any capacity whatever.

Very respectfully,
Your obedient servant,
JOSEPH WHEELER.

HEADQUARTERS CAVALRY DIVISION,
SANTIAGO DE CUBA, July 25, 1898.

TO COLONEL E. J. MCCLERNAND,
Adjutant General Fifth Army Corps:

SIR: I particularly request that five or six army physicians, five stewards and twelve hospital corps men, to be detailed for service with this Division as soon as practicable. Drs. Newgarden and Bailey are both sick and unable to do duty, and Dr. Havard, our Chief Surgeon, had been ordered away on other duty. This leaves us practically without medical officers, which is very undesirable, as we have among the troops a great deal of what we call " four or five day fever," which needs careful medical treatment to prevent relapses.

I enclose a report of the Inspector-General of this command, in which these matters are alluded to.

Very respectfully,
JOS. WHEELER,
Major General U.S. Vols.

HEADQUARTERS CAVALRY DIVISION,
SANTIAGO DE CUBA, CAMP HAMILTON, July 24, 1898.

ADJUTANT GENERAL CAVALRY DIVISION:

SIR: I have the honor to submit the following report of an inspection of the Cavalry Division.

The officers and soldiers are in urgent need of almost everything except arms and ammunition. The former can supply themselves when the transports are unloaded and their baggage is transported to camp, which is going on now.

I have verbally already reported the condition of the enlisted men as to clothing and I understand requisitions are being prepared — they have no reserve supply on the transports and have only what they have on their backs. The articles most urgently needed are shoes, stockings, trousers, lightweight underwear, leggings and hats. On the first day of the fighting the men put aside their packs and in most cases lost them. Yesterday some fresh beef was issued to the Division — the first since leaving Tampa on the 13th of June. A more varied diet is urgently needed; beans and rice even, owing to limited transportation, having not been regularly issued, and since leaving transports the command has been living on hard-tack, bacon, sugar and coffee.

It has been and is now extremely difficult to get any officers' stores, and such as have been gotten have been in very limited quantities. In this climate, with so many enervated men, canned fruits, oatmeal, &c. should be added to the ration irrespective of cost. The commissary should also have meat extracts for sale.

As already known from other sources, this inspection discloses a very large sick list. The surgeons report about ninety per cent. as malarial fevers, rest ordinary camp disease — no serious cases; but the men uniformly

appear weak, enervated, tired — need as near absolute
rest as possible, and change to a cooling, nourishing
diet.

The Chief Surgeon reports the hospital medicines
limited in variety. Five additional surgeons, five
stewards, twelve hospital corps men and six hospital
tents and flies are needed. In the first brigade the
hospitals are consolidated under the supervision of Capt.
Harris, Medical Department. On the 23d there were
201 cases in hospital. There was no tentage except
shelter tents; no cooking utensils except two camp
kettles and the meat ration can; no food except straight
rations. It is hard for sick men under such circumstances. At this hospital there is not sufficient stimu-
lants and calomel and soda tablets. The hospital is
well located near a good spring.

In the second brigade there are regimental hospitals.
The 1st Cavalry has one conical wall tent, but is
expecting supplies from Daiquiri; this hospital is very
much in need of a cook, who is absent in Daiquiri.

In the 10th Cavalry there are three A tents and one
wall fly. The surgeon in charge reported practically
no medical supplies, needs one medical field-chest and
one surgical field-chest; also acetate of potassium,
chlorate of potassium and an apparatus for the examination of urine. The 1st Vol. Cav. has a paulin.
The surgeon reports that he requires 500 cubic centi-
meters of Wasburg's tincture. The troops have been
without cooking utensils, but are being gradually
supplied as the transports are unloaded. The question
of transportation is a very serious one, and if the number of pack mules assigned to this Division cannot be
increased from those now on the Island, and it is contemplated to keep the Division here for any length of

time, at least two hundred and fifty mules, with proper number of civilian packers, should be shipped from the United States at once. As the matter now stands only one day's supplies can be furnished, without taking into consideration any change of camp, stores or anything that would interrupt the ration supply.

The most important questions now to be considered are a nutritious diet suited to building up constitutions weakened by battle, fever, and exposure; rest for the command; proper shelter from the rain and sun; suitable clothing, and sufficient transportation. The matter of supplying officers' stores, including mineral water, should be adjusted as soon as possible and the Division Commissary be furnished such articles for sale.

None of the regiments, except the 1st Vol. Cav., which has one wagon, has any transportation.

> Very respectfully,
>
> E. A. GARLINGTON,
> *Major, Insp.-General Cavalry Division.*

HEADQUARTERS CAVALRY DIVISION,
NEAR SANTIAGO DE CUBA, July 24, 1898.
To MAJOR GENERAL WM. R. SHAFTER,
Commanding U.S. Forces:

DEAR GENERAL: I have just received your message through my daughter. I would feel terribly mortified to go back to the United States until the war is over, and feel certain that they will need you and all of us at Porto Rico; but if we cannot go there I want to stay with my men who have fought so bravely. I could not bear to leave them here and go off to the United States. If we do not go to Porto Rico we certainly will be put against some other enemy, and I am anxious to stay and fight under you anywhere I may be put.

I am glad to say that the change in food and getting up tents has already had a good effect upon the health of the men. I beg that you will not order me to go to the United States, and I also beg that you will take good care of your own health.

I thank you a thousand times for sending my daughter out this morning. I am in the very best of health and I am glad to say that my son, who was very sick yesterday, is now better. Every Officer of my Staff who is with me has now been through his attack of fever except Mr. Mestre, who is a native Cuban and acclimated.

The Cavalry Division will be ready for any kind of service when called upon.

With very high regards,

Your obedient servant and friend,

JOSEPH WHEELER.

HEADQUARTERS CAVALRY DIVISION,
SANTIAGO DE CUBA, July 25, 1898.
To HON. SECRETARY OF WAR,
Washington, D.C. :

SIR: We are laboring under great difficulties on account of the very few officers we have on duty. To illustrate, the 10th Cavalry went into action on July 1st with 19 Officers ; two of these Officers, Lieutenant William E. Shipp and Lieutenant William H. Smith, were killed and nine Officers were wounded, leaving but eight Officers on duty with the Regiment.

The 1st Regiment is now commanded by Lieutenant Colonel Charles D. Viele, the 3d by Major Henry

Jackson, the 6th by Major Thomas C. Lebe, the 9th by Captain E. B. Dimmick, and the 10th by Major S. T. Norvell.

This deficiency of Officers would be in a measure relieved by retiring a number of Field Officers who have not done duty in this campaign, who are really unfit for duty and who ought to be retired. This would promote the senior Captains who have been distinguished for gallantry, fortitude and endurance in this campaign.

I urgently request that early action be taken in this matter.

Very respectfully,

JOSEPH WHEELER,
Major General U.S. Volunteers.

CAMAMENTO RIO SAN JUAN,
27 Julio, 1898.

ECMO. SR. MAYOR GENERAL JOSEPH WHEELER:

MY DEAR SIR AND OF MY MOST DISTINGUISHED CONSIDERATION: In answer to yours of yesterday in which you asked me for several dates relative to the march of the columns under my orders, I have the pleasure of participating to you that I left Manzanillo in the afternoon of the 22d of last June at the head of five battallions of Infantry of the regular army, one section of Mountain Artillery (two pieces of 8 centimetres) and a small group of Caballery irregular; with which columns I arrived in Santiago de Cuba on the 3d of this month, having sustained on the march several combats with the insurrects, of which the important one was that of the 1st of July in the hill of Aguacate;

this combat occasioned me 27 dead and 67 wounded that I left on my pass in the hospital of Palma Soriano.

At the same time that I give these dates to you, I have the honor of manifesting that I should like to see very much that you would kindly give me on your part the following : —

Number of the American forces that attacked the positions of Sevilla the 24th of June, number of which attacked the hill of San Juan and the place of "El Caney" on the 1st of July. Number of which did the same with the Plaza of Santiago de Cuba on the 2d.

And the last the number of cannons that the American army placed against the city of Santiago de Cuba the following days to the 3d of the inst.

With the anticipated thanks,

Remains yours very truly,

FEDERICO ESCARIO.

HEADQUARTERS CAVALRY DIVISION,
SANTIAGO DE CUBA, July 31, 1898.

To MAJOR GENERAL NELSON A. MILES,
Commanding the Army:

DEAR GENERAL : The Cavalry Division having now been isolated for ten days, I am in a position to deny the rumors that have been current as to the existence of yellow fever among us.

I am sure a short sea trip would put the men in this command in excellent health, and we feel that we could be of very great service to you in Porto Rico.

With great respect,

Your obedient servant and friend,

JOSEPH WHEELER,
Major General U.S. Vols.

HEADQUARTERS CAVALRY DIVISION,
SANTIAGO DE CUBA, August 1, 1898.

To MAJOR GENERAL NELSON A. MILES,
Commanding the Army:

DEAR GENERAL: I am glad to say that the Cavalry Division is improving in health.

I believe that a sea voyage to Porto Rico would put the Division in good order for service. I am confident the Division would be of great value to you.

The surgeons assure me there is not and has not been any cases of yellow fever in the Command. If for any reason you should not deem it advisable to order the Cavalry Division to Porto Rico, I am confident I could be of service to you and I would be more than delighted to be in the campaign under your command.

With great respect,
Your obedient servant,

JOSEPH WHEELER,
Major General U.S. Vols.

HEADQUARTERS 5TH ARMY CORPS,
Aug. 6, 1898.

GENERAL WHEELER: Send in the regiment that is nearest 500 strong. Do not exceed 550 in the first detachment. 500 will do better. Use your wagons to bring sick and convalescent to Cavitas.

The men set aside by the doctor as suspicious cases must be left and cared for by you. Bring only ammunition in belts. Leave the rest piled up. The train will be at Cavitas early this afternoon. The exact hour will be telephoned as soon as known.

W. R. SHAFTER.

[*Endorsement:*]
Official Copy respectfully furnished to Commanding General 1st Cavalry Brigade, for his information and guidance.

By command of Maj. Gen. Wheeler,

J. H. DORST,
Assistant Adjt General.

HEADQUARTERS CAVALRY DIVISION,
Aug. 6, 1898.

COMMANDING GENERAL 1ST CAVALRY BRIGADE:

SIR: The Commanding General desires that you have five hundred and fifty men at Cavitas at one-thirty P.M. to-day.

Please send me word how many Officers and men will march with the 3d and 6th Cavalry.

Respectfully,

JOS. WHEELER,
Major General U.S. Vols. Commanding.

HEADQUARTERS 5TH ARMY CORPS,
SANTIAGO, Aug. 6, 1898.

To GEN. WHEELER: A train sufficient to carry 550 men will be at Cavitas this afternoon at 1.30 P.M.

J. D. MILEY,
A.D.C.

HEADQUARTERS CAVALRY DIVISION,
Aug. 6, 1898.

COMMANDING GENERAL 2D CAVALRY BRIGADE:

SIR: The Commanding General directs that the 1st United States Cavalry and 1st United States Volunteer Cavalry be ready to join the ship to-morrow.

Further information will be supplied later as to the time of the embarkation.

Respectfully,
JOS. WHEELER,
Major General U.S. Vols.

HEADQUARTERS CAVALRY DIVISION,
SANTIAGO DE CUBA, Aug. 6, 1898.

COMMANDING GENERAL CAVALRY BRIGADE:

SIR: The Commanding General directs that all tentage be left standing when the troops commence to move to the transports.

He advises that just before the commands leave camp to embark on transports, that the men destroy their bedding, and as much as possible of their oldest clothing that has been worn by them during the campaign, in order to reduce to a minimum the danger of infecting the ship.

Very respectfully,
JOS. WHEELER,
Maj. Gen. U.S. Vols., Commanding Cavalry Division.

HEADQUARTERS 5TH ARMY CORPS,
SANTIAGO, Aug. 7, 1898.

GEN'L WHEELER: How many men to go in 1st Cav., Roosevelt's Regiment, 2d Battl. of 3d Cav.?

SHAFTER, *Maj. Genl.*

HEADQUARTERS 5TH ARMY CORPS,
Aug. 6, 1898.

To GENL WHEELER: Genl Shafter asks how many men there are in the four regiments of your division ordered to embark first; they will all go aboard to-morrow.

J. D. MILEY,
A.D.C.

Aug. 6, 1898.

To COL. DORST:

SIR: Pursuant to General Wheeler's orders, the 6th Cavalry will go first, and will be ready by noon and await telephone order. The 6th is the strongest numerically, reason it is selected.

Strength 6 Cav., 391.
3 Cav., 368.

Very respect'y,
S. S. SUMNER,
Bg. Gen. Vol.

HEADQUARTERS 5TH ARMY CORPS,
SANTIAGO DE CUBA, August 7, 1898.

GENERAL ORDERS, }
No. 32.   }

Regiments about to go north will take with them only clothing and blankets; all tents will be left standing. 100 rounds of ammunition, in belts, will be taken; all other is to be packed up and left in camp, where it can be gathered up by the Quartermaster's Department. The day before, or on the morning of, embarkation, careful examination will be made of each regiment, by a medical board, and any man whose case appears likely to develop yellow fever will be sent to hospital.   Notice will be given from day to day to each command as ships are ready to transport them.   Regimental officers will see that their commands are supplied with 10 days travel rations, to be drawn at the wharf when they go on board.   The most careful attention must be given to details by every officer as to looking out that convalescents are properly cared for.

By command of Major General Shafter,

E. J. McClernand,
Assistant Adjutant General.